BIOG
Stein
Steinbach, Alice.

Educating Alice :
adventures of a curious

Educating Alice

Educating Alice

Adventures of
a Curious Woman

ALICE STEINBACH

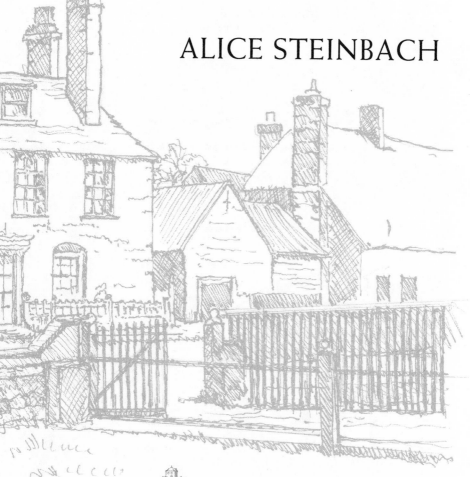

RANDOM HOUSE
NEW YORK

Printed in the United States of America on acid-free paper

Random House website address: www.atrandom.com

246897531

FIRST EDITION

Book design by Carole Lowenstein

*This book is for Irvin Steinbach
and for Maggie Thompson Dundas,
in memory*

To learn of the pine, go to the pine.

—MATSUO BASHO (1644–1694)

Contents

Introduction

I've been trying to remember what started me on the path to this book. Perhaps it began on the hot summer afternoon when I played my first passable rendition of "Who-o Goes the Wind" in the front parlor of the Miss Pearl Evans School of Piano. I was five and my ability to read correctly the little black dots with the squiggly tails thrilled and excited me. Or perhaps it started at Carlins's ice rink when I learned to skate backward, sort of, for the first time. Or maybe the genesis of this book was when Grandmother taught me how to use the old Singer sewing machine, the one with the foot pedal. I must have made a half dozen very plain handkerchiefs that day, gifts for Mother, my third-grade teacher, and my best girlfriends.

As a child I was interested in learning about everything. Animals, tap dancing, tombstones, weaving potholders, hair braiding, the stars and planets, roller skating, rocks, ironing, and painting—the back fence kind of painting, not the kind called art. I am told by those who knew me in those formative years that I constantly pestered family, friends, and unwary strangers asking such things as: How do you get to Mars? How do birds fly? How do you do a time step? Why does gasoline make cars go? How do you iron a dress? Why doesn't a red skirt go with an orange blouse?

I now call this period of my life: A Portrait of the Reporter as a Young Girl. Back then, however, I had quite a different profession in mind.

Given my insatiable curiosity and intense admiration for Nancy Drew, my future plans hinged on entering the detective profession. I saw myself as Nancy Drew aging into Miss Marple. It was the perfect life for me, I thought then, one that would require me to constantly ask questions, find out the answers, and along the way learn a lot of new things.

Although the detective thing didn't work out, I wound up almost in the same place. If you throw in travel and adventure with the items listed above in my Nancy Drew fantasy, what you end up with is a newspaper reporter.

In my twenty years of reporting I got to ask successful writers, dancers, artists, actors, scientists, and quite a few political figures such questions as: How did you learn to write-dance-paint-act-think-vote like that? I can honestly say I learned something new from every story I wrote, including the concept of string theory from one of the smartest physicists alive.

For two decades the job of reporter fit me perfectly. But some careers, like some marriages, are not meant to last forever. After taking time off from my newspaper job to write a book that allowed me to travel around the world, I found it difficult to return to my old routine. So after much deliberation I quit my job and set out to find a way that would allow me, personally and professionally, to combine three of my passions: learning, traveling, and writing.

This book is the result of my decision to travel around the world as an informal student, taking lessons in such things as French cooking in Paris, Border collie training in Scotland, traditional Japanese arts in Kyoto, and the architecture and art of Havana. The premise behind the trip described in these pages was simple. I wanted to study things that interested me in places I found interesting. Some of the lessons were taught in organized classes; others were learning experiences where the approach was more about teaching learnable rules in unstructured settings.

Those who embrace the philosophy that you study, say, cooking or Border collie training for the sole purpose of becoming a chef or a shepherd will be disappointed to hear that I am neither. Nor will the reader be equipped to apply for such positions after putting down this book. Instead, I offer a story about what I set out to learn and what I came back knowing.

Yes, I can tell you what an artist's life is like in Havana, but I also learned about the lives of two Cuban women, teachers, who live with great dignity on very little money in a crumbling apartment building. And, yes, you will meet a young apprentice geisha in Kyoto and find out why a modern Japanese girl enters such a profession, but you also will meet a Japanese woman who tries to help other women in her country find their "undiscovered" abilities in the workplace.

My hope is that by the end of our journey together, you will share with me what my role model, the late Richard Feynman, called "the pleasure of finding things out." Feynman, a Nobel laureate who was a legendary physicist, accomplished bongo drummer, and expert safe-cracker, summed up his lifetime of learning this way: "I was born not knowing and have only had a little time to change that here and there."

I offer here stories of my efforts to add little bits of knowledge here and there to what I was born not knowing.

Educating Alice

Cookin' at the Ritz

A LIGHT SNOW was falling as I left my hotel and hurried across the narrow rue Cambon to the employees' entrance of the Hotel Ritz. It surprised me that I had learned only two days earlier that such a door even existed. How, I wondered, in all my years of exploring the streets and passages of Paris had I missed it? After all, back doors were a major interest of mine. And so were side doors and courtyards hidden behind green gates and anything else that concealed the private Paris from me. Once, I spent two years writing letters and making phone calls before being allowed to visit the mysterious Maison de Verre, a house on the Left Bank designed in the late 1920s by the French architect Pierre Chareau. Compared to that heroic effort, gaining entrance to the back door of the Hotel Ritz was a snap: I had simply enrolled as a culinary student in the Ritz Escoffier École de Gastronomie Française.

Now here I was, on a snowy morning in February, about to enter the hotel not as an outsider but as an insider, a thrilling prospect. After all, I told myself, anyone willing and able to pay seven hundred dollars a pop to stay overnight could walk through the Ritz's imposing place Vendôme entrance. But only those carrying an employee's identification card were allowed through the back door on rue Cambon. Still, as eager as I was to begin what seemed an adventure, the truth is I was nervous about what to expect on the other side of the door. A French security officer who would turn me away? A snooty chef who would laugh at my limited French vocabulary? Classmates who would criticize my chopping and dicing techniques? A sudden, humiliating announcement from the school's *Directeur* that, for undisclosed reasons, he had revoked my student status?

It was in this Kafkaesque frame of mind that I pushed open the plain unmarked door and stepped into a small vestibule. A security guard sitting in a small room behind a counter stood up and carefully gave me the once-over. Immediately his stern appraising demeanor made me think of my root canal dentist.

"Bonjour," I said with fake nonchalance, holding out my photo ID in such a way that my thumb covered any evidence of a very bad haircut. He nodded and reached for the card. I watched as he looked at it and frowned. Was it my bad haircut that offended? "Is something wrong?" I asked. His response was to look at my face and then at the photo, comparing the two. He repeated this twice. Face-then-photo. Face-then-photo. Just as I started to explain that I'd drastically altered my hairstyle—for the better—since the photo was taken, a buzzer went off. A clicking sound followed as the gate to the long basement corridor unlocked and, with a wave of his hand, the guard motioned me through.

So this was it, then, the moment when I became a part of the venerable Hotel Ritz. After descending a flight of stairs, I looked down a corridor so long I couldn't see the end of it. What I could see, however, was a small army of employees engaged in a whirlwind of activity. Fascinated, I watched as men in crisp white uniforms picked up crates containing hundreds of bottles of Evian water and florists pushed carts filled with lavish arrangements of lilies, tulips, and irises. As I moved deeper into the corridor I saw workmen carting off worn pieces of Persian rugs and cabinetmakers moving a hand-painted Chinese chest marked "For repair." Service staff carrying covered silver breakfast trays entered and exited the service elevator. Some of the employees nodded to me in a collegial way as they passed by. I nodded back, trying to conceal my excitement at witnessing all the daily routines necessary to run a world-class hotel.

I continued on through the long corridor, past the sparkling white tile and stainless-steel kitchen classrooms of the cooking school, to the locker rooms where students changed into their uniforms. After a few minutes of struggling with the key, I unlocked the door on the right marked "Women." When I opened it a blast of hot, steamy air hit me; it

smelled like the warm dampness I breathed as a child when changing clothes in the locker room of the YWCA pool.

Inside the small, L-shaped room there were thirty-five bright blue lockers, a few narrow benches, and an adjoining space with a toilet, a shower stall, two sinks, and a mirror. On a small table in the corner someone had left a hair comb and a large roll of Tums—a bad omen, perhaps, to find in the locker room of a cooking school. After locating the locker assigned to me—Number 210—I opened it and saw hanging inside the uniform I'd been fitted for on the previous day. The room was empty so I began to undress quickly, hoping to finish suiting up before my classmates arrived. Call me insecure, but I preferred not to meet my colleagues for the first time wearing only my underwear.

The uniform was formidable. First, I removed the sturdy closed-toe shoes students were advised to wear and stepped out of my khaki pants. Then I pulled on a pair of heavy cotton houndstooth-check trousers. My sweater came off next. It was replaced by a starched white double-breasted chef's jacket with double rows of buttons and the name of the school embroidered in blue on the left. Then came the napkinlike neckerchief that had to be tied in a very specific way. Next, I wrapped a starched white apron around my waist, tied it in front, and then tucked a thick white side towel under the apron string on my left side. By this time I was perspiring heavily.

Finally it was time to don the flat, starched white hat worn by students. I approached the hat with some trepidation. I still had not gotten over the humiliation of being told by the sympathetic French laundress who fitted me that I would require a very large hat. "A size 21," she said sadly. "There is no larger." Also I had no idea of how to wear this hat. Pushed back on my head like a beanie with hair showing? Or pulled down over my forehead, just above the eyebrows? Either way, it was not a becoming look. I decided to wear it in the more severe position: very low on my forehead, almost to my eyebrows, with all my hair covered. Somehow, it seemed more professional that way.

I looked at my watch; it had taken twenty minutes to suit up. I made a brief detour to the mirror and stopped to stare at myself. The person staring back, the one who was supposed to resemble a culinary student, looked in fact like a Red Army nurse, circa World War II. Actually I sort of liked the look. I fancied myself as looking very much like the Hemingway heroine in *A Farewell to Arms*, despite the fact she wasn't Russian and the story had nothing to do with World War II.

To complete the uniform I pinned on the nametag, which, I had been warned at my fitting, "should in all cases be worn every day."

With half an hour to kill I headed for the employees' cafeteria, where I was entitled to eat at a student discount. The pretty, softly lit room was almost empty, so I sat down with a cup of latte and studied the dishes we would prepare over the next four and a half hours: sole fillets with a mandarin sauce; boeuf Bourguignon, waffle potatoes, souffléed potatoes, chocolate and orange mousse. We would also learn to prepare meat glaze and demi-glace. I flipped the pages containing the recipes, trying to familiarize myself with the conversion of measurements and weights from the European metric system into its American equivalent, a daunting task. Added to that was the further hurdle presented by having the course conducted in French with simultaneous translation into English. Between the foreign metric conversion and the foreign language translation, I saw the potential for big mistakes.

Indeed I had spent the night before worrying about whether I would measure up to the standards of the Ritz Escoffier Cooking School. After all it had been more than twenty years since I'd studied classic French cooking and almost as long since I'd cooked at that level. So, to be on the safe side, I had enrolled in a course listed in the school's brochure as designed for the "beginner to intermediate student." Still, the name alone—"The César Ritz Course," named after the hotel's founder—was intimidating to someone who grew up in a Scottish household where Grandmother dragged out the *Wee Scottish Cookbook* when company was coming and a fancy dish like steak pie or leek soup was called for.

I worried too about meeting my nine classmates, all of whom had started the six-week course together, beginning in Week One. I, on the other hand—having neither the time nor money for the full course—chose the option of starting halfway through the course in Week Four. What this meant, of course, was that I was the New Girl in Class, subject to all the disadvantages accruing to such an identity.

Kitchens are dangerous places. Within minutes of beginning our classroom work, two students caught on fire. Or to be more precise, their long side towels caught on fire. Real chefs, it turned out, don't use potholders. When something hot has to be handled they use their sturdy side towels. Which is exactly what Bruce and Paulina were doing—removing a huge stainless-steel pot of fish stock from the gas burner—when flames erupted. The blaze was put out quickly and no one seemed concerned. Except me.

"Does this happen often?" I asked Paulina, a young Mexican woman with bright hazel eyes and a wide smile.

"Oh yes," she said cheerfully. "I think we've all caught on fire at least once."

I was sorry to hear this; almost as sorry as I was to have arrived in class with my nametag pinned obediently on my chef's jacket. Neither Paulina nor Bruce nor any of the other students were wearing nametags. They didn't need to. After three weeks of cooking together my classmates knew not only each other's names but their nicknames as well. I felt branded by my nametag, the Hester Prynne of culinary class, defined by a bad first impression. I was not alone, however, in my unhappiness about being the only one to follow the rules.

Chef Philippe Moreau, our instructor, made clear his annoyance before starting the cooking preparations. His assistant and translator, a tall, smart Frenchwoman named Laurence, conveyed his sentiments. "Chef says why is no one wearing nametags but Aah-leeze? He says how is he supposed to know who anyone is? Chef says to please start wearing them."

To tell the truth I had mixed feelings about my sudden alliance with Chef, as everyone called him. It carried a pejorative whiff of being "the good student who caused all the trouble," a role repugnant to me. A voice, heavily accented, interrupted my thoughts.

"Aah-leeze," said Chef, raising his eyebrows and pointing to the top left side of my jacket. "Please button." As quickly as possible my fingers forced the button I'd accidentally missed through the tight, starched, empty hole. As my classmates watched, I felt relieved to be rid of the "good student" label. "Now we continue," Chef said, turning his attention to a large pot of fish stock simmering on a gas burner.

Chef Moreau, who cooked for ten years in the Ritz Hotel's main kitchen before becoming the school's chief instructor, was a man whose personal and professional demeanor combined two ingredients not usually thought of as compatible: discipline and charm. In his forties, he was handsome, with thick dark hair, pink cheeks, and a large expressive face. He looked a lot like Alec Baldwin, or, to be more precise, the way Alec Baldwin might look if he were a lot slimmer and dressed up like a chef. Chef Moreau was dressed exactly like us, except for one thing: instead of a flat starched cap he wore a twelve-inch toque that resembled a pleated white soufflé on steroids. Wearing it, he appeared to be seven feet tall. But Chef wore his toque with a certain insouciance, which negated any suggestion he was a contestant in the "my-toque-is-bigger-than-your-toque" competition that exists among the very best chefs.

I had already seen Chef in action. The day before my first practical class, he conducted one of the school's twice-weekly demonstrations. The "demos," which students were required to attend, were open to the public for a fee of about fifty dollars. Attended mostly by American, European, and Japanese tourists, the sessions drew a smartly dressed group of women—and a few men—who took lots of notes and asked many questions. The demos were given in one of the large, fabulously equipped kitchens used to train students.

Watching Chef in action was like watching Marcel Marceau perform, particularly for those with shaky French. It didn't matter that everything he said was translated simultaneously into English; Chef did so many things so fast that even the linguistically agile Laurence sometimes fell behind. In the two-and-a-half-hour session he prepared stuffed chicken legs, brown veal stock, various bouillons, Breton pudding cakes, dessert syrups, poaching syrups, and consommé with mixed vegetables. As he went along he downloaded bits of valuable practical information that Laurence translated:

"Chef says egg whites act as a filter to take out impurities so consommé is clear."

"Chef says sauté mushrooms until they release all their moisture and are slightly crispy. He says mushrooms full of water are not good."

"Chef says deglaze with cognac, then with dry white wine."

"Chef says he wants to hear a lot of sizzling from the meat when it's browning."

"Chef says always cook vegetables in copper pots; aluminum will give them gray color."

"Chef says herbs should never be washed."

Something about Chef's culinary dictums reminded me of the famous fashion pronouncements issued by the late great Diana Vreeland. "Pink is the navy blue of India" was the one that popped into my mind while listening to Chef say "The more you cut herbs, the more you lose flavor."

A woman in the audience wearing a mink hat, her full-length mink coat draped over her chair, leaned forward and raised her hand to ask a question. "This recipe isn't the same as what you're doing," she said, pointing to the recipe printed in the handouts given to us as we entered. Chef's riposte was immediate. So was Laurence's translation: "Chef says you have two recipes for the price of one. The one printed and the one Chef is doing."

As Chef continued chopping, dicing, clarifying, peeling, slicing, and boning I began counting the utensils used to prepare certain dishes. At one point I counted twenty-nine pots, pans, skillets, and bowls in use, as well as seventeen slotted spoons, wooden spoons, whisks, knives, and spatulas, and five sieves and pastry cones. Even the efficient *plongeur,* the dishwasher in the tiny cleanup kitchen behind the demonstration counter, wound up like the Sorcerer's Apprentice, barely able to finish one batch of saucepans and stockpots before another batch marched toward him.

Chef, however, seemed in complete control. Only once did he lose his place. In the middle of preparing stuffing for the chicken legs, Chef smelled something burning. "It's the butter you have melting in the oven," Laurence reminded him. He answered her in rapid-fire French that to my untutored ear sounded a bit defensive. Any such emotion however was lost in Laurence's translation: "Chef says you can't chat and work at the same time. But Chef says it is his job to chat and work at the same time. So he keeps up a running repartee with his assistants and the demonstration group."

It was the sign of a perfectionist, I thought, becoming upset when you let one small detail slip. I wondered if such perfectionism would extend to what he expected from his students.

Now, on my first day in class, it became apparent immediately that Chef's approach to teaching the ten uniformed students gathered around him was quite different from what I'd observed in the demonstration. For one thing, Chef was no longer performing for an audience; he was teaching students who had committed a fair amount of time, energy, and money to study with him, so he jettisoned some—with emphasis on the "some"—of the showman's persona. For another, Chef's perfectionism now extended to us. In every task, large or small, he demanded we be perfect too. And of course the biggest difference was that we were the ones doing most of the actual cooking. At the end of class we would sit down together to eat what we made and critique it.

Before we began, Chef drilled into us the importance of *mise en place*, the French term for organizing all the food and equipment needed to prepare a particular dish. Ten chopping blocks, along with knives and stainless-steel bowls, lined the sides of a long rectangular table, and each student chose a workstation. I chose the station between Nathalie, an amiable young Frenchwoman who, because she was French, was likely to be a skilled cook, and Bruce, who I'd learned at the demo class was an Irish psychoanalyst. It was my way of assuring that, should the need arise for cooking advice or therapeutic intervention, I had covered my bases.

Then we began what turned out to be a daily routine: preparing all the ingredients for the recipe at hand—in this case boeuf Bourguignon. First, we made the marinade for the beef. Then for the next twenty minutes we peeled, cut, and sliced vegetables, chopped garlic, cut 3½ pounds of chuck roast into pieces, and prepared a bouquet garni, an herb bundle made of peppercorns, bay leaves, thyme, and parsley tied in cheesecloth. It was very basic work but, Laurence translated, "Chef says uniformity in cutting is very important."

The room fell silent while the group worked. Except for Chef's instructions and Laurence's translations, which occasionally overlapped, there was little socializing. The work was hard, the pace fast, the knives dangerous, the students serious. While we chopped, diced, and sliced, Chef walked around the table, sometimes answering questions, more often pointing out a better way to do something.

Already I could see he ran his kitchen with precision, strict rules, attention to detail in both preparation of food and personal appearance, and a philosophical approach that included criticism as an important learning tool. As a critic, Chef had two powerful weapons: the ability to maintain the hint of a quizzical look on his face at all times and eyebrows able to express instant approval or disapproval. I found the quizzical look particularly unnerving since it gave the impression he was always about to ask why you were doing something the way you were doing something.

Chef's goal, it became clear, was not to teach specific recipes but to see that we worked in a methodical way and understood the basic techniques used in each dish. My goal, on the other hand, was to keep a low profile and avoid doing anything dumb. To help achieve this I kept an eye on Nathalie, a cook who clearly knew what she was doing. Her peeled baby onions were tiny masterpieces, perfectly shaped without a nick or layer of skin anywhere on the surface, and her sliced mushrooms a marvel of fungal uniformity.

When I saw Chef approaching our end of the table, I asked Nathalie, who spoke excellent English, for her opinion on my knife skills. She studied the vegetables on my cutting board. "Chef won't like those mushrooms," she said, not unkindly. "Mushrooms have to be cut in eight even-sized pieces." I was crestfallen; I knew my onions were bad—full of nicks and bumps—but I actually thought the mushrooms had potential.

Nathalie was right. Chef, I could tell, was not impressed with my knife skills. He expressed this by asking me to do a few more cuts before moving on to fish filleting. He also suggested, in a nice way, that I might want to remove my watch while preparing food. I nodded, removed my onion-studded watch, and started cutting. I wanted to tell Chef that I wasn't normally this clumsy in handling a knife. And I wanted to point out that I knew how to cut the French way—by holding the tip of the knife on the board with my left hand while cutting in a circular motion. But he was gone before I could remember whether the French word for "knife" was masculine or feminine.

While we were waiting for the fish filleting to begin I asked Bruce, who seemed quite capable in the kitchen, why he was taking the course. "Do you like to cook?" I asked.

"No, I like to eat," he said. We both laughed. But there was another reason. Bruce told me he and his English wife, an interior decorator, planned to open a bed-and-breakfast north of London, one that would feature an outstanding menu. Bruce's plan was to complete the longer, six-month training course at the Ritz Escoffier School and then do an internship in the hotel's main kitchen.

I told him that sounded something like signing up for active duty in the army.

"Actually, becoming a chef is a lot like being in the army," said Bruce who, it turned out, was from Belfast and had once served as an army infantry soldier. "It's all about discipline, about a precise way of doing things, about working you hard."

I was surprised to hear he'd been in the army. Actually, I'd been surprised to learn that he was Irish. When I first saw Bruce at the demonstration a day earlier I was certain he was French. Not only was he wearing an elegant tweed jacket cut in the European style, he also had on square, black-rimmed glasses that gave him the look of a French intellectual and accentuated his facial resemblance to Yves Saint Laurent. The last thing in the world he looked like was a former infantry soldier.

I was about to ask Bruce how he went from being an infantry soldier to a psychoanalyst when Chef began to talk about something called the "BF-15." For a second I wondered if, while I was talking to Bruce, Chef had moved on to a discussion of World War II aircraft. But no, he was talking about different kinds of potatoes, and one of them was called BF-15. It was the potato we were to use in preparing the potato soufflé. Chef described the BF-15 as a "middle-aged potato," a term I found especially resonant.

"Chef likes the BF-15 because it's an older potato and doesn't contain as much water," Laurence translated. We would need two deep fryers, she said, one for a first frying and another for a second frying. "Chef says it is very difficult to make souffléed potatoes using just one fryer."

We peeled the potatoes and, after washing them under cold running water, cut them into ⅛-inch slices. "Chef says never wash potatoes after cutting."

Working with deep fryers containing hot oil was not one of my favorite things. Of all the accidents possible in a kitchen—stabbing yourself with a fish knife, catching on fire, throwing out your back while lifting a five-gallon pot of water containing ten pounds of meat—of all these possibilities the one that spooked me most was the idea of accidentally boiling myself in oil. My timidity resulted in potatoes that didn't puff up to Chef's standards.

Quickly we moved on to chocolate mousse, using an especially rich recipe that incorporated whipped cream rather than egg whites. Then came the dish I couldn't wait to eat: sole fillets with mandarin sauce. I loved every ingredient in it: fish, spinach, Grand Marnier, whipping cream, and mandarins, a type of orange that is small and sweet with a loose rind.

By this time I was tired and hungry and my feet hurt. I wiped the chocolate mousse off my watch, which was now hanging from a buttonhole in my jacket, and saw that it was close to seven P.M. We'd been cooking for four hours with another thirty minutes to go before sitting down to dinner. Even the air-conditioning that ran year-round in the kitchen didn't prevent the room from becoming very warm; the heat made the cap on my head feel like a gladiator's helmet. Although I could hear Laurence translating Chef's dictums on meat glaze and demi-glace—"Chef says when stock is reduced by half, you have demi-glace; for glaze you reduce it by three-quarters"—I was only half-listening. My thoughts had drifted to a darker place where one question kept spinning in my mind: Can I really get through another two weeks of this?

Finally, dinner was served. As we sat eating and drinking wine around the long table elegantly set with china, silver, and fine crystal, the group loosened up and started talking—in English, fortunately, since keeping up in French with so many people speaking so quickly would have been impossible for me. Most of the conversation was about food, although I noticed the words most often used by Americans when talking about food—words like calories, margarine, cholesterol, Dr. Atkins, low-fat, Diet Coke, saccharine—were absent. Mostly the conversation had to do with an exchange of opinions on the hot new restaurants in Paris (L'Avenue and Spoon); the best food markets (Marché Maubert and Saxe-Breteuil); the best shops for kitchen equipment (Dehillerin and La Bovida); and the new bar everyone was talking about, Le Fumoir.

Although such tips about food and bars interested me, what I really wanted to know had more to do with who my classmates were. However, I refrained from asking too many questions, a real challenge for a former reporter. I decided instead to concentrate on listening, a valuable learning tool that I sometimes overlooked. My plan worked. By the time dinner was finished I had pieced together some shorthand sketches of several classmates.

First there was Paulina from Mexico. Friendly and effervescent, she was a recent law school graduate who'd come to Paris to study French and take the cooking course. Next was Caren, a smart, good-looking American who had recently moved with her husband to Paris from Brittany, where they'd lived for a few years. And then there was my cooking neighbor, the appealing, very direct Nathalie, a Frenchwoman who lived in Paris with her husband and young children. A conversation I'd overheard led me to believe Nathalie was an actress. Missy from Kuwait had no profession as yet. Just eighteen, she had received the cooking course from her parents as a graduation gift.

By the end of the first day I also had learned something about myself: that I was the least competent cook in the class. Part of it, I rationalized, was beginning in the middle of the course and not knowing where things were or how to operate the scary stove or instantly convert measurements. But let's face it, even Pedro, a dashing young Mexican who seemed to have little background in cooking, turned out to be naturally gifted in the kitchen.

By the time I reached my hotel it was close to nine. The task of cleaning the kitchen after dinner had added forty-five minutes to the four-and-a-half-hour class, and changing from my uniform back into street clothes another fifteen. I was exhausted. All I wanted to do was shower the grease out of my hair and soak in a hot tub. My room at the hotel revived me, however: it was charming. In the soft glow of the lamps left on by the hotel maid, I saw my bed waiting, the covers turned down, and on the plump feather pillows two chocolates in shining foil.

I climbed into the tub, unwrapped one of the chocolates, and closed my eyes. Instantly my eyelids became little screens on which scenes from my past were projected: *Grandmother in her homemade red-and-white flowered apron cooking a strange Scottish version of hamburgers. The day in high school when I accidentally started a fire in Mrs. Parlett's home economics class. The first time I cooked chicken duxelle for my husband and sons, a dish received with, how shall I put it, extreme* apathie.

A sudden jerk of my head made me open my eyes; the water in the tub floated just below my nose. I must have dozed off. No reason to panic, I told myself; it wasn't even a close call. Still, I could just imagine the obituary headline in the next day's *International Herald Tribune*: AMERICAN WOMAN, LEAST COMPETENT STUDENT IN COOKING CLASS, FOUND DEAD IN HOTEL TUB, CANDY WRAPPER CLUTCHED IN HAND.

I had arrived in Paris four days before the start of my cooking classes, the idea being to shake off any jet lag and spend time checking out my hotel and the surrounding neighborhood. It was the first time in a dozen years of frequent visits to Paris that I'd stayed on the Right Bank. "I'm a Left Bank person," I told friends whenever they recommended a hotel on the north side of the Seine. The truth is, I'd become something of a Left Bank snob. Never mind that I crossed the river almost every day to indulge in the rich cultural life of the Right Bank, I still clung to the notion of Left Bank superiority.

My decision to stay on the Right Bank while taking cooking lessons was based mostly on proximity. The hotel I picked was as close as I could get, just steps away from the Ritz's back door. That way, I figured, if it was raining or snowing or classes began at eight in the morning or at eight in the evening, it would take only minutes to run across the rue Cambon from one place to the other. The hotel also offered a very agreeable winter rate that included a full breakfast. As far as I knew, none of the other students were staying in hotels. A few lived in Paris; others had taken apartments or were living with relatives.

I began my Right Bank education by exploring the rue Cambon, a street that begins at the rue de Rivoli near the Tuileries, crosses the fashionable rue St.-Honoré, and ends at the busy boulevard de la Madeleine. From there I branched out into the area around the Opéra Garnier and rue de Miromesnil. Mainly I was searching for hangouts to replace the ones left behind on the Left Bank. A bistro where I would be comfortable dining alone. A bar where I could sit reading a book while nursing a glass of wine. A café with the right ambience for a long Saturday or Sunday breakfast with my newspaper. A bookstore where I might hang out on rainy nights. A market where I could buy fruit and cheese for a late-night snack.

Jeanine, a receptionist at the hotel who knew I was studying at the Ritz Cooking School, was very interested in what went on in the classes. She was, I learned, an accomplished cook, as many French-women are. "We learn from our mothers and grandmothers," she said. "Everything from how to kill a chicken to shopping for the perfect melon." Jeanine and I talked more about eating than cooking, however, and she became interested in my quest to find little places in the neighborhood. "Any luck today?" she'd ask, handing me my room key. Sometimes, since she was a native Parisian, she would recommend a place.

"You might like taking lunch in the upstairs café at Hédiard," she said one day. "They have a fine menu that's based on what's in season, and all the ingredients are from their shop." Although I knew of the famous Hédiard, a luxury food store on nearby place de la Madeleine, I'd had no idea it contained a restaurant. "And since you love coffee so much," Jeanine added, "you'll be happy to learn they offer a choice of eight different coffees."

Jeanine also knew a lot about the neighborhood and its history. "Did you know that this hotel was once the Ritz Annex?" she asked one day. "And that the Faubourg-St.-Honoré was named after the patron saint of pastry chefs?" Jeanine also pointed out that the young Henry James had lived for a time next door to the hotel on the third floor of a building that was now the Chanel atelier.

With some trepidation I offered up the only bit of history I knew about the rue Cambon. By this time I trusted Jeanine enough to take a chance on not being put in my place vis-à-vis *l'histoire française.*

"Did you know that Herminie Cadolle, the woman who invented the brassiere in 1889, opened her custom corsetière shop on rue Cambon about a century ago and that her great-great-granddaughter still runs it in the same building?" I said. Just as I was about to tell her of the time I interviewed this same great-great-granddaughter, Poupie Cadolle, who told me stories of her grandmother fitting Mata Hari for underwear at the Ritz, an arriving guest cut short our conversation.

On the evening before my course started I decided to have a drink in the Ritz lobby. It was Sunday and as the winter light faded, twilight slipped in, *l'heure bleue.* I watched as the delicate color stained the sky and thought suddenly of the blue Waterman's ink I used in fifth-grade penmanship class. Although it was a mild evening for February, very few people were out on the street and the city seemed eerily calm. I walked the few blocks to the hotel's place Vendôme entrance thinking about the history that resided still in the stones beneath my feet and of the stories that kept their secrets in the massive walls around me.

If travel is a means of visiting other centuries, as some French philosopher observed, then Paris offers a spectacular trip to the past. Of course, in terms of French history the Hotel Ritz might be considered nouveau Ritz. It was founded in 1898 after established hotelier César Ritz learned that 15, place Vendôme was for sale. Once the lavish eighteenth-century town house of the Duc de Lauzun, commander of the French cavalry at Yorktown in 1781, the property offered Ritz the atmosphere he wanted for his hotel: the intimacy of an aristocrat's private house rather than the public ambience of a grand hotel. Over the next fifteen years, two adjacent buildings were purchased, adding 153 rooms to the 85 of the original hotel.

To me, Paris is the most beautiful city in the world. I never tire of walking its streets and never lose my awe of the city's architectural order and coherence, a tribute to the genius of Haussmann. When I drew near the hotel it began to rain. It was a soft, slow rain, and as each drop passed under the lamplight circling place Vendôme, it shimmered like a streak of silver in the damp air. *It smells like a spring night at home,* I thought, as I climbed the hotel steps and stepped inside. Since there is no real lobby at the front of the hotel, I headed for the opulent lounge just past the Bar Vendôme. There, seated on a plush sofa near a crackling fire, I ordered my favorite aperitif, Lillet Rouge, and began searching the room for signs of deposed royalty or British rock stars.

From my cozy perch I could see the rain outside, a slanting rain that slid down the glass windowpanes. I tried to imagine what the Duc de Lauzun did on a rainy evening at home. Did he sit in this room and tell stories of the charge he led at the Battle of Yorktown? I wondered. Or perhaps he sat reading Rousseau or Molière. Warm and content, I sat sipping my Lillet. The book I'd brought with me—a used copy of *Parisian Sketches* by Henry James, found in a shop on rue de Miromesnil—lay unopened on the table before me. Although I was eager to read the book—Jeanine had raved about it but warned it was hard to find—my companion for the evening turned out to be someone other than Mr. Henry James.

My imaginary visitor arrived wearing her best clothes: a cape woven in the tartan of her clan—Buchanan—and a dark green tam-o'-shanter topped with a navy pompom. "My special events outfit," Grandmother always told me when she wore the cape and tam on our trips downtown to shop at The Carry On Thrift Shop or listen to the piano player at Kresge's Five-and-Dime. She must have been in her sixties then—a long time ago—but here she was now, in memory, looking not a day older than I remembered her from our shopping trips in Baltimore. It was odd, too, because I'd been wondering what Grandmother—who liked simplicity almost to the point of severity—would make of a place like the Ritz. "Too grand," I imagined her saying. "I'll not stay here, not even if you paid me."

Still, even though it wasn't her cup of tea, how nice it was to have Grandmother, appropriately dressed in her special events outfit, sitting next to me in Paris at the Hotel Ritz. It was her first visit to the city and to the hotel. Well, I thought, Paris is entitled to its history and I am entitled to mine. And like Paris, my history is always with me.

When I returned to my hotel that night, the concierge motioned me over. "I have a letter for you," he said, handing me an envelope fashioned of rice paper, the address written in a very fine, almost printed, hand. I knew immediately it was from my Japanese friend, Naohiro. "Thank you," I said, trying to keep myself from ripping open the envelope and devouring its contents on the spot. Instead I carefully placed the letter inside my handbag and hurried to my room. Once there, I threw myself across the bed like a teenage girl settling in for a long telephone talk with her boyfriend. For me, though, a letter is always better than a phone call. People write things in letters they would never say in person. They permit themselves to write down feelings and observations using an emotional syntax far more intimate and powerful than speech will allow.

For the next half hour I sat reading and laughing and sighing at Naohiro's sharp humor and elegant observations about everything. His letter began with an amusing description of returning to his Tokyo apartment only to find that his college-age daughter, Mizue, had moved in with her two cats, explaining she was fed up with the idea of becoming a physician and wanted to try her hand at acting. And, oh, yes, in addition to being fed up with her studies, she'd had a big fight with her boyfriend over the cats. But if her father were willing to keep the cats, she'd be willing to go back to school. After he reminded Mizue that he lived half the year in Paris and had no desire to transport the cats back and forth, she reluctantly agreed to go back to school and take the cats with her. At the end of his letter, Naohiro wrote that after our last meeting in Paris, he'd actually gone back to the very expensive square where we had laughed about taking an apartment worth two million francs. "It's still available," he wrote of the place des Vosges apartment, "and still too expensive."

When I read this, my mind raced back to that visit. I thought: The last time I saw him, where were we? Then I remembered. It was in a small art gallery on the rue de Beaune, one that specialized in avant-garde Russian art, a style we both loved. He was returning to Tokyo on a business trip that afternoon, and I walked with him to the Pont Royal where we said good-bye. For a long time Naohiro and I stood close to one another, our bodies touching as we watched the glass-roofed tourist boats move slowly along the Seine before disappearing under the bridge. It was an awkward parting, neither of us able to express our feelings in public. His letter, however, was neither awkward nor reserved. I liked it very much.

· · ·

By the middle of my first week I felt at home in my Right Bank neighborhood. For one thing—and it was a big thing—I'd found the right hotel. With its warm staff, comfortable rooms, great breakfasts, and good location, it answered all my needs. It was also a hotel without attitude. And a hotel in Paris without attitude is not so easy to find.

"What did you cook yesterday?" Jeanine asked as I headed off to class one morning.

"Salmon with endives and parsley butter sauce," I said. "It was wonderful. The only bad part was that I had to scale, gut, and fillet a very large and very slippery salmon. But it wasn't as hard as I thought it would be." I didn't mention to Jeanine that on my way back to my workstation with the heavy salmon, I dropped it on the floor and had trouble retrieving it; when I tried to pick the fish up, it just slid away. Fortunately, Chef hadn't witnessed this cartoonish caper.

"And what are you cooking today?" she asked. I thumbed through the pages of the elegant blue-and-gold folder containing the week's recipes. "It says roasted quail with green peppercorn sauce, potato soufflé, and diamond cookies." I handed Jeanine the book so she could see the recipes and names in French.

She looked over the recipes and said, "Ah, later I must copy down the potato recipe."

"I think we made that recipe on my first day in class, so I'm not sure why we're making it again."

"Because it was good?" Jeanine said, laughing. "That's why I make things more than once."

Chef began the day's session with a lecture on tardiness. He reminded us that we had a lot to accomplish in our classroom time and, glancing at the three students who had straggled in late, suggested we plan our time more carefully. Cooking successfully at this level, I was learning, is all about organization and time management—not only in preparing food but also in programming yourself to meet the unending demands facing a chef. And while my future plans did not include becoming a professional chef, there were several students in the class who hoped to work as chefs or open restaurants. Some, including Bruce and Caren, whom I'd gotten to know a little better, were likely to continue on through almost eight months of advanced courses. Elisabeth, a young strawberry-blond Lebanese woman who was a star in the class, was also planning to go the distance. For their efforts they would receive the Ritz Escoffier Superior Diploma in French Cuisine and Pastry-Making, the school's highest award.

Finally Chef turned his attention from tardiness to the day's lesson. As we moved over to the long worktable, I saw that each student's cutting board had something feathery lying on top of it. Something feathery and small, with a petite beak and bright little eyes that still looked startled, just as they must have looked at the moment its neck was snapped. Next to each bird lay a very sharp knife. Well, I thought, at least I won't have to kill it with my bare hands.

Then I heard Chef explaining in French what he wanted us to do. Since Laurence didn't seem to be in the kitchen I translated Chef's instructions for myself: "You are to *something-something* the quail's top, clean *something-something* out, hold it over *something-something* feathers, and move back the quail hot."

"What did Chef say?" I whispered to Caren, who stood next to me at the table.

"Chef said you are to behead the quail, clean out its lungs, pluck it, and hold it over the flame to remove all feathers."

"That's what I thought he said," I replied. Which was partly true. Even without understanding the words I often could intuit from Chef's gestures what he was saying.

I could see that Caren, who had a soft spot for animals, was hesitating, reluctant to begin the beheading. So was I. Nathalie, while sympathetic to such feelings, had no such hesitation. "But then I'm used to seeing my grandmother chase down a chicken and kill it for dinner," she said in her amiable but direct manner.

"And I was used to seeing my grandmother make rhubarb pies," I said, picking up the knife. It took longer than I thought. *Do quails sing?* I wondered, as the sharp blade finally separated the small bird into two parts.

"Chef says to save the necks and wing tips for the stock," said Laurence, who had reappeared in the classroom. After eviscerating the quail, plucking it, and flaming the leftover feathers, we moved on to trussing. A cinch, I thought, remembering all the capon legs I'd tied together for long-ago Sunday dinners.

I was wrong. Trussing the quail in Chef's class meant sewing with a long threaded pick, not tying. It also involved about seven steps that Laurence recited as Chef moved around the students at the table. He stopped to look at my work and then spoke in a low voice. "The pick goes in between the thighs diagonally, then bring it through the closed legs."

Remarkably, I was able to follow Chef's instructions, by concentrating really hard on the French words while watching him pantomime every step. I did as he asked.

"Now turn it upside down and go through the skin of the wing and neck."

My hands were shaking as I pushed the long pick through the bird's skin.

"Now, tie."

I tied, feeling all thumbs.

"A double knot, please."

For a minute I couldn't remember what a double knot was. Then, without thinking, I tied one.

Although Chef said nothing about my finished "truss" I could tell from his eyebrows it wasn't a disaster. When something was really bad, Chef's eyebrows always shot up to just beneath his toque. Either that or he would say something in a tone that was dangerously polite. I was thrilled to have passed the eyebrow test and my energy level zoomed up as though I'd just downed a double *café express.*

Before continuing with the quail recipe we made the cookie dough and placed it in the refrigerator to chill. Then we prepared the complicated batter for the potato dish, which was not at all like the potatoes we had prepared in our first class. After that we returned to making the green peppercorn sauce and rice with currants for the quail. Then came the real test: timing everything precisely so that no dish arrived on the table too early or too late. Even with ten of us scrambling to bring all the last-minute pieces together at the right time, there was a frenetic atmosphere in the kitchen. The whole scene reminded me of a Three Stooges comedy, the way we kept bumping into one another racing from the stove to the refrigerator to the oven. The fact that there were ten stooges involved in the commotion—instead of three—made it even funnier.

I tried to imagine putting together a meal like this in my kitchen at home. I couldn't. For one thing, when I opened my refrigerator I saw containers of low-fat cottage cheese and yogurt, sliced chicken from the deli, wheat germ, Egg Beaters, and a few pieces of softening fruit. Here, when the refrigerator door opened, I saw buckets of homemade stock, pans of freshly grated gruyère cheese, bowls of ready-to-use demi-glace and *crème fraîche,* along with containers of *coulis,* a strained fruit sauce used to decorate desserts.

And here in this kitchen, unlike mine, everything Chef needed miraculously appeared, handed to him by an assistant, while everything used up or dirty disappeared, delivered back to the hands of the waiting *plongeur.* To prepare the fifty-step quail dish, more than twenty different utensils were needed. I didn't even want to think about the twelve hours it would take to prepare a proper consommé. In my kitchen consommé came out of a can. But the French cook is not concerned with the number of steps or length of time it takes to prepare a dish correctly. It made me wonder: Does food define a culture, as popular theory has it, or does a culture define its food?

Still, cooking in the two kitchens—Chef's and mine—had one thing in common: after tasting and smelling food for more than three hours my appetite always lost its edge, whether here or cooking for guests at home. Some of my classmates seemed to suffer from the same syndrome, sampling the food as critics rather than eating for pleasure. It occurred to me that while we all like to eat, we like it more when someone else does the cooking. Sometimes I wondered how Chef felt about sitting down to eat after cooking all day, every day. Did he still enjoy it? Or was it too much of a good thing? I knew very little about Chef and had a lot of questions I wanted to ask him but probably never would. Despite his charm, Chef intimidated me. Not in a million years could I imagine going up to him and saying something like, "Chef, when you're alone at home, what do you like to eat for dinner?" In food-besotted cultures such as Paris's, chefs were stars with egos as big as the Ritz, celebrities to be gossiped about.

When not cooking with Chef or attending the demo classes, I spent as much time as possible exploring the Ritz Hotel. For me it was the French version of *Upstairs, Downstairs,* though on a much larger scale. And, of course, that was how César Ritz originally envisioned his hotel: as a large house in the country for aristocrats. As I saw it, the main difference between the British television series and life at the Hotel Ritz was that the "upstairs" people here were wealthy guests instead of an aristocratic family, and the "downstairs" folks were called employees instead of servants. Other than that, the similarities were striking. Each of the two tiers of life at the Ritz offered its own pleasures, complexities, and rules—just as they did at the Bellamys' London mansion—and I enjoyed observing both.

I loved, for instance, putting on my street clothes after class and riding the employees' elevator upstairs to the lobby. Every time I emerged from the service elevator into the long corridor known as "Temptation Walk," I experienced a moth-to-butterfly moment. Designed to connect the hotel's two wings, "Temptation Walk" is aptly named, at least for walkers who can afford, say, a $10,000 diamond necklace or $900 cashmere sweater, which are among the fabulous items displayed in one hundred tall glass cabinets lining a hall about the length of a football field. Since examining the contents of each case—and the people peering into each case—could become an addiction, I was forced to apply my "chocolate rule" to Temptation Walk: I allowed myself to sample only six of the glass cases a day, then closed the box.

Upstairs, I also liked to poke around the hotel's gift shop and the little museum that housed historical photos and artifacts relating to the Ritz. Of course my chief pleasure came from observing the rich and famous as they went about their daily rituals. Often I would do this while having a *citron pressé* in the lounge, where I would engage in occasional conversation. Once or twice, after working up my courage, I entered the intimidating Bar Vendôme, my faux Hermès "Kelly" bag swinging at my side, to have a salad and glass of wine for lunch. Even though it was way over my budget, I rationalized the expenditure by telling myself that lunch was costing me about the equivalent of a theater ticket to see a Molière farce.

Although being privy to the world upstairs had its moments—such as watching a guest arrive with four wizened Pekingese dogs wearing pearl necklaces, each perched in a white wicker basket carried by a bellboy—what I most enjoyed was exploring the downstairs world. I never tired of snooping around the hotel's three-story basement or, as the Ritz referred to these below-ground floors: minus 1, minus 2, and minus 3.

On my forays into the sub-basements I carried a little list of what was on each level:

1. The main kitchens, the cooking school, the cooking school's library and locker rooms, and the Ritz Health Club.

2. The swimming pool that connected to the sumptuous health club by a glamorous winding staircase right out of an old MGM musical, the pastry kitchen, florist rooms, employees' cafeteria, and the *Laboratoire*

Chocolat, which made all the chocolate for the hotel and the cooking school.

3. The laundry and cleaning operation—a major player, responsible for all linens, staff uniforms, and anything else that gets dirty—and the wine cellar where more than one hundred thousand bottles of wine are stored.

I liked to imagine that even Chef would be impressed by my well-organized attempts to catch a glimpse of the engine that powered the Ritz. Only once did my plans go awry: when I pressed the minus-2 button on a service elevator and bright lights suddenly lit up every corner of minus 1—the floor I was on—causing me to hightail it up a nearby ramp to safe ground as fast as I could.

When prowling around downstairs I made a point of wearing my student's uniform, the idea being that a person in civilian clothes might raise eyebrows. But no one seemed concerned to see me wandering around; in fact everyone was friendly. One day after standing shyly—and maybe a bit slyly as well—at the door to the hotel's main kitchens, craning my neck in a desperate attempt to see inside, a chef approached me.

· "Would you like to come in?" he asked.

"Ah, yes, that would be nice," I said, trying not to pump my arm into the air in an American-style victory salute.

I followed the chef into the spacious blue-and-white tiled kitchens, gleaming with copper pots and high-tech stainless-steel equipment. Chef explained how the kitchens, which operated twenty-four hours a day, were organized. "They are separated into areas that service the different needs of the hotel: the restaurant Espadon, the Bar Vendôme, and room service."

In the *boulangerie* there were hundreds of loaves of rising bread waiting their turn to join the hundreds of loaves baking in huge ovens. I stopped to watch a pastry chef work on a concoction featuring peaks of snow-white chantilly encircled by a shiny crown of caramelized cream puffs.

"Does it have a name?" I asked.

"It is called *Saint-Honoré,* Madame. A specialty of the Hotel Ritz."

Another specialty of the Ritz was the flower arrangements created by the hotel's florists. More than once I'd marveled at the carts filled with flowers to be delivered to guests or placed somewhere in the hotel's public spaces, everything from yellow and purple pansies in tiny white faïence pots to spectacular displays of full-blown roses, elegant lilies, and exotic orchids. One day after seeing a particularly grand arrangement in the lounge I descended the two floors to compliment the florist.

"Merci, Madame," said the young woman cutting stems behind a counter in the flower-scented room. Tall and slender, her short golden hair elegantly cut into spiky layers, she reminded me of a bright yellow chrysanthemum exploding from its long stem. She didn't seem to mind the intrusion, so I stayed to chat, which in my case meant asking questions.

"We try to honor any request from a guest," she said, responding to a question. "But if you want ikebana, we won't do it. We are a classic florist." She paused. "Once we had a call from an assistant to the Princess of Thailand, a guest at the hotel. She wanted the entire suite filled with flowers, but there was one condition. None of them must have any fragrance." I was dying to find out what flowers were used, but a man wearing a white coat and white gloves came in and began loading white pots of tiny nosegays onto a cart. I left, determined to come back and find out the answer.

One night after class I sat in a small café near the Palais-Royal and began writing a letter to Naohiro:

Dear N,

You asked me to tell you more about my classmates and I will try. You already know about Bruce, Paulina, and Caren, so let's see what I can say about some of the others.

Well, there's Elise from Boston. She moved to Paris two months ago and lives with her French boyfriend. In her late twenties, I think, she is rumored to be living on a trust fund. Elise is one of the best cooks in class but is very moody. ("I have a bad attitude," she says repeatedly.) She often looks tired in the morning and is prone to shooting a don't-even-think-about-it look in the direction of anyone approaching her before noon. It's the way I imagine the young Dorothy Parker to have been: not a morning person. Maybe that's why I find Elise appealing.

Then there's Pedro, a good-looking guy from Mexico, probably in his late twenties or thereabouts. He's said to have worked as a management consultant in New York before coming to Paris. When the course ends he's on his way to Rio for Carnival. Very glamorous but very enigmatic, at least to me.

A person I really like is Nathalie. She's French, lives in Paris with her husband and young children. She works as a radio actress, which is a shame since she has such an expressive face. She's an excellent cook. Chef turns to Nathalie—and to Elisabeth, a twenty-one-year-old native of Lebanon who's already done a stint in the kitchens of Portugal's Ritz Hotel—when he needs help in the kitchen. Nathalie's also an excellent artist; her notebook is filled with extraordinary drawings of various knives, pots, kitchen equipment, and carving techniques. It's the kind of notebook Leonardo might keep if he were a culinary student.

Do you remember the first dinner we ever shared? At Tan Dinh, the Vietnamese place on rue de Verneuil? Chef cooked a dish yesterday that reminded me of the lobster we ate there. I think I will go there for dinner this weekend—for the lobster and for the memories of that night.

On an afternoon when Chef Moreau was to give a demonstration I had lunch in the employees' cafeteria: pumpkin soup, bouillabaisse, blanc-mange. Thanks to my employees' discount card, it came to a little under ten dollars. Afterward, with time to kill before the demo, I decided to do some reading in the cooking school's library. When I turned the corner that led down the hallway to the library, I almost bumped into a man dressed in a white chef's jacket. He was leaning against the wall, one knee bent, his raised foot acting as a brace behind him as he talked to Laurence. Suddenly it dawned on me that the man standing about two feet away from me was Chef without his toque! I was shocked. He looked much younger. Shorter, too, though still tall. Less formidable. He seemed almost like a different person. It reminded me of the time many years earlier when I was a part-time waitress in a French restaurant and the maître d' unwittingly seated my psychoanalyst at one of my tables. When we recognized each other, neither of us knew what to say. So I said, "*Bonjour. The coq au vin is excellent ce soir.*"

While I was wondering how to revise this line so that it might apply to Chef and me, his assistant, Laurence—whom I liked a lot—motioned me over.

"*Bonjour,*" I said.

"*Bonjour,*" Laurence said.

"*Bonjour,* Aahleeze," Chef said.

I didn't know how to respond so, emboldened by their friendly overture and the absence of Chef's toque, I asked him a question, using Laurence as my translator: "Chef, I've been wondering—when you're alone at home, what do you like to eat?"

Since Chef's English was about as good as my French, Laurence translated his surprisingly long answer. "Chef says that like all cooks he likes to eat the things that are easy to cook. Pot-au-feu. Boeuf Bourguignon. Blanquette de veau. Cassoulet. Chef says he holds on to the cooking of his mother. His mother cooked a lot of typical country dishes."

I asked where Chef was born. His answer was to motion me into the demo kitchen where we stopped before a large map of France. I noticed that before entering, Chef put on his toque. Then he pointed to a spot on the map halfway between Paris and the city of Lyon and started to speak. "Chef says he was born outside Nevers, north of Lyon. And he says he started cooking at sixteen in a two-star restaurant in Pouilly."

Since my next question was a personal one, I tried to put it as diplomatically as I could. "Chef, after watching you for over a week, I'd say that you have one of the most demanding jobs around. How long can you go on being a chef?"

Chef smiled and said, "I'm still a young guy—in my forties. I like to think I'm going to be a young guy forever." He held out his ample square hands. "See, my hands haven't started to shake yet."

By this time every chair in the demo kitchen was occupied; about fifty people were waiting for the demonstration to begin. I thanked Chef profusely—"*Mille mercis*," I said over and over again—and told him how kind he was to answer my questions. Then I took a seat next to Bruce at the back of the classroom.

Chef, aware that he was beginning a few minutes late, shifted into high gear and took off like an Air France Concorde. He boiled regular milk, he whipped cream, he made almond milk, he soaked gelatin, and he diced and sliced strawberries, all for the *blanc-manger aux fraises*. He chopped vegetables, he soaked fish bones for fish stock, he chopped off the claws and tail of a lobster, then cut its head in half lengthwise for lobster à l'Américaine. Finally, he put the lobster pieces in a flat-sided pan containing oil and sprinkled in chopped shallots and garlic, flaming it with cognac before adding white wine, fish stock, meat glaze, chopped tomatoes, and tomato paste.

Sometimes Chef hummed a little as he worked. Sometimes after tasting a dish he would grade it, saying "Pretty good." Sometimes after

doing a difficult task with a technique as methodical as a NASA count-
down to liftoff, he'd announce, "Nothing easier." But the thing I liked
best was the way Chef would stop in the middle of a cooking demo to
express his pleasure over a new piece of equipment—a new knife,
perhaps, or a new piping bag.

"I see so many similarities between chefs and surgeons," Bruce said as
we listened to Chef rhapsodize over a special pan. "Chefs delight like
surgeons in new and good equipment, and they share the same precise
organization. And then there's the way they're always thinking a step
ahead—like surgeons." Bruce, it turned out, was in a position to make
the comparison; he had gone to medical school in London after leaving the military. That, along with his natural talent for cooking, made
Bruce the perfect candidate, in my opinion, to become an accomplished
chef.

Of course, not all chefs at the school taught in the same way as Chef
Moreau. Once or twice when we had some other teaching chef, we
were exposed to a completely different style. At our first class with Chef
Philippe Girard, a staff member from the upstairs office introduced him,
saying, "This is Chef Girard's first demo for the Ritz Escoffier cooking
school. But he is a chef who gives demos and classes everywhere in the
world and has worked in many different restaurants in Paris and
Provence."

Chef Girard, a man as long and lean as a Giacometti figure, was just
as precise, self-confident, and authoritative as Chef Moreau. But his
teaching manner was totally different. A man with a reserved, low-key
personality, Chef Girard never engaged in the kind of repartee with his
assistant that Chef Moreau did. And it was hard to imagine Chef Girard
deviating from a printed recipe as Chef Moreau did several times. Still,
there was something very clean and elegant about Chef Girard's
straightforward method of teaching.

Since it was Valentine's Day, Chef Girard was teaching a very romantic dinner-for-two menu: foie gras with caramelized apples, sole and
salmon, Black and White Tears of Love. This last item was an amazing—and in my view far too complicated—dessert that involved white
chocolate mousse, chocolate chantilly cream, vanilla custard sauce,
white chocolate ganache, shiny chocolate icing, and chocolate sauce. It
also required making tear-shaped molds from semi-rigid plastic strips, at
which point I bailed out and began studying the audience.

I noticed there were no men in the audience except students and that the majority of women taking the class were Japanese. I wondered: Was there something about a "romantic dinner-for-two" that appealed more to Japanese women than to, say, American or British women? I decided to put the question to Mariko, a Japanese pastry student with whom I'd become friendly, when we met for tea the next afternoon.

"No, I don't think the reason Japanese women came to the Saint Valentine's demo had anything to do with romance," Mariko said the next day as we walked along the rue Royale, on our way to Ladurée, one of the most famous tea shops in Paris. "Maybe they are there for the chocolate and custard sweets. Japanese people have developed a taste for French pastry. It is why so many of us are in pastry classes."

It was true. I had already noticed that the pastry-making course seemed to be a magnet for the Japanese, women and men alike. In my class, which offered some pastry instruction but focused on fundamental cooking methods and preparation, there were no Japanese students. Curious about this, I asked Monique, who worked in the school's upstairs office, if such a division was generally true throughout the year.

"It is true," Monique said. "Japanese take pastry because they want to open pâtisserie shops or teach. French pastry has to be imported in Japan and it is very expensive. It is also considered quite chic in Japan to serve French pastry at home."

Mariko, who was twenty-nine and single, told me she hoped to open a small pâtisserie upon returning to Tokyo. I had gotten to know Mariko because we always seemed to be the first to arrive in the locker room to change into our uniforms.

"I see we are the early birds again," I said to her the second time this happened.

Mariko looked at me without answering. I was puzzled by her lack of response; I knew she spoke English. Had I offended her in some way?

Then Mariko said, "What does it mean? The early birds? Is it a bad thing to be?"

I laughed. "No, I think it is a good thing to be," I said, explaining to her the story of how the early bird gets the worm.

She listened attentively, in the special way that Japanese people do, then said, "Then I will call us the 'early birds.' " It became a running joke between us.

But even before our first conversation, I'd noticed Mariko working in the pastry kitchen across the hall, her dark hair pulled into a bun at the back of her head and covered with a delicate net of white flour. Lively and smart, with a good sense of humor, she reminded me of Yuko, the Japanese woman who would soon marry my younger son in Tokyo. I found myself drawn to her.

Now we were on our way to Ladurée so that Mariko might taste the pastries made famous by this turn-of-the-century tea salon. Although known for its *royals* (almond biscuits iced with chocolate or mocha frosting) and its classic *financières* (almond cakes shaped like a gold brick), Ladurée is most famous for its crispy, flavored macaroons filled with a layer of rich caramel cream made with salted butter.

Mariko and I had already made a trip to Dalloyau's dessert shop to sample its *Mogador* (chocolate cake layered with chocolate mousse and raspberry jam) and to the Pâtisserie Stohrer on rue Montorgueil to taste everything from cakes to chocolates. A chef in the Ritz's main kitchen had told us about rue Montorgueil, an old cobblestone street closed to traffic. "It is the last remnant of the old Les Halles market, and you still find Paris chefs who go there to shop," he told us. He was right. The rue Montorgueil was amazing. We had spent a whole day there, admiring the stalls of iced silverfish and dark-shelled mussels; the fat, succulent-looking sausages; the fresh pasta hanging on racks; the wheels of ripe cheeses; the bright red cherries and rosy peaches. It was like strolling through a still life by Chardin.

Mariko and I loved visiting the street markets. We had spent a Sunday morning at the organic market on the Boulevard Raspail in the chic quartier of St.-Germain, and a Saturday afternoon wandering through the Marché d'Aligre, where people of all ages, backgrounds, and nationalities mingled together near the busy Faubourg St.-Antoine.

But Ladurée—the original one on rue Royale, not the new one— remained one of my favorite stops for lunch or a mid-afternoon coffee and pastry, particularly in wintertime. How I loved entering the warm shop with its scent of pastry baking and the smell that rose from steaming cups of the richest cocoa I'd ever tasted. After walking through the always-crowded bakery I'd usually try to find a window table in the tearoom. I could have stayed all day listening to the soft buzz of women speaking tête-à-tête across small tables, while at their feet, clipped poodles stirred from their sleep just long enough to sigh their contentment. And I never tired of the scent of hot chocolate escaping from the silver pots carried on trays by waitresses, or the sound of china cups being picked up and put down. I loved it all: the sounds, sights, smells, even the cigarette smoke that curled up into the air. To me it was quintessential Paris.

Once we were seated, I could see Mariko was instantly smitten with Ladurée. We each ordered a selection of pastries and *café allongé*, a coffee that is half as strong as a regular *express* but still strong. "We will drink it to clear our palate between sweets," Mariko joked, "just as Japanese people eat sweets between sampling the different teas."

When the several plates of sweets were set down before us, it was hard to decide which to eat first. As I looked at the lush chocolate desserts and frothy meringue confections, a memory suddenly darted out from its hiding place:

I am eight years old and I am standing in the neighborhood bakery trying to decide between a box of dark chocolate cupcakes and a luscious strawberry shortcake. I point to the chocolate cakes, and the bakery lady wraps the box with a thin white string. At home I go straight to my room and eat every cupcake, sitting alone on the bed I share with Grandmother. Since Father died, only sweets fill the emptiness I feel.

I saw that Mariko had placed on her plate a strawberry tart, a chocolate macaroon, and an almond biscuit iced with mocha. It was my turn to decide. Without thinking I picked up a little cake drenched in bittersweet chocolate and took a bite. I let the dark chocolate melt in my mouth and then slide slowly down my throat, savoring the sensation. It occurred to me that my grieving eight-year-old self had never really tasted her chocolate cupcakes.

I took another bite. *Taste this slowly*, my thinking voice said to both the eight-year-old girl and the woman who accompanied her. *Isn't it delicious?*

The first week of cooking school had blurred by, like a video on fast-forward. There was so much to learn, particularly since I was playing catch-up with the others who, after three weeks, knew the basic techniques and where to find the equipment they needed. By the second week, however, I could see that Chef's training was paying off. My slicing, dicing, julienning, mincing, and chopping skills had improved. Not only did I know what a mirepoix was—chopped carrots, onions, leeks, and celery used to make stocks and sauces—but I knew how to caramelize one. And while still shaky, my ability to use things like a mandoline, pastry bag, knife sharpener, larding needle, and chinois (a cone-shaped strainer), as well as a dozen or so different knives, was growing every day.

My confidence increased as I became more familiar with some of the basic techniques underlying classic French cuisine: preparing brown veal stock and fish stock, poaching, searing, deep-frying, blanching, sautéing, boning poultry, filleting fish, glazing and deglazing. I had learned the importance of *mise en place*, and I was careful not only to orga- nize the ingredients and equipment I would need before starting a particular task but also to bring everything up to the same level in the actual "prepping" of the ingredients to be used. Given a recipe that called for, say, a dozen onions to be diced, the experienced prepper would first peel all the onions, then halve all of them, and then move on to dicing all of them. Such an approach is faster than peeling one onion, halving it, and then dicing it. In pastry class I had learned how to make jams and fresh fruit sauces, chocolate truffles, tulip pastries, mousseline pastry cream, dessert syrup, Caribbean cake, and the famous génoise cake. I had also learned that unless I wanted to spring for a whole new wardrobe in a larger size, the trick was to sample, not eat, what we turned out in pastry class.

To my surprise I found myself wishing I could stay through the final week of the course. I would miss my classmates. Even though it was difficult, given the hectic pace of our cooking sessions, to forge any deep friendships, I'd grown closer to Nathalie and Caren and planned to see them when I returned to Paris. I would miss Chef's deconstructing recipes and techniques like a culinary Jacques Derrida while Laurence offered up her Proustian translations. I would miss the locker room that sounded like a miniature United Nations with its voices speaking in French, Japanese, Italian, Arabic, and languages I couldn't identify. I would even miss the friendly laundresses who chatted every time I exchanged my dirty uniform for a fresh one.

But the thing I would miss most was this: the way the act of cooking forced you to live in the present tense, something I often forgot or was unable to do. Living in the present tense meant living like a child, or as I had come to define it, living in the purity of the ticking moment. I was getting better at it, though I still had to remind myself not to ignore the present—right there in front of me, begging for attention—as I care- lessly looked backward and forward. But the unrelenting demands of cooking—particularly under the watchful eye of Chef Moreau—had the power to shut out everything except the reality of the moment at hand.

On the day of my last cooking class I woke up early and, instead of trying to catch another hour or two of sleep, got out of bed, showered, and dressed. Although I'd been out late the night before with some classmates, I wasn't tired. And since a sudden schedule change had pushed back the morning class by an hour—to eight from nine— I decided to treat myself to a farewell *café crème* and baguette at the Ritz. For the last time I crossed the narrow rue Cambon to the back entrance of the hotel, and as I drew closer, a remark made by a hotel employee popped into my mind. "It was from this very door that Princess Diana and Dodi Fayed left in their limousine," she told me, referring to that August night in 1997 when the couple's car crashed in the tunnel near place de l'Alma. Now in the early morning light, the one-way street was almost deserted. With no traffic and no pedestrians, a lovely quiet spilled down like a silent waterfall into the space between the shops and buildings that lined the narrow street.

But at 38, rue Cambon, the employees' entrance was hopping with an army of vendors unloading crates of fruit, vegetables, bottled water, flowers, meat, fish, paper towels, furniture, rugs, and anything else needed to get one of the world's grandest hotels ready for the day. I stood in the long corridor and watched them, thinking I might never see this again. Then I got on the service elevator and made my way upstairs to have breakfast. After two *café crèmes* and a baguette layered with French butter and raspberry jam, I traveled downstairs to pick up my uniform at the laundry, then hurried to the locker room to change.

Alone in the locker room I stepped out of my khaki pants and into the required houndstooth-check trousers. Immediately I knew something wasn't right. I looked down and saw the trouser hems flapping on the floor, about four inches beyond my feet. The laundress had given me a size long instead of a size medium. It was almost eight, too late for a trip back to the laundry. That left me with two choices: roll up the trouser bottoms and look like a complete loser, or wear my khakis. I went for the khakis. It was risky but I figured the chances of Chef's noticing were small since my apron stopped midway between my knees and my ankles.

I was wrong. Chef was already there, waiting alone in the kitchen when I arrived. Right off, he noticed my khaki pants. Although Chef said nothing, his eyebrows went into full alert mode, a move that elevated his toque another inch. Then he eyeballed me from head to foot, stopping when he reached my legs. Still silent, he motioned toward my ankles. Chef seemed to be waiting for an explanation for the disorder I'd brought into the classroom.

"They gave me the wrong size," I stammered, in a barely audible voice. Immediately I knew it was the wrong thing to say. Not only was it totally irrelevant—a sort of my-dog-ate-my-cooking-trousers excuse—it was counter to everything Chef was trying to teach us. It showed a lack of discipline on my part and, worse, a willingness to ignore the rules. True enough, I thought some of the rules arbitrary and silly and had serious questions about why leaving one button undone or wearing the wrong color of pants made any difference.

But somehow Chef's not allowing me to get away with this latest lapse in my appearance—even though it was my last day and he knew he'd never see me again—triggered something inside me. I suddenly saw that a chef who doesn't care about the importance of appearance wouldn't care if onions were peeled uniformly or stock was prepared properly or mushrooms were sautéed long enough to lose all their moisture. And, I asked myself, would I want to be taught by that kind of Chef?

Before I could finish working through this epiphany—if that's what it was and not a caffeine overload—my classmates straggled in, looking as tired as I did. I wondered if their lateness weighed in on Chef's scale as the equivalent of my lapsed dress code. Chef said nothing, however, launching instead into the day's menu: pork tenderloin with leeks and Meaux (whole grain) mustard, zucchini spaghetti with fresh tomato sauce, apple charlotte, and several kinds of omelets.

First came the dish that required the most cooking time, the apple charlotte. To my surprise, Paulina and I were each assigned to prepare an apple charlotte from start to finish. Since I was used to working in a group of three or four students—an arrangement that allowed me to count on someone to fill in the gaps for me—the idea of working alone made me nervous. But the sense of empowerment resulting from my newly acquired "rules and order" attitude carried me through. And while the finished product wasn't perfect, when I removed the apple charlotte from the oven, a surge of culinary pride sent me scurrying for my camera, eager to record my lopsided masterpiece.

By this time Chef was starting to demonstrate the technique for making omelets. Finally, I thought, something I know how to do well. But my confidence began to erode as Michelle—substituting for Laurence—translated Chairman Chef's Thoughts on Omelets. "Chef says if he were hiring another chef, he'd make him prepare an omelet. It is that difficult to make correctly. Chef says he likes omelets slightly runny and he adores traditional rustic ones—like grand-mère's omelet, put right on the table in a pan."

Then came the moment I'd been dreading. One by one we took turns making a potato omelet—while Chef watched! I hung back for as long as possible, looking on as the others struggled through the more-difficult-than-expected technique of omelet-making. Finally it was my turn. I beat the eggs and cream together with a fork, then added the diced, cooked potatoes along with parsley, salt, and pepper. I poured this mixture into a frying pan with melted butter and using a fork pulled the cooked edges in toward the center. So far, so good: this was how I made omelets at home.

The hard part involved manipulating the very heavy, very hot frying pan. Chef and Michelle talked me through it: "Chef says to fold the omelet over, stir the middle while shaking the pan. Roll it around. Chef says it is important to shake the pan the right way. You jerk the pan forward, then pull back." Although none of this made any sense to me—the steps seemed out of order—I did get the hang of shaking the pan. I found that if I thrust the frying pan out in a lunging motion—the way I was taught to lunge at an opponent in fencing class—it came exactly right. As usual, Chef hovered over us as we cooked, on the lookout for signs of disorder or a lack of methodology.

But today I didn't mind his watchfulness. Still under the influence of my widening epiphany, my attitude had changed. It now embraced order and rules and accepted the French way of thinking, one that posited there were only two ways to do something: a right way and a wrong way. This belief applied not only in their cuisine but in their architecture and manners and daily life as well. It was, I decided, the quality above all others that defined the French and made them who they are.

That night I met Jeanine for a farewell drink at Bar30, an elegant but cozy bar I'd discovered near the place de la Concorde on rue Boissy-d'Anglas. I liked it because it was quiet, friendly, and had a piano player who sounded like Hoagy Carmichael. As Jeanine and I sat on a sofa in front of the fireplace drinking a very good wine, she handed me an oblong box wrapped in pale blue paper. I opened it and there, nestled in chocolate brown tissue, were a dozen little sponge cakes, each one shaped like a shell. I recognized them as madeleines.

"My favorites," I said. "And, of course, Proust's favorites, too." She laughed and I did, too. Jeanine knew from our discussions of French writers that I admired Proust in a way that approached idolatry. "*Merci, Jeanine. Mille mercis.*"

"My mother made them," Jeanine said. "She's quite a good pastry cook. I thought you might like to take them on the plane with you tomorrow. A good little snack, no?"

"A great little snack, yes." I paused, uncertain about whether to say what was on my mind, fearful it might strike Jeanine as too intimate, too much the expression of a naïve American. But, despite my fear that Henry James might appear at any moment, I said it anyway: "And you, Jeanine, have been a great friend to me. I'll take that on the plane with me too."

Later, as I walked backed to the hotel, I found myself wondering what the madeleine in my life might be—the one taste with the power to instantly transport me back to the past, back to a place, a person, a childhood. We all have them, madeleines. So what was mine? The answer came to me a few blocks later: my madeleine was Grandmother's strange brown candy. Cooked in cake pans, it was a cross between caramelized sugar and a hard fudge. Grandmother always cut pie-shaped slices of it right from the round aluminum pan.

But sadly I would never experience that taste again. For unlike Proust's madeleines, Grandmother's candy could not be found in a cook-book, and no one knew the recipe. Several times I had tried to re-create it but with no success. Now, as I walked along the rue Royale, a Paris street redolent with history, I suddenly tasted the candy again, tasted its sugary caramel flavor melting in my mouth. Then, like a genie let out of a cake pan, Grandmother appeared. It made me smile, the sight of her standing at the entrance to the elegant Maxim's wearing, as usual, her sensible, laced-up shoes bought in Stewart's Bargain Basement.

As I packed to leave the next morning, I carefully placed a few things in a suitcase I planned to carry on board, things I didn't want to risk losing. The box of madeleines from Jeanine. My notebook from class.

My address book with all its new entries. The gold-embossed certificate—presented to me by Chef—that had my name written in black ink just below the words *Ritz Escoffier École de Gastronomie Française, Paris*. And the official Ritz Escoffier paper toque—the tall version worn by Chef—that I'd bought in the gift shop for a little under ten dollars. I'm sure I'll never try the toque on, much less wear it while cooking. To me, it would be like playing Yo-Yo Ma's cello while he was out of the room.

Dancing in Kyoto

IT WAS DARK when I arrived at Kansai Airport, just outside of Osaka. Although I knew from pictures that the soaring modern terminal looked spectacular in the daytime hours, it seemed cavernous and depressingly empty at this time of night. Just the sort of scene Edward Hopper might have painted, I thought: the image of a tired, solitary figure, late at night in a deserted place, dragging luggage behind her while wondering what to do next. In my case, I knew what to do next; I just didn't know how to get there. I needed to find the train that would take me to my final destination: Kyoto.

I studied the directions I'd copied down before leaving for Kyoto. *After customs, go to lowest level in building. Get on Haruka Express, the Green Car. Train leaves two times every hour.* Of course, now that I was actually here, the directions were of no use at all. The map, which had seemed so clear before arriving, suddenly was incomprehensible. Lowest level? Where was that? The ticket office for the Haruka Express? Not where the map showed it to be. And my trusty little *Tourist's Japanese Language Handbook* was all but useless since no one understood my painfully slow pronunciation of the questions I'd written out in phonetic Japanese:

Excuse me, do you speak English? Excuse me, where is the train station? Excuse me, where do I go for the Haruka Express to Kyoto? Excuse me, I don't speak Japanese.

But for the grace of a Japanese porter who'd worked at a New Jersey train station for two years, I'd still be wandering around Kansai Airport like a gaijin spirit trapped in a foreign afterlife. "Train ticket?" the porter asked, pointing to the ticket in my hand. "Please, may I have?" He looked at it and motioned me to follow. I did, thinking if ever there was a time to depend on the kindness of a stranger, this was it. I followed him the way a child follows her mother in a big department store, even wanting now and then to grab his sleeve. Quickly he guided me through the airport, across footbridges to small hidden elevators, then down an escalator, then through another concourse, and finally to a train platform. "Stand here, please," he said, bowing.

"*Arigato*," I said, bowing in return. Then I handed him 2,000 yen, which I believed was about $15 but could have been $150 for all I knew. Whatever it was, he deserved it. He bowed again and left just as a train pulled into the station. I jumped on, praying it was the Haruka Express to Kyoto. If not, I'd just go wherever it took me, which, I figured, couldn't be too far out of the way since Japan is a small country.

The train was sleek and comfortable, and I breathed a sigh of relief as I settled back into my seat. Another step taken in the long road from my home in Baltimore to Kyoto, I thought. Only a few more hurdles remained, including one I really dreaded: negotiating my way out of Kyoto's train station. "It is far more difficult than getting out of Kansai Airport," a Japanese friend had warned me. "Kyoto Station is like a city of its own." Oh, well, at least I knew I was on the train that would take me to Kyoto. I knew this because the white-gloved conductor who, after bowing to the occupants of the entire car, had turned to me, bowed again, and asked to see my ticket. "Kyoto, yes?" he asked. "Kyoto, yes," I replied. He nodded his head, bowed, and left. I took this as an affirmative response.

Through the window of the train I watched as an utterly foreign terrain slowly revealed itself, emerging from the dark the way a city does when you fly into it at night. From my vantage point on the elevated tracks I could see the bright, garish lights and illuminated bill-boards of Osaka spread out around me like a neon jungle. Jumbled streets ran like crooked streams throughout the vast city, and wooden teahouses mingled with gas stations and bars and sad little laundromats where a few people sat silently in front of clothes dryers. Blinking on and off like red tracer bullets against the dark sky were hundreds of lights whose messages, in Japanese, appeared briefly, then disappeared. Off in the middle distance, the outlines of high-rise buildings began taking shape. When the train slowed briefly I could make out the forms of several men leaning over dilapidated desks in an office building.

I leaned against the train window and thought of my son Sam, who lived in Osaka for four years after college, working as a translator. How he loved this city, its food, its language, and, most of all, its people. In a culture notorious for its coolness to a gaijin, or "outside person," my son was able to count among his friends many Japanese people who not only invited him into their homes but also shared their holidays with him. Now looking out at this sprawling, intimidating city of more than ten million people I had renewed respect for him.

I wondered if the group of Japanese women I had arranged to meet in Kyoto would learn to feel even the tiniest bit of such familiarity with me, another outsider. And, just as important, would I be able to relate in a meaningful way to these women whose culture and codes of behavior were so foreign to a Westerner? In some ways, Japanese women seemed more mysterious to me than Japanese men, particularly those old enough to have grown up in a more traditional society. But I was heartened by my correspondence with Michi Ogawa, the woman who had taken charge of arranging lessons for me in traditional Japanese culture. After several months of exchanging e-mail letters, there was something about the way she described her work and her life that made me feel Ms. Michi Ogawa and I might have a surprising number of things in common.

As promised, Kyoto Station turned out to be an ordeal. For ninety minutes I searched for a way out of the sixteen-story train station, stopping at every information booth that advertised "English spoken." At each booth I ran into a variation of the same obstacle. The English-speaking attendant was away from the desk. The English-speaking attendant spoke English only a little better than I spoke Japanese. The English-speaking attendant spoke English but gave directions so unclear as to be useless. By this time I hadn't slept for almost thirty-six hours, and the urge to express my frustration by screaming out "I can't take it anymore!" was growing. Then through an open door I spotted a line of taxicabs. I rushed out, jumped into the backseat of one, and handed the driver a piece of paper my Japanese friend Naohiro had given me with the name and location of my hotel written in Japanese kanji—the Chinese characters that form the basis of written Japanese. Twenty minutes later I was in my hotel room.

After unpacking I sat down at a low table in front of the shoji screens covering the window. I was about to slide them open to get my first look at Kyoto when I noticed the white porcelain bowl with its masses of purple freesias and tiny pink lilies. When I leaned over to inhale the intoxicating scent of the freesias, I saw a card tucked inside. I opened it and read: "A good welcome to Kyoto from Michi Ogawa."

Cheered by the thought that at least one person in Kyoto knew I existed, I pushed open the screens. For years I had waited for this moment, this first glimpse of Kyoto, a city that my father had described to me when I was little. Once he brought home to me a souvenir hair comb of ivory with dangling plum blossoms; I wore it to school every day until the plum blossoms broke off. But tonight Kyoto was covered with darkness and mist and I could see nothing from my window. Or perhaps it was my eyes—so tired, so heavy—that were covered with darkness and mist. It didn't matter, really, since stored in my head since childhood was my own imaginary Kyoto.

Exhausted, I crawled into bed and fell into a deep sleep, dreaming of a city of silver and golden pavilions, of exotic geisha and Zen rock gardens, of moon-viewing and ponds filled with golden carp, of little girls wearing in their hair ivory combs with dangling plum blossoms.

When I awoke the next morning at six-forty-five, I was ravenously hungry and still exhausted. After wolfing down a Calcium Blitz Energy Bar, packed for just such an emergency, I showered, dressed, and went down to the hotel dining room, where a dozen or so people were in line for the buffet breakfast. On the spur of the moment I decided to have a Japanese-style breakfast. I loaded up my plate with grilled fish, rice gruel, miso soup, salad, and pickles. Given the upside-down time cycle my body was adjusting to, the choice seemed exactly right.

At a little before nine I headed back to my room. The food had helped but despite three cups of coffee, I still felt very tired. Not that it mattered. I purposely had made no plans for the day, figuring I would just read and nap and maybe take in a museum for a couple of hours. Then, by the next day, I'd be ready to hit the ground running.

As I entered my room the telephone rang. "This is the front desk, and I have a message for Miss Alice Steinbach," said the voice at the other end of the line. "Miss Michi Ogawa says she will meet you in the lobby at ten o'clock and go with you to the Festival of Ages." Then I heard a click and the voice was gone.

The message puzzled me since I knew of no such arrangement. Had I completely forgotten about some important event arranged by Michi? And what exactly was the Festival of Ages? I searched through my travel material and found an entire booklet on Kyoto's *Jidai Matsuri*, which means "Festival of Ages." The introduction explained the event's significance:

> This festival well deserves its renown as one of Kyoto's three greatest fêtes. Kyoto was the capital of Japan from 794 to 1868 and mirrored many changes in various ages during more than ten centuries. You will find the main feature of *Jidai Matsuri* in the unique procession, consisting of more than 2,000 participants clad in costumes representing each important historical epoch during which Kyoto was Japan's capital.

It sounded fabulous. But the idea of reliving ten centuries of Kyoto's history in my current jet-lagged state was formidable. So I grabbed my camera and notebook and rushed downstairs to throw back as many cups of coffee as I could before Michi-san arrived.

As I stood waiting in the lobby I thought back to what I had learned about Michi Ogawa. I knew she was married to a mathematics professor and that after staying home to raise her four children and run the household—as most Japanese women now over the age of forty had done—she decided to look for a job. But Michi found that there were no good jobs for Japanese women of a certain age, even for someone like herself, an educated and well-traveled woman. So she decided to see if she could change that and, in the process, create employment not only for herself but for other women as well. Using her own savings plus a loan, she and eleven other women—most of whom had lived abroad and taught Japanese to foreigners—formed the Women's Association of Kyoto in 1997. Known as WAK, its purpose was to "introduce foreign visitors to Japanese culture in daily life."

After reading about WAK in a travel newsletter I was put in touch with Michi by the Japan National Tourist Organization in New York. It seemed a marriage made in heaven: I wanted to learn exactly what Michi and these Japanese women wanted to teach. Within months, the women—who charged a modest fee for their services—had arranged lessons with experts in origami, flower arranging, tea ceremony, antiques appreciation, traditional dancing, and woodblock printmaking.

Because I didn't know what Michi Ogawa looked like—and vice versa—I stood near the hotel entrance checking out every Japanese woman dressed in Western-style clothes. Since Michi had been described to me as "a woman who is quite liberated in her thoughts"— so much so that she had chosen to drop the customary suffix *–ko*, the word for child, from her name, Michiko—I paid little attention to those wearing kimonos, except to admire them. However, one particular figure drew my attention: a woman wearing a celery-colored kimono splashed with flowers in subdued tones of pink, blue, and yellow and wrapped with a deep pink obi tied with a pale ribbon. When she walked the pale colors of her kimono flowed together, giving the impression of a watercolor come to life. The woman's dark hair was pulled back in a bun and covered with a midnight-blue hair net; it reminded me of the snoods American women wore in the 1940s. On her feet she wore white split-toed socks and the traditional Japanese shoes called zori. She was the picture of a traditional Japanese woman—except for one thing. The briefcase she carried was a dead giveaway. I knew it was Michi Ogawa.

Almost at the same instant, Michi—who did not know what I looked like—recognized me, probably because I was one of the few non-Asians in the lobby. We eyed one another for a minute or two, then spoke, almost in unison.

"Are you Steinbach-san?"

"Yes. Are you Ogawa-san?"

"Yes."

We bowed to each other, a move I'd practiced in front of the mirror many times. Then Michi suggested we sit in a nearby lounge to wait for the arrival of a woman named Noriko, who would accompany us to the Festival of Ages. I thanked Michi for her gift of flowers. She smiled. Then, somewhat awkwardly, I presented her with a gift: a small black leather case meant to hold business cards. In Japan, I had been told, it was customary to give a gift to those whose hospitality you accept. And since I knew that most introductions and meetings in Japan involve a routine exchange of business cards, it seemed a good choice for Michi. When I bowed and handed her the small package wrapped in thick, glossy sand-colored paper and tied with a purple silk ribbon, she smiled and thanked me, saying she would open her gift later.

Then Michi said something that surprised me: "I thought you would be older."

I laughed, secretly pleased that Michi's remark had none of the formality I expected at this first meeting. "I *am* older," I said. "But I'm wearing a lot of makeup this morning, trying to hide the jet lag." She smiled, an expression I would come to recognize as a more refined Japanese version of laughing.

As we spoke, a Japanese woman dressed in a tailored navy blue suit and navy pumps approached our table. It was Noriko Kasuya, a successful career woman who held a high-level job with the Kyoto Tourism Bureau. Her organization often collaborated with Michi's group to promote the city, especially to foreign visitors. She sat down and over tall glasses of iced orange juice, we engaged in small talk. *How was the flight? Have you ever been to the United States? Is this your first trip to Kyoto? Did you like New York when you visited?*

Of course what I really wanted to know was more about Michi's life, and Noriko's too. What their daily life was like, where they lived, how they felt about the role of women in Japan, about geisha, about old traditions that were dying out, about marriage customs and child raising, about the spread of Western culture into their country. What I was looking for were all the details that might offer a glimpse into their lives. It was the way a reporter attempts to catch the shape of a story through a slightly open door. But I had come to Kyoto as a student, not a reporter. Still, old habits die hard. So whenever I felt that old reportorial urge coming on, I thought of the advice Naohiro had given me: "Remember, Japanese people do not ask direct questions or answer questions directly."

We began to talk about the difficulties involved when a Japanese woman creates a business from scratch, and what it was like to go from being, in Michi's words, "an ordinary housewife with no experience of working outside until I was forty years old" to a position of leadership. I asked what her husband's reaction had been when she broke out of the housewife role.

"At first he agreed I should do it," said Michi. "He said, 'Sometimes when you were a housewife you often spoke the same thing every day. Only about children and the neighbors. And your conversation was sometimes tired.' I was very, very shocked at what he said. I had no time to go out. I had to take care of children and prepare the breakfast and prepare the lunch and then I had to drive him to the university where he lectured because he didn't drive. Then I waited for him and prepared the tea and then children came home from school."

Michi's answer stunned me. It was so direct and revealing, almost a perfect summing up of how many American women felt about their lives until the 1960s. I turned to Noriko, who, at thirty-nine, is unmarried and a generation younger than fifty-one-year-old Michi. "Do you find such a description of marriage old-fashioned?" I asked Noriko, who began her working career when she was twenty-two.

"My generation preferred to use our time for ourselves," Noriko said. "Many of us wanted to have careers and put off marriage. My friends who did marry and have a family often go to work when the children are about ten years old—although they do not have such big families as Michi's. Even in her generation it was very unusual to raise four children. But it is even more unusual for a Japanese woman at such a late age to start a business like Michi."

Michi smiled and said, "Some of the women in my group began to work after age fifty. But some of them only want to work two or three days a week. My group wants to be individual from husband, but our generation also wants to keep peace at home."

Emboldened by the forthright answers of both women I asked Michi if her husband had come to admire what she was doing.

"No!" she said emphatically, softening the answer slightly with a smile. "When I worked only two or three days as a Japanese teacher, he helped me. Even so I usually got up at six-thirty and only at night after the children went to bed studied until two o'clock in the morning. But when we women work outside, our family can't continue the same way of life."

As I listened to Michi it occurred to me how many of the messages she had sent me during the planning of my trip to Kyoto were written at two in the morning, after her children were in bed and her house in order.

I saw Noriko glance at her watch. "It is time to go," she said. "The festival will begin soon."

And then the three of us set off for the spacious park and gardens surrounding Kyoto's Imperial Palace, where for the next several hours I watched, awestruck, as ten centuries of history unfolded before me like a gorgeous painted scroll. It was as perfect a lesson in Japan's traditions and history as anyone could hope for. Especially if I included what I had learned from my earlier conversation with Michi and Noriko.

Later that night I sat in my room rereading Arthur Golden's novel *Memoirs of a Geisha*, which is set in Kyoto. I thought about Michi, trying to figure out why she had worn a kimono to our first meeting. It struck me as out of character for a woman with such modern views. Not only that, but the day had been very hot and Michi earlier had mentioned how difficult it was to move when wearing a kimono. Most of the Japanese people sitting near us at the Festival of Ages were dressed in casual Western clothes; only the painted paper fans they used to cool themselves in the ninety-degree heat hinted at traditional Japan. Perhaps, I thought, Michi wore a kimono because it was a festival day. Or perhaps she dressed that way because she knew that many foreigners expected to see Japanese women in kimonos and would be disappointed by their absence. Most of the women I had seen at the festival wore Western-style clothes; some dressed in Nike sports clothes, others in fashionable designer outfits.

At about eight o'clock, despite all my efforts to stay awake, I fell asleep sitting up in bed, reading about Sayuri, the fictional geisha whose memoir captivated millions of Western readers. When I woke up it was still dark outside. I looked at the clock and groaned: it wasn't even midnight. Of course now I wasn't sleepy since it was really one-thirty in the afternoon—yesterday afternoon—for me. Instead of fighting it I decided to get up and write in my journal. Without much thought I wrote down the words, "Haiku for a Festival." Then, quickly, almost as if it were being dictated to me, I wrote:

> *A very hot day:*
> *The sound of paper fans still*
> *Flutters like soft wings.*

It was with great excitement and some trepidation that I set out in a taxicab for my first dancing lesson in the *Wakayagi* style. Although I had no idea what the *Wakayagi* style was, I loved to dance and fancied myself to be rather good at it. My only fear was the condition of my knees. How on earth did Japanese women manage to kneel on tatami for hours with their legs folded back beneath them? I could do it for about twenty minutes and then my legs started drifting into a sidesaddle position. I could see already that even the giant-sized tube of Ben-Gay I'd packed was not going to last very long.

Still, I consoled myself by embracing my newly acquired tallness. In Japan I towered above most of the women, and many of the men too. I liked being tall. In some perverse way it encouraged me to stand up even straighter, the way I was taught to, but never did, as a teenage student at Miss Walters Charm School in Baltimore.

When Michi arrived at the hotel to drive me to the dance instructor's home, I hardly recognized her. Instead of a kimono she was wearing a very stylish khaki suit with a crisp white blouse and red beaded necklace. Although her dark hair was still pulled back into a neat bun, she had allowed a few wavy strands to frame her face. The look suited her. I suspected she preferred wearing such Western-style clothes not only for their comfort but because they did not reflect what Michi referred to as "old Japan"—a concept based on age-old images of Japan as a place of geisha and samurai—while overlooking modern Japan. Michi, along with many Japanese women, wished to update this tourist's version of her country so that foreigners might learn to appreciate the new Japan as well as the old one.

When we arrived at the dance instructor's home in the Nakagyo area of central Kyoto, my translator for the lesson, Tomoko, greeted us. With her was the thirty-four-year-old woman who was to be my dance teacher. "She has two names," Tomoko said, introducing the dancer, a slim, elegant figure dressed in a yellow silk kimono and black obi delicately embroidered with colorful butterflies. "Her real name is Junko Kawakzatsu. But her stage name is Ouka Wakayagi, which means 'form of cherry.' Wakayagi is one of the three major schools of dance, and because Ouka-san is a diplomate of that school she is authorized to use 'Wakayagi' as her stage name."

Ouka-san lived with her parents in a charming old-style wooden house, or *machiya*, the Japanese word for a town house. On a colorful street of traditional wooden row houses that contained both homes and workspaces, Ouka's *machiya* was a two-story structure with slatted wooden grillework covering the windows that faced the street. Her house, like most of those adjoining it, was built close to the edge of the street, leaving room for only a narrow sidewalk.

Inside the small entrance, we stopped to remove our shoes and then followed Ouka upstairs to a large tatami room with a raised platform at one end. The platform served as a stage for her dance pupils, including the one about to be instructed.

But first, I had to suit up for my lesson. With Ouka-san's help I donned a white cotton *yukata* (a lightweight kimono) patterned with large blue leaves that looked like stars. Then a wide orange obi was wrapped around my waist. Next came the white, split-toed socks, fastened on the side by snaps, that I would wear while dancing. To my embarrassment the socks, known as *tabi*, were too small for my American-sized feet. But like Cinderella's stepsisters I managed to squeeze into them anyway.

Ouka, who began dancing at the age of two, chose to instruct me to the music of "Gion Kouta," a famous Japanese song. Tomiko explained the choice: "Seasons are very important in Japan, especially in Kyoto. So Ouka will teach you the Spring part of the song." But before my turn came I kneeled awkwardly on the tatami and watched the graceful dancer perform. I listened as Tomiko explained the meaning behind Ouka's movements: "The story is about an apprentice geisha who dreams to have happy family and happy wedding. She adores her lover but can't meet him whenever she wants to. Sorrow passes over her face as she waits for her lover. To perform this dance well, the dancer must deeply imagine her sorrow."

In Ouka's dancing every movement seemed to express sorrow. Sorrow was there in the slow turning of her body, in the slight movement of her silver fan, in the tilt of her head. She seemed to inhabit a world of sorrow, of loss, of longing for her lover. As I watched her moving interpretation of "sorrow deeply imagined," I thought of Yeats's haunting question: "How can we know the dancer from the dance?"

"This is not easy to do," Tomoko said of Ouka's performance. "It takes about three years of study to even approach what this dancing should look like."

My heart sank at the thought of dancing under Ouka's watchful eye, not to mention the eyes of Michi and Tomoko. Of course my first hurdle was to get the blood circulating in my legs again after spending twenty minutes in a kneeling position. *A profile in courage,* I thought, as I attempted to rise from my sitting position on the floor. Miraculously I made it. I climbed onto the stage and positioned myself next to Ouka, who handed me a small painted fan.

The music started and for the next thirty minutes I tried to follow Ouka's slow, graceful movements. But after ten minutes of trying to imitate the effortless skill of her hand and arm movements—particularly those involving the silver fan—and the delicate tilting motion of her head, I realized it could take thirty years for me to reach an approximation of what Wakayagi dancing should look like. Still, I continued on, surprised that I felt little embarrassment about my awkwardness. For some reason I felt protected in this environment where the mood of my hosts seemed completely nonjudgmental. Instead of shame, what I felt was a reawakening to the essential humility of learning. Being a student meant always looking up to someone wiser and always measuring yourself against that wisdom and knowledge. But being a humble student also meant experiencing the thrill that comes from adding a new piece to the puzzle of where and how you fit into the larger world.

When the lesson was over, we shared green tea and sweets shaped like chrysanthemums and maple leaves, in honor of the autumn season. Then Ouka introduced me to her mother and father and their adored pet terrier, all of whom posed graciously for a photo. As I looked through the lens at the four smiling faces—yes, even the terrier, a breed not always known for its sunny disposition, seemed to be grinning—I saw, or thought I saw, a family whose faces expressed something rare: contentment. Quickly, I snapped the picture, hoping to capture that look.

Before leaving we all stood on the narrow sidewalk outside the house, chatting in English and Japanese, although even with a translator I had no idea of who had said what. But it didn't matter. I played with the terrier—at my own risk, given the nature of the beast—and just talked while Michi or Tomoko translated back and forth. Perhaps the feeling I had of being understood was not so surprising in a family that had a dancer at its center, someone who communicated, as her parents did, with gestures, her posture, and above all her eyes.

Afterward, still wearing her yellow silk kimono, Ouka walked like a slant of sunlight with us to Michi's car. I found the neighborhood entrancing with its warren of narrow streets, which were lined with interesting shops and elegant *machiya*. As we walked the several blocks, neighbors called out greetings, shopkeepers bowed, teahouses beckoned.

So charming was the neighborhood—and so appealing was Ouka, who waved good-bye until our car disappeared down the long street— that I found myself thinking, *I could live here.* But before making any decision about moving from Baltimore to Nakagyo-ku, I needed to go back to the hotel and ice down my aching knees.

I had just started wrapping ice cubes in a towel when the phone rang. It was Naohiro calling from Tokyo. I had tried not to think about him, about our plan to meet in Kyoto in two days. I'd told myself: Compartmentalize. Focus on the purpose of the trip, on what you've come to do. Of course my thinking voice always interrupted such good intentions. *Fat chance*, it would say, summing up succinctly the odds against forgetting about Naohiro. Now he was on the phone, just three hours away by bullet train.

"*Kon-nichiwa*," he said, knowing I'd understand the word for "Good afternoon."

"*Kon-nichiwa*," I replied, pronouncing it just as he'd taught me to.

"Are you well?"

"Very well. Although I'm having a little problem. Too much kneeling on tatami for these American knees."

Naohiro laughed. "And how are you dealing with being the object of attention in a place where you look so different? This must be a new experience for you. I can't wait to walk with you through Kyoto where I look like everyone else and you don't. Are you prepared to be the exotic one for a change?"

I laughed, although it was something I'd thought about. "I'm sure it will take some getting used to. But even in Kyoto, you still will be the exotic one to me. That won't change. I wouldn't want it to change."

"If that is what you wish, I will do my best to see it never changes," Naohiro said. Then he spoke in Japanese, just one or two short sentences, which of course I didn't understand. I called him on it.

"You know it's not fair to speak in a language I don't understand," I said, faking petulance when in fact I loved hearing him speak Japanese, loved the way his voice shifted in timbre, becoming lower, more musical. "So tell me, what did you just say?"

"Ah, you will have to wait. I will tell you in person my thoughts when I see you on Friday. Do you think you can wait that long?"

"No. But I have no choice. I will just put you out of my mind for the next two days and concentrate on ikebana flower arranging."

"And I shall do the same," Naohiro said. "Forget to think about you and the many things I want to show you in Kyoto."

We talked for a few minutes more, flirting as we always did on the telephone, then reluctantly said good-bye. Naturally my mind was racing, wondering what Naohiro had said to me in Japanese and why he refused to translate it over the phone. It seemed to have something to do with my telling him not to change. A dozen crazy things went through my head, ranging from some kind of wry observation—which he was very good at—to some intimate personal declaration of the possibility he would forget what he said and have to make up something. Since waiting was not my strong suit, it would take all my powers of concentration to stay focused on my lessons while ignoring the static that was bound to be given off by my intrusive thinking voice.

The next morning I awakened to find a note had been slipped beneath my door. It was a handwritten fax from Michi:

> Dear Alice,
>   Today, we have arranged for you a meeting with a geisha and a maiko—an apprentice geisha—at Miyagawacho Dance School at 11 o'clock. Ms. Noriko Kasyua and WAK's interpreter (Ms. Kominami) are waiting for your coming. Please show the next paper (a map) to a taxi driver. When you have any troubles, please call me soon. Have a nice day.

I felt a little flutter of excitement, knowing that this meeting was actually going to happen. It was one thing to pass the occasional geisha or maiko on a street in Gion—the part of eastern Kyoto that is the setting for *Memoirs of a Geisha*—but this was different. After all, how many times in one's life does the opportunity arise to actually sit and talk with a woman who has led the kind of life that has inspired countless exotic fantasies among Westerners?

First, of course, I had to get to the Miyagawacho Dance School, a challenge much more difficult than it sounded. I had learned this the hard way after venturing out a few times on my own, only to find myself hopelessly lost. After all, how does a stranger find her way around a city where most of the streets have no names? And where the ones that do— mainly the major thoroughfares—have names impossible for a tourist to remember? I gave up the notion of using a guidebook after trying to follow these directions: "Concentrate on Shijo-dori between Yasaka Jinja and Karaum Eki as well as Kawara-machi-dori between Sanjo-dori and Shijo-dori."

To complicate matters further, the numbers on buildings and houses—if indeed they have a number—are meaningless; only Japanese postal workers know the rationale of why No. 52 is next to No. 854. And since my Japanese language skills consisted of about thirty basic phrases—things like *Good morning! Good evening! Do you serve cappuccino?*—

it was not possible to just stop someone on the street and ask for directions. The resulting confusion left me feeling like a two-year-old who,
upon venturing a block away from home, has no idea where she is,
where she wants to go, or where she came from.

Which is why on the morning of my meeting with a geisha I found
myself in the back of a taxi, clutching a note written by a hotel receptionist in hiragana, one of two Japanese character sets. It was a system
used by most non-Japanese-speaking tourists to Kyoto. I found the
concept eerily similar to one used in grade school when I handed over
to my teacher a note from Mother giving me permission to go on a class
trip. It was frustrating to find myself suddenly illiterate and in a country
where even my four years of Latin were of no use when it came to figuring out the roots of foreign words. The note I had just handed the taxi
driver supposedly instructed him to take his passenger to the Miyagawacho Dance School. But for all I knew, the note could say: "Take this
woman to River Kamo and throw her in."

One look at the driver quickly banished such thoughts. In his fifties,
perhaps, the driver wore a gray suit, black silk tie, and white cotton
gloves. His dark, silver-flecked hair was stylishly cut, and the wire-
rimmed glasses he wore added a certain gravitas to his appearance. He
looked like an Asian Richard Gere, I thought, or possibly a Silicon
Valley venture capitalist. In any case I felt in good hands, secure enough
to relax and enjoy the ride.

I leaned back and rested my head against one of the immaculate
white lace doilies that are a fixture in most Kyoto taxis. I was excited
about the meeting ahead of me but worried, too. What could we possibly talk about? I wondered. After all, my life was as foreign to these
women as theirs were to me. I knew I would be meeting a retired geisha
who now manages a maiko house where she is "mother" to a number of
young apprentice geisha, and also a maiko, as apprentice geisha are
called. In some ways I was more interested in the maiko. Why, I wanted
to know, would a young modern Japanese woman choose a geisha's life
over that of going to university, as many Japanese women now do? But
in a country where direct questions are considered rude, I was not too
optimistic about learning what really went on in the interior lives of
these women.

Still, I drew some comfort from knowing that my translator for the
day would be Etsuko Kominami. Etsuko-san, in her forties and married
to a businessman, was smart and modern and in previous encounters had

expressed her ideas in a very forthright manner—a result perhaps of living for seven years in Lebanon, Ohio.

Etsuko had made quite an impression on me a day earlier when I had shared lunch with her and Michi after my origami lesson and before our visit to the home of a Japanese collector of Asian antiquities. It was Etsuko who pointed out that native Kyoto people pride themselves on their refinement of manner and appreciation of aesthetic beauty. "But they are very hard to know if you are from somewhere else," she explained. Etsuko had moved to Kyoto from Tokyo after marrying. And it was Etsuko who took issue with the "geisha mystique" depicted in *Memoirs of a Geisha*. She dismissed the book as "soap opera" and said, "The idea of geisha represents the past."

Memoirs—translated into Japanese and published as *Sayuri*, the name of the book's heroine—elicited strong feelings, mostly negative, from both Michi and Etsuko. As women who are trying to expand the options open to Japanese women, they were particularly put off by the "geisha mystique" that still surrounds Japan, especially Kyoto. "Geisha are there only to serve rich men," Michi said.

But by the time we had finished our soup and salads, another reason emerged to explain their dislike of the geisha depiction in *Memoirs*.

Etsuko explained: "In the era that the book is set, most geisha were from poor families who sold them into geisha houses when they were just children. We don't like to think about that."

"But why would a young, modern Japanese woman want to become a geisha," I asked, "when so many other choices are open to them?"

"They want to wear beautiful kimono," Michi explained. "And they can meet many rich and famous persons, especially Japanese politicians and big company presidents. To us, they're like the bunny women are in America."

"You mean Playboy bunnies?" I asked.

"Yes, the bunny women," Michi said. The three of us looked at one another and then broke into smiles.

"We are here," said a man's voice, startling me out of my reverie about Michi and Etsuko. It was the taxi driver, announcing our arrival at the Miyagawacho Dance School in eastern Kyoto. Because I had allowed almost an hour for a trip that took twenty-five minutes, I was early and my escorts, Etsuko and Noriko, were not yet there. We were meeting at the dance school because it was where maiko came to take classes in music and dance. Mastering these skills, I had been told by Ouka, my dance teacher, is crucial if an apprentice wants to advance to geisha status. Completing the rigorous training can take longer than earning a university degree. Or at least it used to.

Nowadays, the training necessary to become a geisha—or *geiko*, as they are called in Kyoto dialect—is less demanding than it was in the years before World War II. Even so, the number of genuine geisha, schooled in the art of conversation as well as singing and dancing, is dwindling. Unlike pseudo-geisha, whose main function is to dress in kimonos and pose for photos with politicians and company chairmen, genuine geisha are hired by a man as a companion for an evening. Genuine geisha are not prostitutes, although some may have a special patron.

The number of maiko is dwindling, too. At least that's what a nice man at the Gion Teahouse Association told me. According to him, there are fewer than two hundred geisha in Kyoto who are still practicing entertainers and only fifty-two maiko. He had no figures for the number of retired geisha living in the city. In any case I was about to meet one of those retired geisha: Tomiko Sasaki, seventy-nine, now the "mother" at a nearby maiko house.

A soft musical voice disturbed my thoughts. "Hello, Alice-san," said Etsuko, who had just arrived with Noriko. "Shall we go in?"

We entered the building and walked past a group of stalls that seemed to be ticket desks, then moved into a large sitting room with sofas and tables; on one side were several desks where two or three women were working. After being served green tea we were told Tomiko would see us in a few minutes. I already knew exactly what retired geisha Tomiko would look like: a small woman, old, but still wearing an elegant silk kimono, porcelain makeup, and, arranged in her graying hair, two mother-of-pearl combs with dangling plum blossoms.

The real Tomiko turned out to be quite different. The woman we were waiting for appeared so suddenly that it startled me; it was as though she had been dropped down from some mysterious place reserved for retired geisha. But instead of the Tomiko of my imagination this one wore tailored black slacks and a boldly patterned apricot silk tunic. She looked twenty years younger than I expected. Her pale unlined skin was artfully tinted with normal makeup, and her eyes, behind the large glasses she wore, were unwavering and shrewd, like those of an astute businesswoman. Which is precisely what Tomiko turned out to be.

With Etsuko translating the introductions, Tomiko and I bowed to one another, then exchanged business cards. Etsuko explained that the retired geisha was not only a housemother to maiko but also the head of the corporation that runs the dance school. For some reason, I was not surprised—perhaps because something about Tomiko reminded me of my Camp Louise diving instructor, who, in retirement, became a wildly successful real estate broker.

But as I listened to Etsuko translate Tomiko's story of how she became a geisha, the businesswoman soon vanished, and in her place appeared a young girl, one who dreamed, as many young girls do, of a storybook future. In her soft mesmerizing voice, Tomiko spun a tale worthy of Scheherazade:

I was born in 1921 in Kyoto, a city famous for its legendary geisha district, Gion. In the 1920s and '30s, Gion was home to many glamorous geishas who attracted the attention not only of rich and famous men but also of many little girls in Kyoto. I was one of those little girls. Even in elementary school I longed to be like the beautiful, kimono-clad maiko who lived next door to me. My dream became reality when I began my apprenticeship at the age of fifteen. I lived in an *okiya*—a geisha house run with an iron hand by the "mother" of the house. I still live in the same house, a beautiful old wooden house near the dance school. But now I am "mother" to young maiko living there.

Like all maiko I took courses in music, dancing, and how to reveal just the right amount of bare wrist while pouring tea. I learned to apply the heavy white paste that turned my face into a porcelain mask, always leaving a border of untouched skin around the edge. And I learned to wear the lovely but heavy kimonos and long, confining obis while walking in the high wooden shoe called *okobo*. At first I found no pleasure in being a maiko. I had to practice my artistic skills from morning to night. Even after becoming a geisha, my life seemed to be nothing but practice, practice, practice. What I liked best about being a geisha was performing my artistic skills. Dancing and playing the stringed *shamisen* were my specialties.

I had a special patron who was twenty years older. At a certain age a geisha must have a patron, otherwise it's hard to continue being a geisha because of all the expenses. But my relationship was not strictly a business relationship. If it were only business, I couldn't stand it.

As Tomiko came to the end of her story, I noticed a beautiful young maiko enter the room. She was dressed in a black silk kimono embroidered sparingly with red ginkgo leaves; a dark red silk obi embossed with golden rabbits circled her waist. The effect was so elegantly understated that I wondered if Armani had moved to Kyoto and branched out into designing kimonos. The face above the kimono was no less beautiful: a perfect oval, dusted pale white, framed by luxurious dark hair pulled back into winged puffs from her face and arranged with combs in the traditional *ofuko* style.

The maiko's name was Satosuzu, and with one exception she embodied the glamorous geisha mystique. What marred this perfect picture was the global symbol of luxury swinging from her arm: a powder-blue Tiffany's shopping bag. Still, I found this accessory far less jarring than the Snoopy lunchbox I'd seen on the arm of a maiko walking in Gion.

As Etsuko translated, I was surprised to learn that Satosuzu had been drawn to the geisha profession for the same reasons as Tomiko had several decades earlier. Like the older geisha, Satosuzu said she had a strong longing at the age of fourteen to be a maiko. And like Tomiko, she found the idea of wearing "beautiful kimono" and learning "beautiful dancing" very appealing. Her parents did not "disagree" with her wishes, she said, and so she moved from her home near Tokyo to Kyoto and became an apprentice geisha.

Still more surprising to me was Satosuzu's declaration that, even after five years of training, she was not committed to becoming a geisha. "Only half of those who train as maiko go on to become geisha," Etsuko translated. "Some marry instead and some choose other professions. Satosuzu says she has no idea of what she would do if she changed professions."

Just as I was about to suggest to Satosuzu that she should move to New York and become a supermodel if the maiko thing didn't work out, a small elegant woman as delicate as a wren approached us. She was dressed in a black silk blouse and dark pants, and I watched her talking to Etsuko, who, after a few minutes, turned to me.

"Her name is Honjo," Etsuko told me. "She is a retired geisha who is a housemother, and she wants to know if you would like to see her house, which is just down the street." I found the invitation thrilling, especially since I had been told how difficult it was to be received in a maiko house. So thrilled in fact that I answered in Japanese: *"Hai, hai, hai!"* It meant "Yes, yes, yes" and was one of the few Japanese phrases I didn't have to stop and think about before saying.

As I walked with Honjo, Etsuko, and Noriko down the charming old street lined with wooden teahouses, a light rain began to fall. I watched as umbrellas opened up; my eyes followed the bright circles of red and yellow and white as they moved like a festival dragon along the length of the narrow street before me. When we stopped in front of one of the houses, a little dog greeted us from the doorway and Honjo waved us into the entry hall. After removing our shoes—being careful to leave them facing the door, as is customary if one wishes to enjoy good luck—we followed her up the stairs to the second-floor tatami enter-tainment room. I was surprised to see it was furnished with black leather sofas, a sound system, and a bar. Then Honjo showed us into another tatami room, this one elegantly spare, decorated only with paper shoji screens, sliding white cabinets, and a gorgeous deep red kimono embroidered with silver flowers and displayed on a wooden frame. On the wall next to it hung a painting of a lovely young geisha in profile, a pose that allowed the nape of her neck—considered one of a geisha's most erotic spots—to be exposed. The picture was of Honjo in her youth, Etsuko said.

Once we were all seated on the floor, our knees tucked under—I noticed that Honjo at fifty-nine had no trouble assuming this posi-tion—our charming hostess explained the layout of the house to us. Etsuko translated: "Kyoto houses like this are often called 'eel houses.' They are measured for tax purposes by the length of the house's front, but they can be surprisingly large inside. In this house are four stories. On the first floor is the kitchen, the second is for entertainment, the third floor is the living area, and on the fourth the kimonos are stored. The kimonos represent the riches of a teahouse and are often worth millions of yen."

I asked Etsuko why she had referred to Honjo's house as a "teahouse."

"Because in this room we sit in and the one next to it with the leather sofas, male guests are entertained with tea and music and conversation," Etsuko said.

A maid interrupted with tea and sweets. As she poured the tea,

Honjo surprised everyone by asking if we would like to see some old kimonos. I knew it was an unusually generous offer from a geisha and I sensed that Noriko and Etsuko were as delighted by it as I was. My impression was that these two educated and well-traveled Japanese women found Honjo and her world almost as exotic as I did.

The maid was dispatched to carry down from the attic a series of large white boxes, the glossy kind that an exclusive furrier might use to gift wrap a sable coat. Opening the first one, Honjo untied a ribbon circling layers of heavy white rice paper, lifted out a brilliant indigo-blue silk garment, and spread it out on the tatami-covered floor.

"This is a very rare tie-dye kimono, hand-embroidered with gold-and-white patterns," Honjo told us. She turned back the edge of one sleeve to reveal its pale green lining. "You can't find this kind of thing now." From another box she pulled out the long heavy obi designed for this particular kimono. "It is gold and silver with maroon and purple ties," she said, spreading the obi across the robe. "It is all very heavy when you wear together. Some weigh at least ten kilograms. Makes it very difficult to walk on high, thick shoes."

I did some quick conversion from kilograms to pounds—a useful skill left over from my cooking stint at the Ritz—and came up with ten kilograms equals twenty-two pounds. And yes, that could indeed make walking—or even standing—very difficult.

Over the next hour, several more boxes were carried down from the attic, each one containing a spectacular old kimono. I asked how many kimonos were stored in the attic, a room I would have given anything to visit. Honjo thought about it and said, "I do not know. Maybe hundreds of them." But she did know the value of the robes. "Ten years ago they were worth fifteen million yen. Probably more now." As I was trying to convert yen into dollars, Etsuko whispered, "That's about $160,000."

I was curious as to how such garments were cleaned. "They are taken apart and put into different pots to clean," Honjo said. "Then the kimono is sewn back together again."

Encouraged by her openness, I asked Honjo if she had read the Japanese translation of *Memoirs of a Geisha.*

"The answer is no," Etsuko told me, after a brief conversation with Honjo. "She has been told by other geisha not to read the book. They said if she reads the book, she will be offended. Other geisha have told her the book is dramatized too much for Americans. That is why she chooses carefully the person she wants to be interviewed by. Some exaggerate and some don't write correct things—just to attract attention of the reader. She says some writers write a twisted story."

It made me wonder why Honjo had chosen to speak to me. But for reasons of politeness and respect—not to mention fear of what the answer might be—I didn't ask.

As we rose to leave, a pretty adolescent girl with a scrubbed face and dark hair pulled back into a ponytail came racing up the stairs. She wore a short denim skirt and green polo shirt and could have been just your average Japanese teenager. But she wasn't. Katsura, seventeen, whose parents were teachers, had quit high school to come and live in Honjo's house and planned to become a maiko. *How different she will look in a year,* I thought, remembering the exotic elegance of Satosuzu, the maiko I'd met earlier. Some motherly impulse rose up in me suddenly and I wanted to take Katsura in my arms, as though holding her might keep her from entering a life that offered so few choices, choices that I certainly wouldn't want for a daughter of mine.

As we walked back to the car, I asked Etsuko and Noriko how they felt about the visit. It was my impression they'd never really shared this kind of intimacy with a geisha before. And yet these two modern women, whose lives and values were very different from Honjo's, seemed to have related to her quite easily.

"I was surprised by how comfortable I felt talking to her," Etsuko said.

"I felt the same," said Noriko, who lived what might be called an "anti-geisha" lifestyle; she is single, ambitious, owns her own home, loves her job in tourism, and is planning to vacation soon in Egypt by herself.

It didn't surprise me that neither woman asked for my reaction to the visit with Honjo. By now I had a new theory about the Japanese style of communicating. I was discovering it is not so much that Japanese women are uncomfortable *answering* personal questions—although they often make the answers seem less personal by shunning the word *I.* No, the thing that seemed unnatural to them, I decided, was *asking* personal questions.

After saying good-bye to Etsuko and Noriko, I took a walk in nearby Gion, the geisha quarter east of the River Kamo and the setting for *Memoirs.* This was my favorite district in Kyoto. With its mixture of art galleries and eel shops, its old-style wooden houses and fancy boutiques stocked with the latest Chanel bags, Gion was like the Left Bank of Paris. I also liked the mixture of old Japan and modern Japan. On one street where maiko in brilliantly colored kimonos and adolescent schoolgirls in drab uniforms passed one another with no acknowledgment, I noticed how the schoolgirls often stopped to snicker at the maiko behind their backs, imitating the way they walked in their high-platform wooden sandals, called *okobo.* Strange, I thought, since many of the same schoolgirls wore trendy Frankenstein-like boots with four-inch platform soles, occasionally even with their uniforms. Was there an ironic twist in this? I wondered. In the similarity between the school-girls' uncomfortable-looking boots and the treacherous *okobo* thongs that force a maiko to walk in short stuttering pigeon-toed steps?

I thought again of how puzzled I was about why a Japanese teenager would choose to be a maiko. Maybe it boiled down to a lack of options. While many young Japanese women were able to choose a professional career, many others—like Katsura, the high school dropout I'd met at Honjo's—did not have this option. One of the few choices for such women was to work for a large corporation as clerical workers or "Office Ladies." Such OLs, as they are known, serve tea to the men and file and type their reports. It is a thankless, boring, dead-end position with almost no opportunity for promotion. Given such a choice, was Katsura's decision to train as a maiko so puzzling after all?

By then the light was fading, narrowing into just a strip of brightness bordered by deep pink skies. A walk through Gion at this time of evening meant the sight of chattering Office Ladies headed home; it meant the smell of fish grilling in the *ryotei* restaurants and teahouses near the Gion Hotel; and it meant hearing the *click click click* of maiko in wooden sandals crossing the Sanjo Bridge, just as the fictional Sayuri did in *Memoirs.*

It also meant turning onto Shoji Street just in time to see the hundreds of lamps strung beneath its arcades suddenly light up like small moons. I gasped with pleasure. "One hundred views of the moon," I whispered to myself, thinking of the nineteenth-century series of woodblock prints by the Japanese artist Yoshitoshi. Moon-viewing was still a tradition in Japan. Along with painting and poetry, gazing at the moon was thought to nourish the spirit. The idea appealed to me and I planned one night to sit on the bank of the River Kamo viewing the moon just as Emperor Saga did eleven centuries earlier.

Michi and I often drove through the city at night, something I found quite enjoyable. Not only did our long drives give me a chance to see

Kyoto lit up, its streets busy with night people and nightlife, it seemed to bring out another side of the tireless workaholic Michi, who put in long hours, seven days a week. "We call her our Iron Woman," said Hisako, a WAK translator and teacher, when Michi's name was mentioned. Perhaps it was the dark cocoon of the car that allowed a more intimate side of Michi to emerge on our drives. Or perhaps she talked to me because I was an "outside person," a gaijin, who would not judge her by insider standards. Or perhaps—and this was the option I hoped was true—perhaps Michi felt a sense of connection with me, as I did with her.

On one such ride to my hotel from Michi's home, she began to talk about her family life. Earlier that night, at dinner with her family, I had caught a glimpse of how Michi lived: a comfortable house tucked into the picturesque hills of eastern Kyoto, two charming teenaged sons, a gorgeous white cat named Shiro, a little garden outside—this was the private life of Michi Ogawa. Her two older daughters, one of whom was in medical school, no longer lived at home. And neither, for the most part, did her husband; he had a university teaching job that took him out of town from Monday to Friday.

Dinner was a family affair, with Michi cooking while the boys and I sat at the kitchen table talking in English about school and sports and their future plans. As I watched the easy interplay between Michi and her sons, it occurred to me that Michi might not mind her husband's absence during the week. That feeling grew stronger on the ride back to my hotel.

As a driver Michi was fearless. In a country where many women do not learn to drive, she drove with all the daring moves of a New York City cabdriver. When I told her this she seemed pleased. "I learned to drive because my husband never learned," she said, not adding what I already knew: that it was Michi who chauffeured the entire family, including her husband when he worked in Kyoto, to and from school and university and everywhere else anyone needed to be. She also managed the household finances and proved to have a head for business. She found a way not only to purchase the house where her family now lived but, with help from her parents, to invest in a few other properties as well.

Her frugality expressed itself in other ways, too. Once when I complimented her on the way she dressed—her style was very original, an unusual combination of colors and accessories that expressed an artist's sensibility—Michi told me her clothes were all hand-me-downs from her sister. It was an answer that fit my profile of Michi; I couldn't imagine her spending time on buying clothes. It must also have helped out the family's finances, something a good Japanese wife would keep in mind, especially one with a large family.

"When I was an ordinary housewife, people admired me," Michi said as she drove through the city, her face illuminated under each neon sign we passed. "They said, 'You are a perfect Japanese wife.' My husband was pleased also. I did everything for him." But things changed when she started working two days a week teaching Japanese to foreigners, a choice that disrupted her family's routines.

"If my work was only to get money, I stop," Michi said, in what seemed like an apology for the changes brought about by her decision to work outside the home. "But I believe the work I want to do is for Kyoto City and all Japan. I had the feeling this was something I could do, and that I could do it by giving talented Japanese women a chance to show their abilities."

As she talked I studied her face, which I thought beautiful. Beneath the beauty was etched a look of stoicism; it was a look that suggested the acceptance of harsh truths learned by facing life's realities. But I also saw, or thought I saw, in that small, heart-shaped face the trait that defined Michi's character: her idealism and wish to do good. I worried a little about Michi—worried and wondered whether she was too vulnerable in a world not always hospitable to such goodness. But then I remembered Hisako's words: "We call her our Iron Woman."

On the morning Naohiro was to arrive I stood waiting in the hotel lobby. Always, just before I was to meet him after a long separation, there was a brief interlude when my uncertainty stepped center stage, like a character in a play. This was the moment when my thinking voice would go into its soliloquy, asking the same old questions about my relationship with Naohiro. *Where is this going? Where do I want it to go? Where does he want it to go? What if his feelings have changed since we were last together? What if mine have?*

The truth is, the questions were getting a bit tired. Naohiro and I already had answered most of them, both independently and with one another. Still, there was always the chance that during our time apart, Naohiro had experienced a change of heart. After all, he had been a widower for almost ten years and perhaps he'd met someone new, someone more suitable. A Japanese woman, for instance, with whom he could share his everyday life. Or perhaps he'd met someone in Paris— one of those stunning Frenchwomen with enough intellect and charm to make him forget about me. I wondered if he ever thought about me in this way, about the possibility I might have met someone else. It was strange, I suppose, but we never talked about such things.

But now as I watched Naohiro step out of the taxi and enter the hotel, my uncertainty disappeared. Everything about the man I saw walking toward me seemed reassuringly familiar. The slightly amused look that softened his dark eyes; the lithe body and athletic walk that gave him the look of a dancer; even the clothes he wore—black trousers and a black linen shirt open at the neck—summoned up such a strong feeling of connection that I immediately moved toward him, until we stood face-to-face.

Naohiro put down his briefcase and, as usual, greeted me in a formal way. "I am happy to see you again," he said, bowing slightly. "You look well."

"Thank you," I said, bowing back. "So do you."

"And do you enjoy your stay in Kyoto?"

"Very much. I find Kyoto to be all I hoped for in my childhood fantasies."

"Well, we shall try to update those fantasies a bit in the days ahead," he said, smiling.

I hesitated, then said, "Perhaps we could even add a few realities to the mix."

Naohiro laughed. "Reality is good," he said. "Even better than fantasy."

And with that exchange, all formality departed. Or as Naohiro once described this ritual of dancing around one another for the first few minutes: the ice had been broken.

It was National Culture Day in Japan, a holiday, and many Kyoto people and tourists were spending the day visiting temples and shrines. Naohiro had suggested we spend the afternoon making our way up the Sannen-zaka Slope, a steep, winding street of traditional pottery shops and teahouses that leads to Kiyomizu Temple. Located near Gion, the temple sits in a park, on a hill overlooking the city.

"It is one of the best ways to see Kyoto—from the large wooden deck of the temple's main hall," Naohiro said as we began to climb the narrow stone-paved section of the slope lined with pottery shops. "The deck is supported on an intricate seven-story-high wooden structure of pillars, and standing on it gives you a different perspective on the city. I remember being surprised to see how much greenery there is in Kyoto."

Our walk took us past an old *machiya* with a façade of delicate wooden grillework facing the street. I stopped to examine the thin carved slats that added an element of privacy to the ground floor of the house.

"In Kyoto the latticework you see was cut thinner than in other cities, a bow to Kyoto's taste for refinement," Naohiro said. "And the windows with the slits that are cut into the second-floor wall above are called 'cricket windows.' In the olden days, many samurai would march up these streets, making a pilgrimage to the temple. Those of the shop-keepers' class were forbidden to look at the samurai and, if caught doing so, could be arrested for impudence. The vertical slits of the cricket windows allowed them to secretly look down on anyone passing by."

As he spoke I thought of how, in my Nancy Drew days, I secretly viewed through the Venetian blinds of my bedroom window anyone passing by who seemed mysterious or out of the ordinary. I asked Naohiro, who once had planned to be an architect, to explain more about the old-style wooden houses.

"For a long time houses made of wood were considered ideal in Japan because they were warm in winter, cool in summer, and flexible enough to withstand earthquakes. By the 1800s the craftsmen who built these traditional wooden houses had refined their techniques to the highest level. Sadly, after the war, many of the *machiya* were torn down to make way for development. But I hear that now there are efforts to save Kyoto's historic wooden neighborhoods."

It was a fine day in early November—sunny but not too hot—and the streets leading up to the temple were crowded with vacationing families, flirting teenagers, groups of laughing Office Ladies, a number of *Chanelah* (women who favored expensive handbags by Chanel), and clusters of young geisha and maiko in brilliant silk kimonos, high plat-form sandals, and stark makeup. I suspected there were also a number of "fake geisha" among the strollers.

"Fake geisha?" Naohiro said, when I mentioned this to him. "What is that?"

"I've read there are several places in Kyoto that will turn you into a geisha for a day. And that many women visiting Kyoto—including

Japanese women—are willing to pay up to three hundred dollars for a geisha 'makeover.' It's a head-to-toe transformation. Painted white makeup, full silk kimono, split-toed socks, wooden sandals, and an elaborate wig made of human hair that I'm told weighs five pounds."

Naohiro smiled. "You seem to know a lot about this. Have you been thinking about becoming a fake geisha?"

"Would you like me better that way?" I joked.

He stopped walking and leaned in close to me. I breathed in the familiar pine scent that surrounded Naohiro. Then he put his head next to mine and whispered, "No, you are what I like."

"Say it in Japanese," I commanded.

He did. Then he asked, "Do you like it better in Japanese?"

"You know I love the sound of your voice when you speak Japanese," I said, "but I think I like knowing what you're saying a little bit more."

The view from the balcony of the temple was just as Naohiro described it: breathtaking. But I was uncomfortable standing on the seven-story-high deck, supported only by wooden pillars; it triggered my latent fear of falling. Although I'd once thought of this irrational response as a fear of heights, it was really my fear of falling *from* some high place that spooked me. Naohiro knew of my fear, which began when I was a child. Not only had we talked about it, he'd witnessed it more than once. Now, as he saw my reaction on the temple deck, he moved quickly to my side and put his arm around my waist, pulling me close. I was always surprised by Naohiro's physical strength. And I always found it thrilling. I don't know how long we stood there like that, not moving or speaking. What I do know is that being physically close to Naohiro was so enjoyable that even after my dizziness passed, I let many minutes go by before announcing my recovery.

After leaving the temple grounds we walked back down the sloping lanes to Shinmonzen Street in Gion, often called "Art Street" because of its many fine art and antiques shops. The shopkeepers on this historic lane of two-story wooden buildings had a reputation for being trustworthy, selling only authentic goods. Since Naohiro knew I was looking for a woodblock print by the artist Yoshitoshi, he suggested we visit some of the Shinmonzen Street galleries.

For the next two hours we popped in and out of various shops that specialized in painted scrolls, lacquerware, ancient netsuke (small carved ivory or wooden figures once attached to clothing), Imari pottery, painted screens, and woodblock prints. It was in one of the last shops we visited that I found a Yoshitoshi print I wanted to buy. Part of a series done by the artist in the late nineteenth century, it depicted a young samurai standing under a cherry tree on a moonlit night. I asked the shop owner several questions about the date it was printed, who printed it, and whether it was from the original woodblock or a later one. He answered all my questions and then wrote down the price of the print.

I noticed that while this was going on, Naohiro, who knew about such prints, seemed unsettled by some of the shopkeeper's answers to my questions and, particularly, by the price quoted me. He waited politely for the man to stop speaking and then addressed him in Japanese. Although I didn't understand what they were saying, I sensed the two were arguing. The shopkeeper grew visibly angry. Although Naohiro displayed little emotion, I saw he was angry too, a more dangerous anger, I thought, because it was so controlled.

Finally, Naohiro turned to me and said, "You should not buy anything from this man. Please, let us go now."

Outside, I asked him what happened. He explained that the shopkeeper had been dishonest in answering my questions and that the price he asked for the print was outrageous. "I hope you don't mind that I stepped in, but the man is a jerk and not to be trusted," he said. For some reason, Naohiro's use of the word *jerk* was so out of character that it made me laugh. When I told him why I laughed, he smiled, then said, "I apologize again for intruding, but sometimes you must let me take care of you."

I wasn't sure how I felt about this last remark. On the one hand I prided myself on running my own life. But there was another part of me that thrilled to the idea of letting Naohiro—every now and then—take care of me.

It was still too early for dinner but we both were hungry. So we walked to a small teahouse nearby where we ordered tea and a platter of tofu covered with miso sauce. Although I had thought off and on all day about Naohiro's promise to translate for me the mysterious comments he had made in Japanese during our phone call, I decided not to bring up the subject. At least not yet. Naohiro wanted to know all about my cooking classes in Paris—what we'd cooked, what Chef was like, more details about my classmates. Then he wanted to know about the Japanese women I had met in Kyoto. Then I wanted to know what his new apartment in Paris was like and how his work was going. Then the food arrived and we started to eat and he asked if I had gotten any better at using chopsticks, and I said no and asked him if he had gotten any better at making a good cup of espresso and he said yes.

Then, suddenly, he said: "You told me once that you were not the type of woman a Japanese man would like. That you were too direct, that Japanese men like women who are more reticent, less aggressive. Do you still believe that?"

I hesitated, surprised at the turn our conversation had taken. "I believe that *you* like me. But I still think most Japanese men would not."

"When you told me on the telephone that you wouldn't want me to change, I spoke in Japanese. What I said was that I *have* changed. I have changed because of you. In Japan it is not usual for a man and a woman to have emotional intimacy. But I believe I have learned to share such feelings with you."

Then I did a risky and completely un-Japanese thing. I leaned across the table and kissed Naohiro.

On the morning that Naohiro left, I climbed into a taxi and headed for my tea ceremony lesson. I hoped it would go as smoothly as my origami lesson, which produced several very professional-looking paper cranes. True, someone had helped me with the beak-making part, but so what? After all, I was a beginner and couldn't be expected to produce perfect little cranes. Besides, when doubts about my ignorance in Japanese arts threatened to sabotage me, I simply recalled the words of the great Zen teacher Shunryu Suzuki: "In the beginner's mind there are many possibilities, in the expert's few."

It was advice sorely needed during my lesson in woodblock print-making. Although I was only allowed to carry out a few of the stages of transferring the color from carved wooden blocks onto mulberry paper, I came away in awe of this particular art form. Each color to be printed, no matter how small the detail, required a separate block, which meant carving as many blocks as there were colors in a given print.

"This carving is very difficult," my instructor said, in what seemed a colossal understatement. "Fourteen to fifteen years is the most suitable time to learn engraving. Each print takes two engravers. One to do outline and a second to do detail."

He explained that the carving, usually on heavy cherry wood, was done from an artist's original drawing. "The engraver puts rice paper on top of drawing, then traces outline first. Outline most important. But only the artist's name appears on print." After the carving, another artisan uses a printing tool called a *baren* to complete the process from drawing to engraving to color print. It was this last step that was the focus of my lesson.

My assignment was to print the three sets of colors required by the first three engraved blocks. The trick was to get each color placed precisely on the paper so that the integrity of the drawing was left intact. Or, to quote my instructor, "No red in the black please." One of the challenges of using the *baren* successfully was the skillful application of just the right amount of pressure to each color. It was as difficult a task as any I'd been asked to perform in my brief fling as an art student many years earlier.

Still, my instructor's assessment of my efforts to get the colors in the right places on the paper was: "Not too bad." Although my work fell far short of a Hiroshige print, I took this as a high compliment, one that in later retelling to friends I would translate into: "Really quite good."

But despite these successes I was physically tired. Even after eight days, the time difference was still affecting my circadian rhythms. I grew sleepy at two in the afternoon, woke in the morning at three regardless of when I went to bed, and always wanted dinner when it was breakfast time and vice versa. *How did Madeleine Albright do it?* I wondered as I watched a documentary on cable television, one that featured the former secretary of state talking from Korea one day, Israel the next. Just where had Madeleine-san found the energy not only to negotiate with world leaders but also to select, day after day, just the right brooch for her suit jacket? Given my state of weariness, a lesson in tea ceremony seemed perfect. A relaxing cup of tea was precisely what I needed.

Naturally things did not go without a hitch. Even though I had given the taxi driver a map sent to me by Michi, he was unable to find the home of Kumi Suzuka, the tea ceremony instructor. Finally, after cruising up and down a lovely street of large houses set apart from one another by gardens without having any luck, the driver got out and began to knock on every door, asking for the Suzuka residence. As I sat waiting, two women, both wearing Western-style clothes, approached the taxi. One of them was Kumi Suzuka, who spoke no English, the other my translator Hiroko Maki. She explained why we had trouble finding the house. "The Suzuka family is very distinguished in Kyoto," Hiroko-san said, leading me into the house, "and there are eleven Suzuka families living on this road."

I followed the quietly gracious Kumi-san into the living room of the spacious, airy house whose décor combined Oriental rugs with a Western-style, upholstered sofa and chairs and large windows covered with the kind of heavy silk drapes and gauzy white curtains found in many American homes. Kumi, a lovely-looking woman in her early thirties, perhaps, was dressed simply in a long dark skirt and pale yellow sweater and wore white socks on her feet. She motioned that I should sit with Hiroko on the sofa. Hiroko then explained that the tea ceremony dated back to the twelfth century and was introduced from China as a monastic custom of Zen Buddhism. Over the years, three different schools of tea ceremony developed, and Kumi, whose name I discovered means "longtime beautiful," learned in the Ura Senke school. "She began when she was very young and still practices once a week," Hiroko told me.

As Kumi prepared to begin the formal ceremony, Hiroko explained the social significance of *chanoyu*, as the Japanese call the whole experience of tea culture. "The tea ceremony is a very good way to master manners and a very good way to communicate with other people in the polite way. It is a kind of preparation for marriage—like a manners school. In daily life we don't have so many chances to do the tea ceremony. It is only for special occasions with a special guest or in the New Year or on some delightful event that we make the powdered green tea."

Although I was delighted to be considered a "delightful event," my appetite for powdered green tea was near its tipping point, the result of too many special occasions that required drinking too many cups of the very bitter brew. Still, I knew that kindness was behind each cup of the foamy green tea—kindness and a desire on the part of everyone I met to see that I was properly fêted.

Kumi began the formal ceremony with a bow. She proceeded to the stylized placing of utensils on a tray, after which they were purified in two stages using a silk tea cloth. "Folding the tea cloth is very difficult and requires a lot of skill," Hiroko explained. Several steps later, the hot water was poured slowly into a bowl over powdered green tea; a bamboo whisk was then used to mix the water into a foamy consistency. But before we drank the tea, sweets were offered.

"We eat the sweets first to balance the bitterness of the green tea," Hiroko said. "Without the sweets first, the tea would be too bitter even for the Japanese." When the old beautiful tea bowl was filled with the foamy tea, she instructed me in the proper way to drink from it. "You must turn it counterclockwise twice before drinking and then wipe the spot where you drink."

I liked Hiroko right away. She was smart and friendly and, when not explaining the complicated tea ceremony, surprised me with her sense of humor. Hiroko was not from Kyoto but from Osaka—about an hour away by train—and had come for the day to be one of my translators. Her small intelligent face telegraphed great curiosity about everything, a trait she managed to express indirectly in the polite Japanese way. Later, when we walked through the affluent neighborhood, Hiroko told me that ten years earlier she had lived in Baltimore with her surgeon husband and two children. And not only that, she had lived only a mile or so from my neighborhood. Within minutes we were talking about streets we both knew, the markets where we shopped, and even the newspaper I had worked for—which she read every day while living in Baltimore. It was difficult, she told me, to return to Japan after living in the United States for two years.

"I was in culture shock when we moved back to Osaka from Baltimore. People thought of me as 'Hiroko' in America. It made me feel as though they saw me as myself. But here I was somebody's wife, my children's mother," Hiroko said with unexpected candor. "But gradually I began to see the merits of my country again, and I was proud of my cultural accomplishments."

That night while eating a bowl of shabu-shabu and rice in my favorite Gion restaurant, I thought of Hiroko's admission of being in "culture shock" when she returned to Japan. Her frankness had surprised me, but upon reflection I wondered if she could only have expressed such feelings to a foreigner, particularly an American woman. When, near the end of our meeting, I'd learned that Hiroko and her husband were fans of Dave Barry, as I was, our disparate backgrounds faded away and we began to laugh like schoolgirls over scenes from his book *Dave Barry Does Japan*.

How reassuring it was, I thought, to learn that no matter how far from home a person might travel, there is always the chance of meeting a kindred spirit. The memory of laughing with Hiroko about Dave Barry, I already knew, would remain with me long after I'd forgotten how to properly fold a tea cloth and whether the correct way to turn a tea bowl before drinking was clockwise or counterclockwise.

But to be honest, what I had really learned from Hiroko was something less formal than the rigid intricacies of the tea ceremony, something that can't be taught, except by example. In Hiroko, I saw a woman who had been altered in a very real way by her exposure to American life, so much so that it required a period of adjustment to her own culture when she returned to Japan. But somehow Hiroko had found a way to be a person of both cultures: proud of her Japanese heritage yet able to see the humor in a book that pokes fun at many of her country's customs. It was quite an accomplishment, this genuine embracing of a foreign culture, and in my mind I bowed with deep respect to Hiroko.

I stayed up late that night, writing a letter to Naohiro, telling him about Michi and how much I was drawn to her:

Dear (very dear) N,

I don't know why but when I'm with Michi I have the feeling of being in the presence of someone special, someone who is guided by fervent ideals and not by ambition or the need for recognition. She reminds me of Dorothea Brooke in the novel *Middlemarch*. Michi, like Dorothea, is an unsung woman who quietly goes through each day adding one small act of goodness to a mostly indifferent world. Every day it becomes clearer to me that Michi is held in high esteem by the women who know her.

At a seminar in nearby Kameoka, one woman who worked with her spoke to me of Michi's deep beliefs. "Michi believes every woman has a certain undiscovered ability," Umeda-san told me, "and she wants to provide these ladies with the chance to discover the knowledge they may not be aware of."

But Michi is a real person, not a saint, and I like it most when she talks about herself as a younger woman. One night while we were driving through the city, Michi told me of moving to Paris with her husband shortly after their marriage. She was very young and didn't speak French; her husband was at work all day and Michi was very lonely during the two years in Paris. It was an unhappy time. What saved her was meeting an old Frenchwoman who lived on the first floor of their apartment house near place d'Italie. "She taught me everything a young wife should know," Michi told me. "How to cook à la Française and how to iron. She ironed everything!" Michi said, laughing at the memory. Laughing, she looked like a young girl.

For some reason I can't seem to get this story out of my head. It's like a movie to me: I see a very young Michi, dressed simply in a crisp white blouse and navy blue skirt, standing at an ironing board while an old Frenchwoman with gnarled hands demonstrates the art of ironing a man's shirt.

Now as I write this, my mind wanders back to the time in Paris when your luggage was lost and you had no shirt for your meeting the next morning. So you washed out the shirt you were wearing and later I ironed it. Like Michi, I learned to iron from an old woman: my grandmother. You said you were impressed; I said, Don't be, it's not that difficult. But I think we were both secretly pleased by this small scene of domesticity, unusual for us.

On a rainy morning I set out alone for the famous Nishiki-koji food market, known as "the kitchen of Kyoto." Before leaving the hotel I fortified myself with two breakfasts: a Japanese one of fish, soup, and salad, and an American one of eggs, bacon, fried potatoes, and toast. I was quite hungry since my day had started early—at 1:43 A.M. to be precise—when an earthquake awakened me from a sound sleep. I sat up, on the edge of my bed, while the room shook. When it stopped I ran to the door and opened it, expecting to see a hallway jammed with people trying to escape. Instead I saw an empty corridor that was eerily quiet. So I went back to bed. The next morning I read in the newspaper that the earthquake had measured 5.7 on the Richter scale, not an inconsequential number. Still, most of the damage had occurred near the quake's epicenter in Mie Prefecture, an area about two hours away by car.

Perhaps because the earthquake made me realize that life is short and one must make every day count, or perhaps because taxis were scarce that morning, I decided to take the subway to the food market. I'd been avoiding the subway for reasons of fear: fear that I'd get lost and never be heard from again. Instead I found it surprisingly easy to navigate, almost as easy as the Paris Metro system. Actually, I was finding there were many comparisons between Kyoto and Paris. Like Paris, Kyoto is a city of small shops, some operated by the same families for more than a century. And like Parisians, the people of Kyoto have refined tastes in food, art, and manners. They also revere their history, which still plays a role in their daily lives, just as French history does in Paris.

As I walked from the subway to the Nishiki-koji food market, I was reminded again that a walk through Kyoto is a walk through more than ten centuries of Japanese history, including the present. Such a walk, however, is not always aesthetically pleasing. Sometimes the jumble and juxtaposition of old Kyoto versus new Kyoto startled me. The jarring experience, for example, of finding McDonald's golden arches just outside the large, glorious park surrounding the Imperial Palace was something that had to be taken in slowly. But I was learning to appreciate the value of the past and present existing side by side. I enjoyed the sight of a Starbucks café filled with young people near an old-style wooden storefront where noodles hung drying over long racks.

When I reached the market, a half-mile-long alley covered by an arched roof, I followed a group of chattering women inside. Instantly, I felt I had entered the beating heart of the city, a place alive with smells and sounds and the energy of shoppers out to find the best eels and merchants determined to attract such shoppers by artfully arranging their fish on fresh beds of ice. I heard the loud buzz of vendors and shoppers haggling, the flutter of birds flying through the covered space, and, somewhere, a dog barking. Merchants who wore dark coats wrapped with colorful sashes bowed—sometimes an entire family bowed in unison—whenever I stopped to examine a piece of fruit or a whole fish still swimming on a sea of ice. Often their stalls were decorated boldly with colorful lanterns or banners painted with black calligraphy, their food arranged in a way that would make the old Dutch painters of fruit and flowers gasp in admiration.

I couldn't shake the feeling I'd been here before, which, of course, was impossible. But the feeling persisted, following me for the rest of the day like a faithful old dog.

That night, while writing in my journal, the reason popped out in the words coming from my pen. "I think that even when we travel alone," I wrote, "we bring along a companion: our past. It accounts for the feeling I had today in the Nishiki-koji market. It was as though I were here in this new place, and at the same time walking through the old Lexington Market in Baltimore, as I did so many Saturday mornings ago with Mother. The newly washed stone floors had the same sharp smell of disinfectant, the unheated building filled with iced fish and meat was just as cold, and, most important of all, it was the same person who walked through both places."

Near the end of my stay in Kyoto, I attended a farewell dinner given in my honor by the Women's Association of Kyoto. Of course by now I thought of the women who had taken me into their homes and shared their culture with me as more than just a group that helps foreign tourists to understand Japan's culture. I considered them friends, women I had come to know and respect during my visit.

The potluck dinner, Japanese-style, was held at Michi's house. When I arrived by taxi, Michi and a few other women were waiting outside to greet me. As we walked to the front door I saw a hand-painted sign: *For Ms. Alice Steinbach. The Women's Association of Kyoto extends a warm welcome to you.* Beneath the words was a delicate watercolor rendering of apple blossoms. Inside the house a low table decorated with an American flag and a Maryland flag was set with platters and bowls of traditional Japanese food prepared by the women, one of whom had brought her three young children.

The only thing missing from this glorious evening was formality and ceremony. Instead, there was laughter and warmth and lots of picture taking. But mostly there was nonstop talking: about politics, children, husbands, careers, art, the relationship between the sexes, food, Hillary and Bill Clinton, and Rush Limbaugh. At some point I forgot that my new friends were Japanese. Or perhaps what I forgot was the reverse: that *I* was *not* Japanese.

As I looked around the room I reminded myself of Henry James's admonition that a writer must be "one of the people on whom nothing is lost." I wanted always to remember this night, this meal, these women. Years from now, I thought, when I have forgotten how to dance in the *Wakayagi* style and make origami cranes, I will remember Michi, Hiroko, Etsuko, Hisako, Tomoko, Michiko, Masumi, Fumiko, Noriko, Junko, Honjo, and all the others.

And when I am too old to remember their names, I will call upon the "person on whom nothing is lost" to remember them in other ways: The woman of the golden cat pins. The woman of the cherry blossom dessert. The woman who loved Dave Barry. The woman of the honest tongue. The woman of the shining intelligence. The woman of the beautiful kimonos. The woman who danced like a slant of sunlight. The woman who made flowers into works of art. The woman—the Iron Woman—who turned a vision into reality.

And, in memory, I will bow to each one with respect and affection.

The Mystery at the
Old Florentine Church

O N M Y W A Y to Florence, I had to change planes in London for a flight to Pisa. It was there, at the check-in counter, that I heard the words every traveler dreams of: "The plane to Pisa is not very crowded," the airline agent said brightly. "Would you like a courtesy upgrade to first class?" The unexpected offer so unnerved me that my first thought was: *Is this a trick question?* I was used to hearing the words every traveler dreads: "Your flight has been canceled, but if you run really fast through three terminals and there's not a long line at the gate, you might catch a plane leaving in five minutes."

Then my inner child took over—the one who still believes Meg, Jo, Beth, and Amy March really exist and are living somewhere in upstate New York—and I felt like jumping over the counter to give my benefactor a high-five. But I restrained myself—this was England, after all—and said simply: "Wow! Would I? You bet I would."

By the time we took off for Pisa I had become quite accustomed to the extra attention, the spacious seats, the French champagne, and the full English breakfast served on white porcelain plates. As I sipped my excellent coffee—a rarity on planes whether coach or first class— I imagined a scenario where real life imitated the airlines. What if one day someone suddenly asked if you would like a courtesy upgrade to a first-class life, including an apartment in Paris, a house in Tuscany, a loft in Tribeca, and a private jet to ferry you back and forth? Just as I began

debating in my mind the different answers that might be given to such an offer by, say, an existentialist and a Buddhist, the man seated next to me tapped me on the arm.

"Are you going to the Renaissance lecture series at I Tatti?" he asked, pointing to the book on my lap. It was a history of the Villa I Tatti, the former home near Florence of the art historian Bernard Berenson. It's now the Harvard Center for Italian Renaissance Studies.

"No," I answered, "but I wish I was. It sounds fascinating. Are you going?"

"Yes, I am. There are quite a few of us on the plane who have come down from London for the lectures," he said, in a voice as clipped and British as a privet hedge. Then he rattled off a list of speakers' names—none of which I recognized—followed by the subject matter of their very scholarly talks, also unknown to me. At the end he paused and seemed to be waiting for me to say something.

"I'm sorry but Renaissance studies are not my field," I said, trying to sound like the sort of person who has a field.

"Well, now, one can't know about everything, can one? Do you go to Florence for business or pleasure, then?"

I thought for a moment before answering. "Both, I guess. I've enrolled as a student at the British Institute. In a course called 'Art in Florence.' "

"Oh yes, I've heard of the Institute. I have friends who've sent off their teenagers to spend a year there before university. They learn Italian, see the great art, drink wine, fall in love, and for a year or so fancy themselves as characters from an E. M. Forster novel—*A Room with a View* and all that sort of nonsense."

"That's pretty much what I plan to do in the next few weeks," I said, not entirely in jest. "But I had a difficult time even finding a room in Florence, much less one with a view. In fact I have to change hotels during my stay, since none could offer me a room for the entire time." I asked if he thought the room shortage had anything to do with the conference at I Tatti.

He laughed. "My dear, everyone knows there is *always* a shortage of rooms in Florence." I studied his face as he spoke. Not an unattractive man, I decided, if your taste ran to a cadaver-thin face and slightly jaded look and if, like me, you were a huge Jeremy Irons fan.

"When were you last in London?" he asked, motioning the flight attendant to refill our champagne glasses. "Have you been to the new Tate gallery? It's frightful," he said, not waiting for my answer to either question. "Despise the building, you know. And the art too." He brushed an imaginary crumb from his beige linen suit. "Florence will be a relief after that. Too bad you're not going to the conference. Lovely place, I Tatti. Perhaps I could get you in." He reached into his pocket and from a black alligator wallet pulled out a card. Engraved on the thick ivory paper was his name: *Simon Langford, Art Consultant.*

His patronizing attitude was beginning to annoy me. For one thing I didn't want more champagne and for another I could have done without the crack about "everyone" knowing—everyone but me, that is—about Florence's permanent lack of rooms. I decided to ignore him and, hoping he'd take the hint, turned back to my book.

No such luck. By the time we began our descent into Pisa, I knew more than I wanted or needed to know about Mr. Simon Langford. What art he "abhorred," where not to eat in Florence, what galleries to avoid, what tourist attractions I should skip. He ended each list by saying something like "Haven't been there in ten years. Not worth it."

I could no longer resist a tip of my own. "Perhaps you should think about wiping the slate clean and starting over in Florence, so to speak. Things change, you know. You might be pleasantly surprised."

"That's what I like about you Americans. Off with traditions. On with the new. Full speed ahead." He said this in a critical way, as though the ability to change was a fault. Then, moving right along, he gave me some advice: "Next time you should think about staying at the Regency," he said. "It's first-rate. I never stay anywhere else."

I didn't tell Mr. Simon Langford that I was familiar with the very expensive Regency and knew it was out of my league. No doubt my "courtesy upgrade" had sent the mistaken message that I too was a Regency Hotel type of person. Just as he began to deliver another opinion on something he liked or more probably didn't, the seat belt sign came on and the captain announced we were about to land. Although I felt like standing and cheering about my imminent separation from Mr. L., I didn't. Instead, I pretended to be interested in his last-minute advice about where to buy the best leather goods.

After we landed, as I stood in line waiting to buy a train ticket to Florence, I saw him drive off in a sleek black sedan, a uniformed chauffeur at the wheel. In less than an hour Mr. Simon Langford no doubt would be at the Regency having a drink with friends while I would just be boarding the train. Real life, I thought, does not hand out courtesy upgrades. Or, at least, not always to the right person.

· · ·

My first hotel was tucked away on a reasonably quiet street between the tourist-packed Piazza della Repubblica and Via Tornabuoni, high-rent home to such designer shops as Hermès, Gucci, and Armani. Ten years earlier I'd been given the gift of a two-night stay at this hotel, which, like the Regency, catered to guests who regularly flew first-class but not on courtesy upgrades. My memories of its charm and peaceful-ness had never faded; to me it was quintessential Florence. On a whim I'd faxed the hotel several weeks earlier to ask for a rate on their least expensive single room. Then I promptly forgot about it, never expect-ing they'd have an available room, much less one I could afford.

Three days later, I received a return fax. It was written in the exces-sively polite and flowery style so typical of Italians writing in English. *My Dear Madam, It is with the most extreme pleasure that we offer you . . . looking forward to your kind visit with the highest anticipation . . . with gratitude and every good wish . . . most sincerely yours.* In between the flattery and politeness—a style that always inspired me to new heights of verbal ingratiation in my response—the hotel informed me that, yes, a small room on the top floor was available in my price range for all but two nights of my stay. This meant I would have to move to another room in the middle of my visit and then move back.

Despite some trepidation about what exactly "a small room on the top floor" might mean, in the end it wasn't even a close call. Not only did I have feelings of the most extreme pleasure and highest anticipa-tion for this hotel, I also knew it was near the piazza where one of the British Institute's two centers was located. I faxed back my reservation immediately and then reserved the two unavailable nights at a nearby hotel.

Now, as the taxi driver from the train station handed my luggage to the hotel's doorman, I had a moment of anxiety. Would it be as I remem-bered it? I stepped inside and saw instantly that the answer was yes, yes, yes! The lobby, even in the heat of a stifling late May morning, was cool and lovely; its polished terra-cotta floors and high ceilings held up by stone columns seemed instantly to lower the temperature by half. With its fresh flowers, large comfortable sofas covered in muted green velvet, and museum-caliber paintings hung on pale walls, the room made me feel as though I were in a private palazzo, not a hotel lobby. No tour groups milling around here, only a few relaxed-looking people reading the morning newspapers. I headed for the reception desk, tucked discreetly out of sight in a small space near the two elevators.

"Ah, Signora, we have been expecting you," said the receptionist, who seemed to be waiting alertly for my arrival. "Welcome to Firenze. While your room is being prepared, may I suggest you relax in the lobby? I will see that someone brings you a coffee."

Delighted to have someone take charge of my life, at least temporarily, I did what I was told. As promised, a *caffè latte* arrived on a little silver tray, along with two small almond biscotti. As I sat sipping coffee and looking through the floor-to-ceiling leaded glass windows at the narrow street outside, I felt sublimely content.

A young bellboy interrupted my reverie. "Madame, your room is ready," he told me. "Your luggage has been taken upstairs."

I followed him into the elevator, then down a hallway to the door of my room. He turned the key, we entered, and suddenly it was as though I were in a different hotel: the room I saw was completely devoid of charm and so small that if the bathroom door was open, the closet door had to be shut. The one window in the room overlooked the busy Via Strozzi, a street that led through the city's historic center and was a magnet for the endless stream of *motorini*, the air-polluting, noisy mopeds that are the bane of Florence. Like giant gas-fueled mosquitoes from another planet, they buzz everywhere, threatening to run down any pedestrian foolish enough to cross the street.

The room was not what I had hoped for, but I decided to live with it. It wasn't so bad, I told myself, looking around at the mismatched collection of furniture. *Liar,* my thinking voice hissed back. *It is very bad. Molto badissima!* Then, without bothering to unpack, I gathered up my handbag and camera, anxious to leave behind the room with its hissing voice. I knew they'd both be waiting for me when I returned.

Florence is a city that had always defeated me. Even after several visits, Florence remained nothing more than a picturesque city that contained many of the world's greatest art treasures. My memories of it were like looking at a rack of picture postcards. Michelangelo's *David.* The sturdy Ponte Vecchio that straddles the river Arno. The Cathedral of Santa Maria del Fiore, crowned with Brunelleschi's rust-red dome. Botticelli's *Venus.* The Boboli Gardens. Verrocchio's *Noblewoman with Bouquet.* The Piazza della Signoria and the impossibly crowded Uffizi art gallery.

Unlike Paris, or even Venice—a destination many tourists think of as a day trip to a museum rather than a living city—Florence had never revealed itself to me as a real place. In Paris and Venice I had a sense of the daily rhythm of people's lives, of the neighborhoods where they shopped and worked and lived. In Florence it was as though the Florentines closed their shops and went home to some other city, one I was unable to find. A part of me suspected I had chosen to attend the British Institute not only for the pleasure of studying the city's art treasures, but to see if I could catch a glimpse of the hidden Florence, the one behind the tourist-attraction façade.

Now as I set out for Piazza Strozzi and the fifteenth-century palazzo that houses the British Institute's Language Center, I was reminded of how much Florence reflects its medieval history. While the art sequestered in museums, churches, palazzi, and out-of-the-way cloisters may reflect the beauty of the Renaissance, the somber, stone, fortress-like palazzi and museums give the city—at least its historic center—a Gothic look.

Although it was Saturday and my classes didn't start until Monday morning, I wanted to pinpoint in advance the building where I was to meet my professor and classmates for the first time. According to my map, all I needed to do was walk to the Via Strozzi from the hotel, then cross the street to the piazza. A snap, or so I thought, until I saw the torrent of vehicles streaming down the one-way street. To get to the other side I would have to dodge mopeds, taxis, bicycles, vans, and cars, all operated by drivers determined never to offer an opening for a terrified pedestrian to dart through. Crossing most streets in Florence, even those with pedestrian crosswalks or traffic lights, was like trying to make your move into a game of double Dutch jump rope: I stood alert at the curb, swaying back and forth, trying to gauge the safest moment to enter the traffic. The moment came; I took it and, holding my breath, dashed to the other side.

From my pocketbook I pulled out the schedule for Monday, which had been sent me by e-mail. First came the orientation meeting at ten in the morning, then a conducted tour of "Florence, Birthplace of the Renaissance." My instructions were: "Meet at reception, British Institute Language Center, Piazza Strozzi 2 (4th floor)." It sounded simple enough. But after wandering about the small piazza for half an hour I could find no sign that said "British Institute" and no building numbered "2." What I did find was an open door leading into a massive stone building; I decided to go inside and ask for directions. Immediately I found myself in the middle of swirling galaxies of dust and the deafening noise of workmen hammering away in what seemed a major structural renovation. Shouting over the noise, I asked in makeshift Italian if anyone knew the location of the British Institute.

Most of the men just shrugged and continued working, but one young man, a carpenter, stepped forward and said, "You must cross the Piazza and go right to the Palazzo Strozzino, where the entrance is very small and hard to find."

He was right. Even with his directions it took another five minutes to find the entrance to the British Institute, which, as it turned out, closed early on Saturday. Still I had accomplished my mission: to assure myself that on my first day I would arrive on time, an achievement I hoped would allow me to make a *bella figura*, a good impression.

But now I was left with no plan for the rest of the day. So I began to walk aimlessly through the narrow streets leading to the elegant Via Tornabuoni, a street where modern designer shops and cafés have been successfully installed in fine old Renaissance buildings. As I walked I memorized the street names, drawing in my head a map of the city. Unlike the enchanting names given to many of the *calli* in Venice—my favorites are the Alley of the Curly-Headed Woman and the Filled-in Canal of Thoughts—the streets in Florence seemed to be named mainly after historical figures and events.

After an hour or so of window shopping and browsing in art galleries and bookstores, I stopped at Giacosa, a caffè-pasticceria that had the look of a place I could learn to like a lot. But even though my intuition was right—Giacosa had great *caffè latte* and a clientele of lively Florentines—something was wrong. For some reason, my usual routine of browsing and walking with no destination in mind wasn't working for me. To be honest, I felt dispirited and disappointed by Florence. At a little before noon the city was already beastly hot, the traffic unbearable, and the tourist attractions logjammed with waiting lines of irritable visitors. I was beginning to feel that everyone in the city was either a tourist or a Florentine who was part of the tourist juggernaut. If only I could think of a calm neighborhood to escape to. Some peaceful retreat on the order, say, of Campo San Barnaba in Venice or square des Peupliers in Paris. But where in Florence was there such a place?

By this time I was approaching the Ponte Santa Trìnita, a bridge that crosses the Arno into the Oltrarno, a neighborhood on the south side of the river. *That's it!* I thought, remembering someone had described Oltrarno as being to Florence what the Dorsoduro district is to Venice: a neighborhood where you could find real Florentines going about their daily lives. It was, as I recalled, a neighborhood of serpentine cobblestone streets lined with old-fashioned artisans' workshops, apartments, and family-run shops that could repair, rebuild, or reupholster anything from centuries-old lace to antique chairs. Suddenly Oltrarno beckoned to me. I almost ran across the bridge.

For the rest of the afternoon I wandered through Oltrarno's lively little streets, listening to the hammering of craftsmen in their *bottegas* and popping in and out of artisans' shops where I watched furniture makers and book restorers work their magic. When the temperature rose high enough to turn the air into undulating waves of heat, I bought a huge cup of pistachio gelato and sat eating it in the dappled shade of Piazza Santo Spirito, beneath a large rustling tree. Later in a café a cute waiter suggested a version of cappuccino unfamiliar to me. "*Cappuccino scuro,*" he said. "It's made with more coffee and less milk than regular cappuccino. It's for people who like to taste the coffee." After serving my *cappuccino scuro,* he stood waiting for me to take my first sip. When I did, a look of joy must have crossed my coffee snob's face. "Ah, I knew you would like it," he said, giving me an endearing thumbs-up.

It wasn't until I stopped to look at an antique watch in a shop that I realized it was almost six o'clock. And it wasn't until I settled myself with a glass of Chianti and a plate of antipasto on the terrace of the nearby Hotel Lungarno, that I realized something else: I'd completely forgotten to reconnoiter the British Institute's library and cultural center, located nearby in the Palazzo Lanfredini, an early sixteenth-century palace. It struck me as a good sign, this spontaneous elision of duty and pleasure.

As I sat enjoying the spectacular view of the Ponte Vecchio and the domes and bell towers across the river, I thought about Florence. Not Florence the city but Florence Harris, my best friend all through grade school. This is what we dreamed of doing, Florence and I, from the time we read about Florence—the city—in a picture encyclopedia at the Enoch Pratt Free Library in Baltimore.

We were in fifth grade and trying to decide where we would live after graduating from college. From that day on, right through the sixth grade when we moved on to junior high school, we planned—plotted might be a better word, since we were heavily under the spell of Nancy Drew—every detail of our lives in Florence. Often these conversations would take place on unauthorized visits to a nearby "island"—more like a small raised mound of dirt and sand in the middle of a narrow rocky stream—where we'd sit and eat our favorite potato salad sandwiches.

We'll study art and become famous painters, Florence would say.

And we'll have a little shop where we sell our paintings and hold cocktail parties, I would say.

And we'll have all our friends in Miss Weller's class come visit us. Except for Bunny and Wanda, she would say.

And we'll live in an apartment with a balcony near the bridge that sells lots of gold jewelry, I would say.

I'd almost forgotten this brief but intense childhood dream. Now as I sat looking at the Ponte Vecchio, I remembered everything. If I squinted—just hard enough to turn the bridge and its jewelry shops into a soft blur—I could see the two of us writing down notes in a spiral binder, Florence's wiry red hair brushing the paper we leaned over. We were writing a mystery story about two teenage girls in Florence. So far we only had the title, "The Secret of the Gold Coin in the Crumbling Bridge," and the heroines' names, Alicia and Florencia. That was the same summer we spent all our time in tap class at the YWCA trying to learn, as Nancy Drew had, how to tap-dance in Morse code.

I imagined Florencia here, sitting opposite me now, speaking the perfect Italian we both planned to learn, mostly so we could read art books and interrogate suspects about secret gold coins. I imagined saying: *It's just the way we pictured it, isn't it?* And Florence replying: *I knew we'd get here one day.*

But not together, I thought, as I finished my wine and asked for the bill. Florence, who died too soon, eventually did open an art gallery and framing shop in Baltimore and, for all I knew, may have visited Florence at some point. And I did work in an art museum, although one far away from Florence. But that's the closest we came to realizing our dream of being together in Florence.

Until tonight, that is, when the two of us sat speaking perfect Italian on a veranda overlooking the river Arno.

On the morning of my first class, after hearing on television that the temperature might hit what I calculated to be ninety degrees, I dressed carefully, as if I were on my way to the Sahara Desert instead of the British Institute. Other than possible heat stroke, I really didn't know what to expect. All I knew was that the class was scheduled to spend the morning walking through "Florence, Birthplace of the Renaissance" and, after an afternoon free to do whatever we wished, to return to the Institute's cultural center for an evening lecture on "Gothic Cathedrals of Tuscany." I'd spent much of the night before lying awake, my mind racing with unanswered questions. Would the class be large or small? Who would teach it? Would there be reading assignments? How much of our time would be spent cooped up in a classroom? Would everyone else speak Italian? Would... *Enough already*, commanded my weary thinking voice. *Go to sleep!*

I paid attention. After all, I wanted to be *sharpissima* for my first day at school. But just to be on the safe side I got up and took half a sleeping pill.

Now, as I entered the British Institute, an attendant on the ground floor directed me to a small, narrow elevator that was definitely not for the claustrophobic. It lurched slowly past the first three floors, then stopped with a frightening shiver at the fourth floor. There, a waiting receptionist greeted me. "Dr. Hoch is meeting the rest of the class," she told me. "She'll be out shortly."

Was I late? I wondered. Or was the rest of the class early? As I rummaged through my purse to check the scheduled time for the orientation meeting, a British-sounding woman's voice said: "You must be Alice. Welcome to Florence. I'm Adrian Hoch. We've been waiting for you." I looked up and saw an authoritative-looking woman with clipped dark hair and excellent posture. She led me back through a hallway to another narrow hallway where a woman—in her thirties, perhaps—sat waiting in a chair.

"This is your classmate, Ilene," Dr. Hoch said. "Ilene, this is Alice."

We were, it seemed, a class of two. Which suited me fine. In fact, I was delighted. The idea of being trotted around to museums and churches with a lot of other people was something that had never appealed to me. The ratio of two students to one teacher would be the equivalent of having a private tutor, the way wealthy young British men used to in the eighteenth century when taking the de rigueur Grand Tour of Italy.

It was a perfect analogy, I thought, as the two of us followed Dr. Hoch—"call me Adrian," she told us—to the elevator and then outside to begin our walk through Renaissance Florence. Adrian began by explaining the history of the Piazza Strozzi, the area that had confused me in my earlier search for the palazzo that housed the Institute. It turned out that Piazza Strozzi was a two-palazzo square: home to the massive Palazzo Strozzi, a Matterhorn of a building with stone walls that rise straight from the street, and to its mini-Matterhorn offspring, the appropriately named but hard-to-find Palazzo Strozzino. The smaller palazzo, begun in 1458 and completed between 1462 and 1465, was where the Strozzi family—second only to the Medicis in wealth and importance—lived while overseeing construction of their big palazzo across the street.

Adrian stopped to point out the rough-surfaced stone used in the lower story of Palazzo Strozzino. The plainness of its masonry gave the palazzo the appearance of a massive log cabin, but one built with stones rather than wood. "This rustic, less sophisticated approach was used by the wealthy so as not to arouse envy," she said. Envy, it seems, could turn friendly rivals into enemies, something quite dangerous in those Machiavellian times or, come to think of it, in current times. I'd seen it happen more than once when a war of home improvements had erupted in my own neighborhood. "But even wealth couldn't make such houses comfortable," Adrian added. "They were hot in the summer and cold in winter. Particularly the children's rooms and the kitchen, which were on the top floor."

Adrian then turned our attention to the huge Palazzo Strozzi across the piazza. "This palace was begun in the 1480s and completed in the 1600s. It is the most famous and largest in the city. In fact, it is so big it was never entirely completed. Inside there is a large walled garden area." She pointed to the stone walls projecting from the ground level. "The Strozzi were private bankers, and the petitioners sat waiting on these stone walls outside the palace." And in keeping with the zeitgeist of fifteenth-century Florence, this grandest of all palazzi went out of its way to avoid "envy" by using heavy rustication in its rough-hewn masonry façade.

Next, we were off to the nearby Piazza della Repubblica, a large square described in one of my guidebooks as "hideous" and "not loved by most Florentines." Although it was only the end of May, the infamous summer heat had already settled into the Arno Valley. The unrelenting sun made walking even a short distance an act of valor; sitting and standing was only a little less daunting. Adrian, who was not immune to the heat, offered a suggestion as to how we might keep cool or, failing that, avoid having a heatstroke.

"Do we all agree we should stay in the shade and stop for cold drinks as much as possible during our walk?" she asked.

Right then and there I knew that Dr. Adrian Hoch was my kind of professor. I already liked her style. For one thing she did not have the annoying habit, as some instructors do, of cramming her students with information overload, although clearly she knew her stuff. Instead, Adrian made fifteenth-century Florence come alive by weaving together stories about the art and architecture and people who once inhabited a city that, for a period of time, was as great as any in history.

"This once was the site of the Roman forum," Adrian said as we stood in the Piazza della Repubblica. "And later, from the middle 1500s through 1860, the ghetto bordered the square on its northern side."

I interrupted Adrian to ask a question: Why does my guidebook describe the square as "not loved by most Florentines"?

"That's true," she said, explaining that at one time this area had been a crowded, colorful neighborhood that included an artisans' center, the Jewish ghetto, the red-light district, and the Mercato Vecchio, a busy market center that for centuries attracted farmers and townspeople and traveling traders. Then in a burst of misguided urban improvement the entire area, along with a big chunk of Florentine history, was demolished in the late 1800s. In its place rose the sanitized, commercial Piazza della Repubblica, a square that instead of charm offered tourists a shopping area and two large noisy outdoor cafés.

Happy to leave the Piazza della Repubblica behind, Ilene and I sprinted after Adrian, who, although short and compact, walked at a fast clip. Over the next hour we worked our way through the city's historic center until we reached the Mount Everest of Florence: the Cathedral of Santa Maria del Fiore, or the Duomo, as it's commonly known. Famous for Brunelleschi's stupendous, physics-defying dome, the cathedral is one of the most-visited tourist attractions in Florence. In fact, the swarms of tourists, many of them young backpackers, seemed a permanent part of the structure. As they sat on the cathedral steps talking on cell phones, punching away at Palm Pilots, eating, sunbathing, and sleeping, they formed an obstacle course for anyone wanting to enter the cathedral. Permesso, permesso, permesso, the tourists whispered like a mantra, as they tried to avoid stepping on someone or something. But it wasn't just the tourists; a carnival atmosphere prevailed as vendors hawked T-shirts stenciled with an image of Michelangelo's David wearing sunglasses and artists tried to sell their wares by setting up easels near the horse-drawn carriages available to tourists. As Ilene and I followed Adrian through the crowds gathered around postcard stands and food kiosks, I listened with only half an ear. I was counting on learning about the Duomo in a more private tour later in the week.

More pleasant was the walk from the Duomo to the Piazza della Signoria, the square that for centuries served as the center for Florence's civic life. As we strolled in the shade along the narrow Via del Proconsolo, we passed small neighborhood markets and bakery shops, where people went about their daily errands. Inside one shop, I watched a woman select a loaf of coarse bread, ripe tomatoes, black olives, and red onions—perhaps for a lunch of *pappa al pomodoro*, a tomato-bread soup. On the narrow sidewalk a woman called out *"Ciao, Natalia"* to an acquaintance. The two women stopped and began an animated discussion. Chatting, laughing, gesturing, the women seemed oblivious to the pedestrians forced to step around them out into the oncoming traffic.

I tried to imagine a similar scene on a Paris street, but I couldn't. You would never find Parisians blocking the sidewalk while chatting away; they preferred conducting their tête-à-têtes in crowded cafés while drinking an *express*. Still, it was one of the things I liked about the Italians: the way their familial approach extended to life in general, making the sidewalk part of their house and the stranger on the street part of their family.

As Adrian, Ilene, and I approached the Bargello Museum, the pleasant street began to branch out into some of the most tourist-clogged arteries in Florence. Then suddenly we were in the crowded Piazza della Signoria, a place that perhaps more than any other is the repository of Florentine history. We followed Adrian through the dizzying crowd of tour groups and schoolchildren to the shady Loggia della Signoria. As we stood in this elegant structure, which was built in the 1370s to provide a dignified setting for the city's elected officials to watch public events, Adrian gave us a fascinating historical overview of the famous Piazza della Signoria. As I listened to Adrian, the restless ghosts of past Florentines seemed to swirl about in the crowded square. Dante. Michelangelo. The Medicis. Vasari. And Savonarola, the fanatic monk who induced his followers to burn their worldly goods in the original Bonfire of Vanities and then was himself burned at the stake in this very square.

When we left the city's historic center to walk along the river Arno, it took a few minutes to leave behind the Medicis' world and adjust to contemporary Florence. I looked at my watch; it was twelve-thirty. Traffic on the streets was thinning out as shopkeepers and workers went home for their midday meal. Although Adrian still seemed as brisk and energetic as she had three hours earlier, Ilene and I were wilting. Ilene, of course, was entitled to wilt; she'd arrived in Florence only that morning and had come straight to class. Her plan, she said, was to go back to the hotel and sleep until our six o'clock lecture that evening. I liked Ilene. She was easygoing and laid-back, and she didn't ask Adrian a million questions about every detail of every place we visited. When she did ask a question, it was always an interesting one.

As the three of us were about to part, I asked Adrian if she knew anything about the Borgo Pinti.

"When I first moved to Florence, I lived there," she said. Adrian, it turned out, was not British after all; she was an American who'd lived in Florence for about ten years. I wanted to ask her more about the Borgo Pinti, but I sensed Adrian preferred to keep her private life private. Besides, she seemed in a hurry to get to the library to work on a research paper.

That was okay with me; I had my own research project waiting. Although it was an unexpected digression that could turn the purpose of my trip on its head, my plan was to see what I could find out about the man I'd met a day earlier on Borgo Pinti.

But first I headed for Caffe Giacosa to have some lunch.

The accidental meeting that threatened to undercut my focus on Florentine art had happened on my second day in Florence. It was a Sunday, and I was having a hard time figuring out what to do. Sunday, in my opinion, is the trickiest day of the week for people traveling alone; for some reason, it seems to heighten the potential for loneliness. As a result I have learned from years of solo traveling to find creative solutions to the problem of Sunday. But on this particular Sunday morning I was striking out. Despite the stacks of brochures and calendars spread out before me I could find nothing open except all the usual suspects: the museums, churches, and historic monuments that would be even more crowded than on a weekday.

Just as I was about to give up and take a bus to the nearby town of Fiesole, a listing in one of the calendars caught my eye. The brief entry read: *Bonsai and suiseki garden. Borgo Pinti, 74. Open every Sunday 9–13. Free.* It sounded perfect. I looked in my guidebook to see if the garden was listed. It wasn't. But there was a small reference to Borgo Pinti: "The most attractive of the medieval streets in Florence is the *Borgo Pinti*, at the far end of *Via degli Alfani*. Tall, narrow, highly picturesque but faintly claustrophobic, it runs all the way from the northern gates to the Santa Croce quarter."

I was both enchanted and puzzled by this description. I found myself picturing not a street but a person. *He was tall and narrow and faintly claustrophobic.* It sealed the deal; I had to go there. I drained the last drops of my cappuccino and headed for the concierge to ask directions.

"I have never heard of such a bonsai garden, but here is Borgo Pinti," he said, circling on the map a long street in Santa Croce. "And I do not know the location of number 74 Borgo Pinti. But it would be my pleasure to call the telephone number to ask."

After several attempts to get through, the concierge told me that yes, the garden would be open until one in the afternoon and that any taxi driver could take me there. "A ride of about ten minutes," he added.

I hopped into a taxi and showed the driver in writing where I wanted to go, a trick learned in Kyoto. Then I leaned back and studied the route we were taking to Santa Croce, an old neighborhood that remained much the same as it was in the fifteenth century. At first glance, the long narrow streets with their stern rows of almost windowless houses seemed more boring than "highly picturesque." At one point we passed the Regency Hotel, home to the annoying Mr. Simon Langford. Just to be on the safe side I ducked my head down below the taxi's windows. A few minutes later, we passed the hotel again. We seemed to be going around in circles.

"*Scusi, dov'e Borgo Pinti?*" I asked the driver, hoping that *dov'e* meant "where is?"

Fortunately the driver's English was better than my Italian. He told me he had been up the one-way Borgo Pinto twice but was unable to find the number 74 address. "I will ask the question of someone," he said, pulling over to a well-dressed couple walking arm in arm along the street. They conversed in Italian, then the couple walked on.

"They say it is back that way, one block," he said. "We must go round again."

After looping back, the driver stopped in the middle of a long block lined with stone walls high enough to hide whatever was behind them.

"Number 74," he said, pointing to a large gated door next to an intercom. I paid him and walked to the intercom to search for a name that might indicate a bonsai garden. There was nothing, only the names of private individuals. I walked up and down the block in the stifling noon heat, looking for another gate or sign that might lead me to the garden. Nothing. There was not even anyone to ask; the street seemed deserted. In desperation, I pushed one of the buttons on the intercom. No reply.

Off in the distance, about two blocks down the street, a small group of people had gathered outside a building. I headed toward them, walking between the tall blank stone façades that lined the street and blocked out most of the sun in a city that sweltered in summer. Oh well, I thought, at least it's cool on the "tall, narrow, faintly claustrophobic" Borgo Pinti, a description that now seemed perfect. I stopped at the double-gated carriage entry, where a group of people stood chatting in Italian. Inside I saw people walking through the covered entry into a courtyard, beyond which was a large garden. From a nearby desk I picked up a brochure and read: "Cortili e Giardini Aperti." In what seemed a genuine miracle I knew what each word meant: "Courtyards and Garden Open."

An Italian man sitting behind the desk asked me, in English, if I needed help. I replied that I was curious about what was going on.

"Ah, you are very lucky, Signora," he said, explaining that each year, for only two days, selected palazzi and their gardens were opened to the public for a fee—the money going to a historic preservation fund. I purchased a ticket, one that allowed me to enter all of the properties listed on an accompanying map. Several of the palazzi were located on Borgo Pinti, including the Palazzo Ximenes Panciatichi, the house where I now stood.

"This estate was bought by Giuliano and Antonio da Sangallo around 1490 and was decorated with paintings by Botticelli and Pollaiolo," said the man who sold me the ticket. "It was remodeled in 1603, and in 1796, Napoleon spent most of the month of June here."

As visions of Botticelli in the living room and Napoleon in the bedroom collided in my head, I stepped out into a garden the size of a small park, then turned around to look back at the house. It was surprisingly spacious, a well-proportioned house whose ochre-yellow façade was interrupted by large windows with faded blue shutters. The size and depth of the property astonished me. From the front I would have guessed it was a small row house, like the others on the street. But perhaps they too were as deceptive in appearance as this palazzo.

The garden had several parts. Directly behind the house was a park-like area where chairs were placed in the shade of large old trees. A woman and two children sat under one of the trees, talking, just as the original owners might once have done. A bird sang out; a church bell tolled the hour, and somewhere a child laughed. I moved from the little park to follow one of the gravel paths that disappeared around a bend. It wound around and around between walls of greenery. I passed a marble table built into a little alcove of rustic stone walls and entered a gravel courtyard circled by huge terra-cotta pots of lemon trees, their scent mingling with the warm air.

It was hard to tear myself away from the perfection of Palazzo Ximenes Panciatichi—despite its unpronounceable name—but the lure of palazzi yet to be visited drove me forward. I didn't want to miss anything since it was unlikely I'd ever have such an opportunity again.

It was about a five-minute walk along the Borgo Pinti to Palazzo Roffia. I had been told by the man at the desk that the Roffia family, who owned the palace from 1646 to the end of the century, had commissioned a skilled architect to design it. "It is considered a rare and important example of Florentine architecture from the end of the seventeenth century," he said.

The façade of Palazzo Roffia was more elegant and original than most of the houses along the street. From the entrance door I walked through a long hall that ended in a cool, shady garden. Again I was startled by how large the house and grounds were. It was like opening a plain cardboard box and finding a Fabergé egg inside.

When I stepped into the garden, what I saw astonished me. Straight ahead, balanced on top of a ladder propped against a tall tree, was a gorgeous painting of a cathedral dome, perhaps the Duomo itself. To the left, farther back in the garden, a painting of cool white columns next to a red tree was perched on top of old bricks turned a rusty pink color. And to my right, another painting, one of flowers blooming, stood next to an old pewter urn. The garden was dotted with paintings, which blossomed like flowers planted by a gardener with an exquisite and subtle sense of color and design. I had never seen anything like it.

I approached a woman standing under the loggia who seemed to be in charge and asked if she had any information about the art. As I suspected, the paintings had all been done by the same artist and were for sale.

Immediately, I imagined the painting of the cathedral dome in my garden, leaning against my crape myrtle tree, the rusty pink cathedral dome shaded under a canopy of deep pink blossoms. For one wild moment I was tempted to ask the price. But I didn't. When it came to buying art I didn't trust myself to do the prudent thing. Instead, I thanked the Signora in charge and left. But not before committing to memory every detail of this garden that I could visit, like Brigadoon, for only one day. And I, through a series of wildly random choices, was lucky enough to have stumbled across it.

On my way to the next palazzo I passed a large open gate. Inside I could see a perfect square of lush grass bordered by pristine columns; at the far end of the square the columns arched high above the entrance of a church. Intrigued, I stopped to read the information on the bronze plaque near the gate: *Church of Santa Maria Maddalena dei Pazzi. Founded in 1257. In 1493–96 Perugino frescoed the Chapter Room with the 'Crucifixion.'"*

As I read this a sudden rush of blood made the skin on my face tingle, the way it always did when some half-hidden memory was trying to erase the fragile line between now and then. What seemed to be the trigger for this detour from the present were the words "Perugino" and "Crucifixion"; they suddenly seemed as familiar to me as the names "Rapunzel" or "Cinderella." And then it happened: I slipped through the imaginary line between past and present, like a diver leaving the air and entering the water. In this case, the water was my Sunday school class, an event Mother never allowed me to miss, despite my repertoire of elaborate excuses.

It was there in a Methodist church—although we weren't Methodists—that I first met Perugino and his fellow artists, Raphael and Fra Angelico. To my surprise, Sunday school class had turned out to be more about art than about religion. We studied glossy magazine pictures pasted on cardboard backing of the Madonna, the Madonna with Child, Christ on the Cross. The various Madonnas always went by in a blur, but for some reason I was drawn to a picture of the crucifixion by an artist with the funny-sounding name, Perugino. I found the idea of being nailed to a cross—coupled with my Sunday school teacher's way-too-graphic description of the event—so terrifying that avoiding such a fate became a part-time obsession of mine. It immediately replaced my obsession of the prior year: worrying about being burned at the stake like Joan of Arc.

Now here on Borgo Pinti, light-years away from Sunday school and its cutout magazine pictures, I stood less than a minute's walk from the real thing. Suddenly the day had the feel of an adventure, one that now invited me to confront in the flesh, so to speak, Perugino's masterpiece. I stepped through the gate and hurried inside.

Almost empty, the church was a perfect place to escape the crowds that sometimes made Florence seem more like a Renaissance theme park—LeonardoLand—than a city of fascinating history and great art. I stood for a moment in the cool silence, admiring the brilliant trompe l'oeil ceiling, then moved toward a small room that seemed to be some sort of information center. It was there I saw him, an attractive man, in his middle seventies, perhaps, engaged in conversation with a well-dressed Italian couple. He appeared to be a volunteer guide, so I approached him.

"*Scusi. Dov'e Perugino per favore, Signor?*" I asked. He answered me in rapid Italian, none of which I understood, then pointed to a stairwell whose steps led down into what I assumed was the church's basement. I started looking frantically through my dog-eared copy of *Harrap's Italian Vocabulary: 6,000 Words and Phrases in 65 Subject Areas,* but I'd already forgotten the few words I recognized.

"Excuse me," said the Italian woman in English. "But we have come also to see the Perugino. It is in the crypt downstairs. Father Domenico says he will lead us to it."

"*Grazie,*" I said, nodding to the couple and to the man I now knew as Father Domenico.

The route to Perugino's fresco in the crypt was exciting in a theatrical sort of way; it reminded me of a scene from *Phantom of the Opera.* First we descended a staircase into the humid, dimly lit vaults where glass-fronted coffins offered glimpses of bones and skulls laid out on purple robes. Then we climbed up a second staircase that led to the crypt, and there it was: the *Crucifixion* by Perugino. The Italian couple let out a sigh of appreciation and immediately sat on a bench to study the fresco. "Such a great artist," the man said. The woman seemed transfixed.

Then Father Domenico began to speak. I watched as he pointed to a part of the wall about six feet above the floor. For several moments he spoke excitedly, his eyes burning, making gestures toward the fresco, then the wall, then the surrounding crypt. His manner suggested a man consumed by memory. Occasionally I would hear a word I understood. Water. Fresco. Perugino. November. The year 1966. When he finished I turned to the couple for a translation.

The woman answered. "The Father says that during the flood of 1966, the church was flooded by the water of the Arno River. He says that by 9 A.M., water was rising on the street outside. By eleven it was inside the first floor of the church and people were frantically trying to save what was possible to save. The church was ruined. He says that in the basement, water rose over six feet high, to the bottom of the Perugino fresco, leaving severe cracks in one panel and destroying other paintings and frescoes."

A swarm of questions buzzed through my head, questions I wanted to ask Father Domenico about the flood and his church, but he already had turned away, motioning us to follow him back upstairs. It was closing time, he said, as we returned to the small room where I'd first seen him. After thanking my accidental translators I turned to Father Domenico. "*Grazie. Molto grazie,*" I said, leaving a donation in a container on the table.

As I turned to leave he put his hand on my shoulder. "Wait here," he said in English, walking over to a desk. He returned carrying a small paperbound book. Carefully he opened it and turned to a picture showing three men wearing overalls and knee-high boots covered with mud and oil. Surrounded by debris, the men seemed to be standing in a church.

"I am that one," he said in English, pointing to a strong-looking man, in his forties perhaps. "It was in this church, in the flood."

Now I really wanted to know more. But I could see he needed to close the church. "*Quanto costa, per favore?*" I asked, thinking the little book was for sale.

He answered in Italian. Again I pressed the Italian woman into service. "The Father says it is his copy," she translated. "But he would like you to have it."

I protested but Father Domenico insisted. I thanked him again. He nodded, then walked us to the outside gate, which he closed and locked. I said good-bye to the Italian couple, then headed for another garden listed as part of the one-day tour. But to be honest all I could think of was Father Domenico and the flood. The man in the photograph, the young strong man digging to save his church and its Perugino, intrigued me.

What intrigued me even more, though, was the mystery of why Father Domenico had given *me* his copy of the booklet. If such an incident happened to Nancy Drew, I thought, it might have started her off on a whole new sleuthing adventure. Which, come to think of it, was exactly what was going on in my head.

Later that Sunday night I went through several guidebooks searching for information about Father Domenico's church. Finally, I found this description: "The church of Santa Maria Maddalena dei Pazzi is perhaps the most lovely yet ironically one of the least visited of the smaller churches in Florence. Founded in the thirteenth century, added to in great style in the 1470s by Giuliano da Sangallo. . . ." I stopped reading at this point. Sangallo? The name sounded familiar. Sangallo. Wasn't the first palazzo I visited owned by a family named Sangallo? I pulled out my notebook and there it was: "The Palazzo Ximenes Panciatichi was bought by Giuliano and Antonio da Sangallo around 1490. . . ."

Immensely pleased with myself for having connected such elusive dots, I dozed off wondering if I would learn as much from my professors as I had from the people I'd met on Borgo Pinti.

Now, as I walked back to my hotel after the first morning of class, I thought about my exciting Sunday on Borgo Pinti, particularly my encounter with Father Domenico. His story had left me brimming with curiosity and I intended to satisfy it. My plan was to make a few phone calls, then begin my hunt for information on the Father, his church, and the flood of 1966. Since the evening lecture didn't begin till six, that would allow me three hours to search the Internet on one of the Institute's computers.

Instead I found myself back in my room, propped up on my bed with the little picture book given me by Father Domenico. I had planned to put off studying it until after the evening lecture, but the suspense was too great to bear.

For several minutes I studied the cover; it showed the church, its entrance door, and columns submerged in what must have been six feet of murky water. Above the photo were the words *ALLUVIONE, 4 Novembre 1966.* When I opened to the first page, there was a grainy black-and-white photo of a woman wearing a dress, hat, and gloves, as though on her way to church, caught in floodwaters that reached almost up to her knees. Its striking composition—not to mention the startling image of a well-dressed woman walking along a flooded street—reminded me of

Cartier-Bresson's "decisive moment" approach to picture taking. The Italian caption was easy to translate: "Borgo Pinti at 9 in the morning of November 4." Below it was a picture of a man carrying what looked like a mattress through water up to his waist. It was captioned, "Last effort to salvage." The next picture records the street at 10:30 A.M.: "Water is still rising." Facing it is a photo of three men rowing a boat through the watery street: "Borgo Pinti at 11 A.M. By this time the water is inside the first floor and firemen are trying to save what they can."

Following this were several pages depicting the flooded, ruined interior and damaged paintings of Father Domenico's church, and the attempts to restore the church to some kind of order.

As I paged through the small book, I realized the photographs documented exactly what happened during the first days of the flood—sometimes from hour to hour—on the Borgo Pinti and in the Church of Santa Maria Maddalena dei Pazzi. To me it seemed a visual equivalent to the Rosetta Stone: a photographic time line capable of unlocking the history of one street's struggle for survival on that November day in 1966.

I knew of course about the 1966 flood that buried Florence in mud and mold; for a brief time it dominated even the American news. What I remembered most about the flood, however, was the reaction to the disaster by those of us who worked in museums. Horrified by the crisis facing those charged with saving Italy's artistic patrimony, several of my friends left immediately for Florence to help restore its irreplaceable paintings and rare books. I was embarrassed, no, ashamed, now to think of this, of how much more we knew about Florence's damaged art treasures than about the damage done to its neighborhoods and the everyday lives of people who lived there.

At a little before six that evening I crossed the Arno and headed down the Lungarno Guicciardini, a street that overlooked the river. When I came to an elegant, four-story building with a courtyard on the side, I pushed open the door and headed up the steps toward the Harold Acton Library. Founded in 1917 as part of the British Institute of Florence, the library occupies three floors of the Palazzo Lanfredini, an early-sixteenth-century palace. The Acton Library's inventory of fifty thousand volumes—all of which are available to students at the Institute—is the largest collection of books in English in Italy.

With its breathtaking views across the Arno of historic Florence,

Palazzo Lanfredini was a far cry from the warren of dreary classrooms and offices that constituted the Institute's Language Center on Piazza Strozzi. Since it functioned as the Institute's cultural center, Palazzo Lanfredini also was the setting for events such as lectures, concerts, and films, which were often open to the public. But not tonight. Tonight's lecture on "Gothic Cathedrals of Tuscany" was open only to Institute students.

The lecture room was still locked when I arrived, so I took a seat in the spacious lounge with its view of the river. The view that interested me, however, was the one inside: the lounge, reminiscent of a British private club, was filled with well-dressed young students. Although the majority seemed to be British, the sounds of various languages ricocheted around the room. There was also a lot of flirting going on, which, of course, has its own universal language. On the whole they were a strikingly attractive group: the girls casually stylish, suntanned, and lithe; the boys handsome in a Euro sort of way with their fashionable haircuts and black polo shirts. "Most of them are 'gap' students," Adrian had told me earlier, "sent by their parents to study Italian or art history before going on to university."

Before going in for the talk I looked around for Ilene. She hadn't arrived. I sat down next to a young British girl who looked absolutely smashing in a sleeveless black linen dress and expensive black sandals that showed off a perfect pedicure. With a stylish flourish, the girl had thrown over one shoulder a long tartan wool scarf. Tartan *wool!* In ninety-degree weather! But it was just right—the kind of offbeat accessory that only the most secure fashionista could pull off. Audrey Hepburn could get away with such a stunt. And so could Bunny Stubbs, voted the Best-Dressed Girl in junior high school. It was Bunny who taught the rest of us when to throw away our brown penny loafers and replace them with black Capezio ballet slippers. Scattered throughout this young audience were a few middle-aged couples and a handful of adult women who, like me, were busy preparing their pens and loose-leaf binders for a frenzy of note-taking.

I had taken an aisle seat in the back; it gave me the option of leaving unnoticed if I started to overdose on details about Gothic cathedrals. Instead, as the lecture progressed I found myself wanting more, not less, on the similarities and differences between the Gothic cathedrals of Florence, Siena, and Pisa.

Of course, a lot of the credit for my unflagging interest went to Dr. Kevin Murphy, who really knew how to make history and architecture come alive. A young Brit with floppy hair and a witty delivery—someone wandering in might think Hugh Grant had quit the movies to lecture on Gothic cathedrals—Dr. Murphy addressed the intense rivalry at the time between Florence and Siena, a neighboring city rich and powerful enough to challenge the Florentines. The relationship between the two cities—which led to numerous wars—sounded not unlike the one between the Yankees and the Mets.

"Siena wanted to model their own cathedral after the Duomo of their archenemy, Florence," he explained. "But they were uncertain about how to do it. So they had to go to their enemy, Florence, for advice. You can imagine it was an awful day for the Sienese when they had to call up the Florentines and ask whether their plan would work. And then were told they were doing it all wrong."

When the talk was over I noticed Ilene sitting nearby and walked over to talk to her. "I fell asleep and almost didn't make it," she said.

"So, are you too tired to go somewhere and have a glass of wine?"

"No. Now that I got some sleep I feel great," she said. "Where shall we go?"

"Well, it's still early, so let's just walk around the Oltrarno and when we find a place we like, we'll stop."

Ilene agreed and we set out. It was a little before eight with at least another hour left before the light would drain out of the sky, the perfect time to stroll through the neighborhood. All along the narrow streets, people on their way home from work stopped to buy cheese and salami or a bottle of wine. In the window of one pastry shop I was tempted by a display of *buccellato*, a fig-and-nut concoction baked in the shape of a bagel, but once inside couldn't resist buying a small loaf of *focaccia Venezia*, sugared on top and baked like a soufflé in parchment paper.

Ilene was good company. She was in no hurry and seemed agreeable to wandering with no particular destination in mind. Like me she was traveling alone. A Canadian, she had taken off six months from her job as a computer consultant to travel through Europe and northern Africa, and had just spent several weeks in Egypt. I liked what she was doing; she was not afraid to be on her own and didn't have rigid travel plans.

As Ilene and I approached the Borgo San Jacopo we seemed to cross an invisible line: behind us was the Santo Spirito neighborhood where working-class Florentines mixed with artisans; ahead lay the high-rent Via Maggio, a street lined with palazzi whose noble tenants had been replaced with elegant antiques shops. In between, on the narrow Borgo

San Jacopo, were unusual shops featuring everything from dazzling Italian lighting designs to handcrafted silverware. One shop in particular stopped us in our tracks.

It was a ceramics shop, and displayed in its windows were the most striking examples of pottery, earthenware, tile, and porcelain either of us had ever seen. Without saying a word, we both headed for the door and walked in. Every piece was a marvel of originality, painstakingly shaped into a work of art. Tables, garden fountains, plates, trays, small hand sinks, decorative cooking grills, candlesticks; each piece reflected an artist's sense of whether its form demanded boldness or delicacy. The shop owner, a man in his fifties perhaps, approached us and asked if we had questions. We did. Although I think he knew we were not customers—these ceramics were only for the very wealthy—he seemed to enjoy talking to us.

At one point, Ilene wandered into a back room. As the owner was answering my question about how he packed such fragile items for shipping, we heard from another room the sound of porcelain breaking. We raced in and saw a small plate in pieces on the floor. Ilene looked horrified. She began to apologize in a major way, offering to pay for the plate. I could only guess its price, but whatever it was, it was too much.

To our amazement the shop owner did not seem upset. He murmured something in Italian—it sounded very sympathetic—and waved his hands over one another while shaking his head, as if to say "No, no" to Ilene's offer to pay for the broken item. Of course, she insisted, but he continued to refuse. Finally, after groveling and thanking him in the most obsequious way—the only appropriate response—Ilene and I left. Outside on the street we looked at one another and shook our heads in disbelief.

"Who ever heard of a tourist breaking something and not having to pay for it?" Ilene asked.

"Only in Italy," I said. "In some places we'd both be in jail." We laughed. The "San Jacopo Caper," the name I gave the incident, seemed an adventure and a good omen for the rest of our stay in Florence. It also confirmed my long-held suspicions about the Italians: their real passion is not for objects but for people and, of course, food.

When I returned to my hotel later that evening I found Naohiro's phone message from Paris on my voice mail. As I listened to his soft low voice, I tried to picture him saying the words: *I wanted to hear your voice before I left for Tokyo. I hope the lessons go well and that you will find the Florence you search for.* If I closed my eyes I could see him in his Paris apartment, his slim taut body sprawled across the bed as he talked, his suitcase packed, ready to leave for the airport.

To head off what threatened to become a bout of wishful thinking about Naohiro and me, I decided to get out of my room. I snatched up several sheets of the hotel's elegant stationery and headed for the lobby. After ordering a glass of *vin santo* and some almond cookies for dipping, I sat at a secluded desk and began writing Naohiro about my trip.

In my usual stream-of-consciousness style, I told Naohiro about Adrian and Ilene and Father Domenico and the Perugino painting and the little booklet on the flood and how I was determined to go back to the Borgo Pinti to see if I could trace the flood's progress by matching the places to the booklet's pictures. And then I wrote of sitting on a terrace by the river, watching the sun slip behind the towers and domes, my head spinning with memories of Florence Harris and our childhood dream of living in Florence:

> When I remember my childhood friend and all the exciting plans we had, I wonder: What is the purpose of memory? Is it a trick to make sure we don't forget who we are by reminding us of who we were? I know this: if I didn't have my Sunday school memories of Perugino or the dreams of two little girls named Alicia and Florencia, I would not be who I am.
>
> In a way, Florence is the perfect example of a city where the past and present coexist. The Florentines live among the monuments of five centuries ago, incorporating them somehow into their daily lives. They buy clothing and medicine from shops housed in fifteenth-century palazzi and live in medieval buildings converted into condos. And yet they love the modern too: the minimalist designs of Prada and Armani, and the cool sophisticated interiors of the elegant shops along the Via Tornabuoni.
>
> It reminds me of the day in Kyoto when we walked from the ancient Emperor's Pavilion to the Hip Hop Café for a club sandwich, passing through centuries of Japan's history in less than an hour. Did you notice there was a full moon that night? Did you know how happy I was to see you? Could you tell?

· · ·

Over the next week my days in Florence took on a routine. In the morning, there were visits to places such as San Marco, a cloister of such elegant simplicity that one could imagine Philip Johnson designing it; or to the Bargello, a grim, fortresslike Renaissance prison that now guards one of the world's most beautiful collections of Renaissance sculpture. Afternoons were mostly free, except for the occasional guided tour given by Adrian, Kevin Murphy, or Marcello Bellini, a Florentine history professor who brilliantly guided us through centuries of Florentine culture up to the Renaissance. In the evenings we gathered as a group at the Palazzo Lanfredini for lectures by the three professors.

It was during one of these lectures that Dottore Bellini gave us the history of the word *artist* as we now use it. "In the 1300s, painters and sculptors were anonymous and were called 'artisans,' " he told us. "You were considered an artist if you were a student of the liberal arts. The first painter to sign a work of art was Giotto; he signed it *Work of Master Giotto.*"

I found this bit of information fascinating. But it made me wonder whether the art world, and all the rest of us, might not be better off if Giotto had never signed that painting; if we just looked at works of art for what they were and not for the name attached. For some reason, this led me to remember how an art teacher of mine liked to rein in the egos of her students by quoting the ancient Greek philosopher Xenophanes: "If horses could paint, they would draw gods that looked like horses." It seemed then, and still seems, a profound commentary on the nature of ego.

On the afternoon I decided to focus my research on the first days of the disastrous 1966 flood, I came up with six thousand entries on the Internet. After hours of going through the various sites and weeding out most of them, I pieced together from firsthand accounts a snapshot of those first days after the flood. Without knowing why, I began typing an outline of sorts into my computer:

In the early hours of Friday, November 4, after several days of heavy rain, the swollen river Arno rushed like a waterfall through the city. Among the first to be alerted to the gravity of the situation were the owners of the jewelry shops on the Ponte Vecchio, who, at two A.M., rushed to the bridge to salvage their merchandise. The 600-year-old bridge itself was in danger of collapsing: a truck that had plunged into the river hit the bridge violently, creating an enormous hole in its wall. But it also created an opening for the floodwaters to flow through, which ironically may have saved the Ponte Vecchio from total destruction.

When the raging Arno finally overflowed its banks, it sent a ten-foot wall of water speeding through the streets with such force that it threw cars against walls, piling them up on top of one another like toys. Shops were destroyed, and the muddy, fuel-soaked water poured into homes, churches, museums, and streets, rising to levels as high as eighteen feet. Hardest hit was the densely populated Santa Croce quarter, the lowest-lying area in Florence and the site of many of the city's galleries, churches, and libraries.

By seven-fifteen A.M. the water inside the Uffizi Gallery was waist-high, and in the Biblioteca Nazionale the slimy water ruined an estimated two million books. The flood-waters raced through Piazza del Duomo with such force that five panels of Ghiberti's Gates of Paradise *were ripped from the Baptistery.*

One firsthand account, posted on the Web by a Florentine art conservator, Professor Umberto Baldini, tells of how he and two colleagues tried in the first hours of the flood to save as many paintings in the Uffizi Gallery as they could. After rushing to get there, they waded with difficulty through the flooded gallery, where the water was already more than three feet deep. "We tried to remove as many paintings as we could to safety: these included works by Giotto, Tiepolo, Mantegna, as well as the Virgin *by Filippo Lippi. We also managed to lift the* Coronation of the Virgin *by Botticelli high enough to prevent the water from touching it, because it was too big to go through the door. Once we had got the paintings to safety, [we] headed for the Vasari corridor above the Ponte Vecchio to try and save the paintings that were in danger there," wrote Professor Baldini, describing the long corridor above the bridge that links the Pitti Palace to the Uffizi. "The bridge shuddered and we thought it was going to fall down. We managed to remove the paintings and immediately returned to the Uffizi from where we were able to see the fury of the Arno from the upstairs windows."*

As the floodwaters began to recede early the next morning, the power went down, leaving the city without light, heat, or drinkable water. After surveying the devastation around the Duomo, an American resident named Horace Gibson wrote: "It must have been as Florence was in the Middle Ages: the narrow streets, thick with mud, no illumi-nation, with the dark palazzi towering overhead."

Something about this vivid observation made me stop writing. The idea of stepping out to find the city you lived in suddenly changed into the place you'd read about in history books made my thoughts bolt from the computer screen and race back to the Borgo Pinti. I could imagine the floodwaters pouring in over the long narrow street, ripping the doors from Father Domenico's church and filling up the crypt to within inches of Perugino's masterpiece. And I could see the wave of water bursting through the gates of the Palazzo Ximenes Panciatichi, flooding the garden where I'd sat so peacefully a week earlier.

It was true, I thought. What we call history is nothing more than a continuum—in reverse gear—of the present.

I liked the format of the Institute's daily schedule, particularly since it left my afternoons free. Usually I'd walk over to the Institute's library to look up information on early Renaissance buildings in Florence, particularly those designed by Sangallo. He, Sangallo—someone I'd never heard of until a week earlier—had become a new interest of mine. Then it was off to the Borgo Pinti to continue tracing the path of the 1966 flood through the neighborhood.

By this time I had started to think of the Borgo Pinti as my neighborhood. I no longer had lunch at any of the cafés near the Institute or my hotel. Instead I roamed around the streets near Borgo Pinti, staking out cafés and restaurants that I liked, a task I found much more fun than reading at the library. I guess I just preferred the role of detective—my version of what others call research—to that of historian. Actually it wasn't unlike the role of reporter: poking into places where I didn't belong and approaching strangers in cafés and bookshops to ask questions.

That was how I met Valeria, in a kosher restaurant near the Borgo Pinti where we both had stopped for our midday meals. When the waitress appeared I took a chance and asked in Italian if there was a specialty of the house. Whatever I said was so off the mark that the waitress mistook it for English. "No English," she said, "only Italian."

"*Si, si,*" I whispered, burying my head in the menu, praying that no one had overheard this embarrassing exchange.

No such luck. "I would try the vegetarian minestrone or the roast chicken with herbs," said the woman sitting at the table next to me. "Both are very good." Although her English was excellent, I could tell from the rhythm of her voice and the wonderful emphasis placed on each syllable of *minestrone* that she was Italian.

"Thanks. I mean, *grazie,*" I said to the woman. After ordering the roast chicken and a glass of wine, I decided to take a chance. "I'm Alicia," I said as easily as someone whose name really was Alicia might say it. "And I'm grateful to you for offering your help."

"And I am Valeria," she said. "And now I am nervous you will not like my selection." She smiled—not with her mouth but with her eyes. I liked her easy smile and her quick-witted answer to my question. They made up for my subliminal disappointment that her name was not Florencia. I also liked the way her chocolate-colored hair was spiked into feathery wisps that curled back from her face like tiny icicles. I made a mental note to find out where she had it cut.

"Do you eat here often?" I asked.

"Quite a bit. I grew up just around the corner and still live in the same street."

A bell went off in my head when she said this. Since I guessed Valeria to be around fifty, it meant—if my quick calculation was right—she must have firsthand knowledge of the 1966 flood. But since I wasn't sure of this, I proceeded cautiously.

"It's so nice to meet someone from this neighborhood," I said, explaining that I was a student at the British Institute.

"And how did you find your way to this neighborhood? Are you staying near here?"

"No. But I wish I were. In fact I've been looking at a hotel on Borgo Pinti where I'd like to stay on my next visit." Then I went into a little soliloquy, explaining how a piece of good luck had brought me here on the very Sunday the palazzi and their gardens were open to the public and about Father Domenico and the little booklet. "Since then, the street has become something of an obsession with me. And so has the flood."

"Ah, yes, I know that church. Santa Maria Maddalena dei Pazzi. It was very badly hurt during the flood and we almost lost the Perugino. That was a very bad time in Florence, particularly in Santa Croce."

I asked Valeria if she would mind telling me her memories of the flood.

"You know one thing I remember very much from the flood? My dog. We couldn't find him. For two days and through the night I walked through the dark streets with a flashlight calling him everywhere. *Aldo. Aldo.* But he never came back. I was seventeen and so was he. I still miss him."

But that was not all Valeria remembered. As we sat drinking our second glass of wine, she called on other memories of that day and the night that followed. Tidal waves of water speeding through the streets and into houses. Total darkness when the electricity quit. Cars thrown against walls or turned on their backs like turtles. The wet coldness in the unheated houses. And the eerie silence throughout the city. "The only sound came from men in rowboats making their way through the streets to rescue us. It was like an atom bomb had gone off. There was no food, no phone, no water. I remember walking through littered streets that smelled of fuel oil to the Piazza Signoria, to carry home water from the Nettuno fountain."

I asked if by any chance she had gone into Father Domenico's church after the flood.

"Only the courtyard," she said. "But I saw into the church where men were working in mud and water up to their knees."

We talked for almost an hour before Valeria motioned for her check. "I must go," she said. "I have an appointment to keep. Perhaps we could meet again, if you like."

"Oh, I wish we could," I said. "But I leave for home the day after tomorrow. But please, write down your telephone number in case I should stay longer."

Valeria and I walked out together and parted near the corner of the Via dei Pilastri.

"*Ciao, Alicia,*" she said, holding out her hand.

"*Ciao, Valeria,*" I said, ignoring her hand to give her a small hug instead.

For a few minutes I stood on the sidewalk and watched Valeria walk away. My head filled with the image of the young girl who called out "Aldo, Aldo," for her lost dog. I wondered if she ever dreamed of him.

Since I doubted I would get back to the neighborhood again before leaving Florence I decided to walk one more time along the Borgo Pinti. At the church I stopped to see if Father Domenico was there. He wasn't. I took out my wallet and counted out just enough lire to see me through the next day and my trip to the airport. I placed what was left in the church's donation box. Before leaving I stood for a while in the garden outside the church, thinking of the day I met Father Domenico. Although I still wondered why he had given me the little picture book, it was a question not likely to be answered. Perhaps, I thought, it was better that way. Perhaps not knowing why allowed me to fold the story into my own history, the one that went back to my Sunday school teacher and Perugino and then forward again to the present.

When I left the church, I continued to walk along Borgo Pinti. It all seemed so familiar to me, this "tall, narrow, faintly claustrophobic" Borgo Pinti, a street that oddly enough felt like home. In my head I had my own vision of the street, of what lay behind some of those closed gates. I imagined the Sangallo family at Borgo Pinti 68, having lunch at the marble table in their garden. And I pictured Matteo Caccini at No. 33, lovingly tending his botanical garden, while further along the street at No. 13 the Roffia family was enjoying the rare frescoed rooms of their palazzo.

I could even imagine the elusive, perhaps imaginary, bonsai garden I had never seen at Borgo Pinti 74. It was a stroke of luck—bad luck I thought at first when unable to find the garden—that allowed me to discover the Borgo Pinti along with its palazzi and courtyards, Father Domenico, Perugino, and the story of what happened on this Renaissance street on the fourth of November 1966.

As I passed by the wall behind which the garden was supposed to exist, something told me that my affair with this medieval street wasn't over yet. Someday, somehow, I was going to come back and find the entrance to the bonsai and suiseki garden at No. 74 on the tall, narrow, highly picturesque, but faintly claustrophobic Borgo Pinti.

Sense and
Sensible Shoes

ON A BRIGHT MORNING in mid-July, I awakened to the smell of new-mown grass and the sound of voices filtered through the tinkle of teacups. For a moment I imagined myself back in the bedroom of my childhood, listening to Mother and Grandmother talking over morning tea and scones while outside my older brother Shelby mowed the back lawn. It was a seductive thought, this memory of childhood mornings when each day seemed a clean slate with yesterday's mistakes rubbed out—so much so that I had to struggle to leave behind the comfort of childhood for the uncertainty of the present. But slowly I allowed myself to remember where I was. *In England, in a small hotel in Winchester,* I whispered out loud, breaking the spell.

Then I recalled the night before. Actually I *saw* it: Driving through the dark, rainy countryside straight from Heathrow Airport to Winchester. Missing the turn. Working my way back to Winchester and then getting lost in the narrow, one-way streets. Stopping pedestrians—what few were out on the streets—to get directions that only added to the confusion. And finally, just after one in the morning, climbing into bed at the Royal Hotel, a weary woman desperately trying to remember why she ever thought traveling was fun.

Now, as I lifted the window in my room and leaned out to look around, my spirits soared on gusts of pleasure at the sight of the garden below. With its long curving borders of tall swaying flowers and perfect rectangle of thick, dewy grass, it was everything an English garden should be. I leaned out a little more and saw that, indeed, everything within view was quintessential England: the hedges along a nearby street, a small church just beyond the garden's end, the Georgian-style brick houses, a tall man dressed like Sherlock Holmes walking a low-slung corgi. My excitement at seeing a new corner of the world jolted me back into remembering why travel was so appealing and important to me. Eager to get out on the streets, I quickly showered, dressed, and headed down the steep staircase for breakfast.

It was my first real look at the hotel. Built in the mid-sixteenth century as a private residence, it was now an appealing combination of historic English charm with just enough updating to satisfy the modern traveler. The glassed-in dining room overlooking the garden was clearly an addition and so was a new wing along one side. But the old part of the hotel was burnished and polished and filled with chintz sofas, antiques, and tall vases of cut flowers. I ate my full English breakfast on a little balcony overlooking the dining room, then toyed with the idea of lingering over coffee on an outside terrace.

But I had no time for lingering. For I was a traveler with a mission, a pilgrim in search of a woman I'd never met but considered my friend. She was the reason for my trip to Winchester, the first stop on an itinerary that would take me through Hampshire, Dorset, Somerset, and, finally, to Exeter University in Devon. So, eager to begin the journey that would lead me to her, I left the hotel and set off to find the first address on my list: 8 College Street.

It was a ten-minute walk to College Street, through streets that contained some of the most historic spots in all of England. But I walked quickly, head down, determined not to get sidetracked. It was particularly difficult to pass the magnificent Winchester Cathedral without stopping. But I didn't. There'd be time enough later to see the sights. Finally, just at the edge of the cathedral close, I came to a narrow cobbled street lined on one side with picturesque houses and small shops; on the other side of the street was a tranquil green park that surrounded the remains of a medieval castle. A few more steps and I arrived at my destination: a modest, three-story yellow brick house, close enough to the cathedral for its inhabitants to hear the tolling of the great bells.

I put down the bag holding my camera and notebooks and stood reading the inscription on a small plaque above the door: "In this house Jane Austen lived her last days and died 18 July 1817." A small sign nearer the street cautioned tourists that this was a private house, not open to the public.

So this was it then. The house where the woman I'd known and loved since age twelve had died in the arms of her older sister, Cassandra. I stood for a long time, looking up at the second-story bow window, wondering if it was the place where the invalid Jane liked to sit admiring the garden across the way. Then my thoughts moved into the house. I pictured the heartbroken Cassandra bending over Jane when the end came, closing for the final time the eyes that once had razor-sharp vision, eyes capable of spotting across a crowded drawing room all the small comedies of personal delusion.

As I stood there, my head whirring with thoughts of Mr. Darcy and Mr. Knightley, of Elizabeth and Emma, a young couple pushing a stroller brushed past me on the narrow sidewalk. Two young boys trailed behind them, tossing a ball back and forth. But none of it really registered; I was somewhere else. I was watching Cassandra stand at this very door, her eyes following the coffin containing her beloved Jane being wheeled away from her, through College Street to Winchester Cathedral.

A car door slammed behind me and three women and a tour guide approached the front door and, despite the privacy sign, rang the bell impatiently. I took their intrusive behavior as a sign to leave and began walking, with no particular destination in mind. Or so I thought until I left College Street, entered the cathedral close, and headed toward the cathedral. Then it hit me. Without knowing it, I was retracing the route of Jane's coffin.

In my search for Jane Austen, it seemed, I had chosen to begin at the end. The end of her life, that is. Why, I couldn't explain. Perhaps it was simply a matter of wanting to pay my respects to the desperately ill woman who died at 8 College Street before setting out to look for the sly, fun-loving Jane who was, and still is, alive on every page of her books.

As I neared the cathedral I stopped to study a well-tended garden at the side of a little house. The lavender was the most beautiful I'd ever seen, tall jagged spears in shades of purple, pink, and violet. At the very moment I leaned over to smell the lavender, a large woman with white hair and a nicely weathered face stepped outside. She was wearing yellow rubber garden gloves and a long green smock over khaki trousers.

"Good morning," she said, nodding. "Are you looking for something?"

"I was just admiring your lavender. The colors are so beautiful together."

"Well, then, you should take a few cuttings home. I suggest you wrap them up in your underwear, so no one's the wiser. Then when you get home, just pop the cuttings into a pot and they will grow."

"I don't think I'd get by the customs officer with plant cuttings, even ones hidden in my underwear. And anyway, you can buy lavender in the U.S., can't you?"

"Yes, dear, you can buy lavender in the States." A dramatic pause followed, one that indicated more was coming. "But it won't be *English* lavender, will it?"

I laughed. Her comedic timing was perfect. And besides, she had an "air" about her—to use one of Jane Austen's favorite words—that suggested a wry skepticism, a quality I found appealing. I could imagine her fitting right into *Pride and Prejudice.*

Right then and there, my mood shifted. I decided to look upon this brief encounter with the lavender lady as a sign that I was on the right road, the one leading to Jane.

"To tell the truth, I don't like any of Miss Austen's books very much; to me they're all the same," said the impeccably dressed tour guide as he led me through Winchester Cathedral to the grave of Jane Austen. The guide's name was Tony Humphreys, and his criticism of Jane caught me off guard. Still, I didn't find it offensive. After all, the critic inside every reader has his or her own taste and standards by which a book is judged. Not only that, but I have always suspected that even those male readers who enjoy Jane Austen's work seldom are as passionate about it as their female counterparts. And Mr. Humphreys—aside from his lapse about Jane—turned out to be quite a charming, erudite Englishman who, upon retiring from business, had become an official city guide.

After a brief walk through the back of the huge cathedral, Mr. Humphreys stopped at a large slab of black marble set in the stone floor. The inscription above the brick-lined vault where Jane is buried reads, in part: "The benevolence of her heart, the sweetness of her temper, and the extraordinary endowments of her mind obtained the regard of all who knew her, and the warmest love of her intimate connections."

It surprised me to find there was no mention in the inscription of Jane's brilliance as an author. I asked Mr. Humphreys if there was a theory about this omission.

"Well, you have to remember Miss Austen wasn't famous when she died," he said, pointing out that two of her novels, *Persuasion* and *Northanger Abbey*, were published posthumously. "But all that's changed. Nowadays, her admirers come from right round the world."

"Yes, I know. In fact, I was told the Jane Austen Society of North America plans to hold its annual meeting here in Winchester next year. Is that so?"

"Yes, they are coming to Winchester. And to tell you the truth, all of the guides are rather frightened by it. Many of the people coming— 'Janeites,' I believe you call them—will know every detail of every week of her life."

I laughed. "I know exactly how you feel. Tomorrow I've been invited to attend the annual meeting of the British Jane Austen Society, and I'm terrified I'll mix up Chawton House with Chawton Cottage or, in a moment of panic, pair off Emma with Mr. Darcy."

"Well, then, we've got something in common, haven't we?"

"We do, indeed," I said, exchanging a conspiratorial smile with Mr. Humphreys. What I didn't say—out of respect for his heritage—was that I found the idea of facing a group of British Janeites far more intimidating than meeting their American counterparts.

For the next five hours I wandered the streets of Winchester, marveling at how much of England's history could be found in this town that began as a Roman military outpost. With a small guidebook from the Visitors' Centre in hand, I followed the Heritage Trail outlined on maps. It was a walk that took me through ten centuries of English history, from the bronze statue of King Alfred, who restored Winchester after the Dark Ages and made the city his capital, to the Great Hall where what is fabled to be King Arthur's Round Table has resided for more than seven hundred years.

Finally I made my way to an area designated on the map as "Keats' Walk." The name intrigued me and so did the brief explanation: "John

Keats wrote his ode 'To Autumn' during a stay in Winchester in 1819. His inspiration was a daily walk past the Cathedral and College and through the Water Meadows." Since I once had been an ardent imitator of Keats—in seventh-grade English class I churned out odes to many things, including a veiled hat of Mother's that I thought gorgeous and the amber eyes of my cat, Mimi—I decided to trace his footsteps.

It was a charming walk that took me through the tranquil green park of the Water Meadows to Winchester College, the oldest public school in England, founded in 1382. Across the road I could see Wolvesey Castle, once a medieval bishop's palace and now used as playing fields. Around the corner I noticed a modest yellow house with a little plaque above the door. Suddenly I realized I'd come full circle; I was back at the house where Jane Austen died. I wondered: When John Keats walked past this house in 1819 on his daily outing, did he know that two years earlier a great writer had died here? Did he even know of Jane? Then it struck me: I was walking through Jane Austen's world. Since most of the buildings and grounds were already centuries old when Jane arrived by carriage at 8 College Street, I was seeing now what she saw then.

The day was cool and misty and a soft breeze rustled through the trees as I entered the cathedral grounds; the sound reminded me of water running over stones in a shallow stream. As I drew nearer an old timber-framed building, I heard the high sweet sounds of boys singing. It was the "Hallelujah Chorus," sung as a band of angels might sing it. Convinced it must be a recording, I took a seat beside a woman on a nearby bench and listened. Then, right in the middle of a "hallelujah," the voices stopped. A minute later, they started again, then stopped again. Obviously it was not a recording. But what choir could sing the way these boys did? I turned to the woman next to me and asked if she knew anything about the young singers.

"It's the boys from the cathedral choir practicing in the music rooms," she said, pointing to an adjacent building. "Lovely, isn't it?"

"That's the famous Winchester Boys' Choir?" I said, unable to believe my good luck.

"Aye, it is. The lads in the choir go to school over there. Pilgrims' School, it's called, after the pilgrims who used to stay there during their travels."

"I'd love to hear them in the cathedral. Do you know if they'll be singing at Evensong tomorrow night?"

"They will. And I hear it will be a special Evensong. One celebrating

Jane Austen's birthday, I believe. I guess she'd be two-hundred-and-something by now, wouldn't she?"

"Two hundred and twenty-five," I said. "Although that doesn't seem possible since she still manages to lurk about in our minds like some beloved aunt we rarely see. Absent but still present."

The woman nodded but said nothing. Perhaps her nod was in agreement. More likely her silence was a way of putting an end to the conversation. It was, I decided, a polite version of the dismissal delivered by one of Jane's characters in a similar situation: "You have delighted us long enough."

That night I had dinner at the hotel and then went straight to my room to prepare for the next day. From my briefcase I took out a folder marked "Friday, July 14: Chawton Village," then upended the remaining letters, e-mails, and faxes onto the bed. Much of the correspondence was from Jean Bowden, the former curator and current archivist of Chawton Cottage, the house in Hampshire where Jane Austen spent the last eight years of her life. For Jane Austen devotees, the Hampshire village of Chawton is Mecca; it was country life in Hampshire that shaped Jane's deepest sensibilities, not to mention the plots of her novels.

Jean Bowden, a woman I knew only through her friendly, helpful correspondence, had played a key role in arranging the Hampshire part of my trip. Not only had she offered to accompany me to some of the festivities planned by the British Janeites at their annual meeting, she had also alerted me to an important, by-invitation-only luncheon at Chawton House, the Elizabethan manor once owned by Jane's brother, Edward Knight. The luncheon was being held to announce the transformation of the manor house into the Centre for the Study of Early English Women's Writing. It was a major undertaking that would allow scholars access to manuscripts and books by women writers, both well-known and obscure, of the seventeenth, eighteenth, and early nineteenth centuries. By following Jean Bowden's tactful suggestions I had managed to wangle an invitation to the event.

Now, as I looked over the guest list, I grew nervous. The forty-seven names included the Austen biographers Helen Le Froy and Deirdre Le Faye; the writers Germaine Greer and Maggie Lane; Joan Ray, the president-elect of the Jane Austen Society of North America; professors from several British universities and colleges; and a few titled guests such as Sir Matthew and Lady Farrer. With such a gathering of respected Austen admirers and scholars, I would need to be on my toes. It occurred to me that I should prepare a small crib sheet to take along. Notes to remind me it was Louisa, not Henrietta, who fell from the Cobb at Lyme Regis in *Persuasion*. Or that it was Jane Fairfax who, when admired by Mr. Knightley, aroused in *Emma* feelings of jealousy— although on second thought maybe it was the other way round. I sighed, knowing that in a room full of true Janeites, I was doomed— with or without a cheat sheet.

I skipped down the guest list to my name; beneath it was the designation, "Author." I prayed no one would ask me whether my work on Jane Austen was a biography or scholarly research. True, I could in all honesty cite my tenth-grade paper on flirting in Jane's novels—a subject of particular interest to adolescent girls since flirting and not consummation was, at that age, the currency between the sexes—but I decided not to. To make myself more interesting I practiced saying my name with an unidentifiable accent, a ploy that would allow me, given a worst-case scenario, to answer unwelcome questions evasively, as though I were not fully fluent in English. But after several tries at various faux accents, I gave up.

Thank God Jean Bowden would be there to save me from myself, I thought, as I climbed into bed and turned out the light.

Although the taxi that was to take me to the Hampshire village of Chawton was not due until ten o'clock, I nervously took up my station outside the hotel door at nine-thirty. Since I had no idea of how to get to Chawton Village or Chawton House or Chawton Cottage—indeed found myself quite confused by so many different Chawtons—I got out Jean Bowden's e-mail advice. "Tell the driver that you want Chawton House, up by St. Nicholas Church (not Jane Austen's House on the corner)," she wrote. "He will be able to drive you right up to the door, I expect. If not, alight at the church and just walk up the driveway. You can see the house from the church."

At precisely ten o'clock, my taxi arrived. I hopped in and rattled off Jean's directions as though I commuted regularly to Chawton. Once out of the city, we traveled through wide vistas of green hills that dipped into lush vales and then rose again like verdant waves. The houses along the road—some with thatched roofs—were framed by old stone walls covered with masses of pink roses. On the rising hills a few sheep grazed, white pointillist dots against a canvas of green. When I looked ahead into the distance, I saw no end to the vista of rolling hills and green fields. Through the taxi's open windows, the scent of roses mingled with smells of the dark rich earth. I leaned my head out of the window and took a deep breath; it was like inhaling England. No wonder Jane loved Hampshire above all other places.

"So, is this your first time to Hampshire?" the taxi driver asked suddenly.

"Yes, it is," I said, without embellishment. For some reason I was not in the mood to talk, and I hoped my brief answer would discourage any further conversation.

"I've been to America," he continued brightly. "Do you know what's the ugliest bit of America I saw? Oklahoma. It's all oil rigs and flat land." He paused briefly to light a cigarette. "My wife and I watch the History Channel. I say, that Howard Hughes was a strange duck, wasn't he? Did you know he invented the bra for Jane Russell?"

Just as the driver's roaming, free-range conversation started to interest me, the taxi lurched to a stop in front of a small country church.

"Well, here you are. Chawton House is just up that road." He pointed to a long unpaved driveway that led from the road to a huge house at the top of a hill.

"Where is Chawton Village from here?" I asked as I handed him the fare.

"You just passed through it. Now, off you go, lassie," he said, politely dismissing me.

I stood in the middle of the quiet road and watched his taxi drive away, wondering what to do next. In my anxiety not to be late I had arrived way too early. Ten-thirty, to be exact—which left me with two hours to kill. There was no one around, either on the grounds or along the street, so I headed for the church, which, like everything else, looked deserted. I pulled at the door, half expecting it to be locked. Instead it opened onto a busy scene featuring a phalanx of middle-aged women in tweed suits and sensible shoes who were cutting and arranging masses of flowers. The scent of fresh flowers hung in the cool damp air of the stone church. So evocative was the smell that for an instant I allowed myself to be a child again, back in Baltimore browsing through wholesale florists' shops with Grandmother, looking for floral bargains.

I picked up a pamphlet about the church's history and was about to read it when a woman working nearby asked if I needed help.

"No," I said. "I'm early for a luncheon at Chawton House and thought I'd just take a look around."

"Oh, you must be one of the Jane Austen ladies. We're arranging flowers for the meeting and for Evensong tomorrow night here at the church." She paused to push a lily into the large vase in front of her. "You know, the Austen family—Jane and her mother and sister—used to worship here. They had regular seats on the south side of the aisle. Over there." She pointed at a row of seats close to the pulpit. "The mother and sister, you know, are buried outside in the churchyard."

"Would you mind showing me their graves?" I asked, my voice rising with excitement.

"Follow me," she said, slipping through a side door. As we walked she pointed out a building. "That used to be the stables. But I hear an American lady is now living there." She stopped before two simple tombstones in the small churchyard. "Well, here we are. And now I must be off. Good luck at the meeting."

"Thank you," I said, wondering—no, *worrying*—about why I would need "good luck" at a meeting. But I brushed aside such feelings and turned my attention to the grave sites. The engraved inscriptions on the headstones were as plain as the weathered markers that framed them, noting only the names, dates of death, and age at the time of death. Unlike Jane, both women lived long lives. Her mother died ten years after Jane's death, at the age of eighty-seven; Cassandra lived to the age of seventy-two. How, I wondered, did Cassandra fill up the remaining twenty-eight years after a life devoted, in large part, to her beloved sister Jane? It saddened me to think of the void such a death must have left in her life.

It was so quiet and peaceful in the churchyard that I stood for a long time, listening to the birds calling back and forth from the trees, feeling the soft grass beneath my feet and the warm sun on my back. I thought of Jane's cold marble tomb in Winchester Cathedral and couldn't help wondering if she might have preferred her final resting place to be here, in the Hampshire countryside she loved, next to her mother and sister.

After walking to the village and back—a walk I'd been told was an almost daily ritual for Jane—I saw that the fields below Chawton House had become a parking lot for dozens of cars. Guests for the luncheon, I assumed. Further up the driveway I saw several television crews, including one from the BBC, unloading equipment. I wasn't surprised to see the media turnout as news of the Chawton House Library's formation of a new women's study center had been on all the TV news shows. While the idea of establishing a place where both scholars and non-scholars would have access to thousands of printed books written by women and published between 1600 and 1830 was exciting, the thought of seeing the inside of Chawton House, usually closed to the public, was a dream come true. Of course, the fifty-room house, set on a 280-acre estate, was long past its prime and in desperate need of restoration. Still, it was the place where Jane spent her days and nights when visiting her brother, Edward, who had inherited the house and surrounding lands. It was Edward who came to the financial rescue of his widowed mother and two sisters in 1809—a bit belatedly, in my opinion—offering them a rent-free cottage in the village.

Now as I entered the regal "Great House," as it was always known, I decided the first thing to do was find Jean Bowden. Working on the assumption she was wearing a nametag like the rest of the guests—mine said ALICE STEINBACH, AUTHOR—I walked through the rooms looking at labels instead of faces, searching for Jean's name. After ten unproductive minutes I gave up and followed the stream of guests through several empty, dilapidated rooms into the dining room. With its large buffet tables set with silver trays of food, chafing dishes, and fine china and its stunning view of the countryside, the dining room hinted at the charm and character of the house in its glory days. Chawton House, some scholars say, was the model for Donwell Abbey in *Emma*.

I moved to a corner of the room and stood watching as the other guests reacted to each new arrival with a warmth as cozy and cheerful as a teapot on the boil. It reminded me of something Jean Bowden had written in one of her e-mails. "The Jane Austen world is a very pleasant one," she wrote. "A shared love of her and her works is an entry into instant friendship in a quite extraordinary way."

She was right, of course. Admirers of Jane Austen seem to recognize each other as kindred spirits. The only flaw in this theory was that none of the luncheon guests were recognizing me as a member of the Austen tribe. I tried to give off kindred-spirit vibes as I stood at a large window overlooking the sloping front hill. To my surprise, it seemed to work. A woman dressed in a precisely tailored dark blue suit came up next to me and said, "That was one of Jane's favorite views." Her accent was of the intimidating—to me, anyway—British kind, very cultured, very clipped. Quickly I looked at her nametag. I recognized the name on it as belonging to one of Jane's biographers.

"Did Jane spend a lot of time here?" I asked, thrilled at the possibility of hearing anecdotes about the great author straight from the horse's mouth, so to speak.

"Ah, an American fan," she said, responding not to my question but to my non-intimidating accent. Leaning forward, she peered at my nametag. "And what are you the author of?" she asked bluntly, her fingers punctuating the air with quotation marks as she said the word *author*.

I tried to project an air of sangfroid as I desperately scrolled through my mind for a suitable answer. The tenth-grade flirting paper was definitely out. Maybe I could cite a published book review of *Pride and Prejudice*, omitting, of course, that it appeared in my school newspaper. However, my panic proved to be unnecessary; Jane's biographer had already moved onto another subject.

"Do you know the lady who's heading up the restoration of the house and the new study center?" she asked. "She's an American, too."

"No, I don't. Is she the same American woman living in the restored stables? Or a different one?"

"The same. Her name is Sandy Lerner and she's quite an accomplished businesswoman. Something to do with computers, I think."

Just as I was about to repeat my question about how often Jane Austen visited Chawton House, the biographer in the dark blue suit waved to someone across the room and after a quick "Nice to meet you," loped off to greener fields.

Left to my own devices, I wandered out to the entry to check out who among the invited guests had picked up their nametags and who had not. Among the few remaining nametags was that of Germaine Greer, seemingly a no-show. Since searching for the intriguing writer and feminist was what had kept me occupied, I decided the only way left for me to look busy was to eat lunch. I quickly filled my plate with finger sandwiches and chafing-dish goodies, then headed for one of the chairs scattered around the room. I felt like a wallflower, sitting alone, watching from the sidelines as the other guests engaged in animated conversation. I amused myself by sizing up the guests as Jane Austen might have in one of her novels. *An exceedingly slender woman whose upright posture and open gaze had no equal in the room. A sensible-looking gentleman of perhaps seven- or eight-and-fifty who has all the advantages of being tall and well dressed. A woman of such a stern and scholarly countenance that one wishes only to avoid making her acquaintance. A gentleman whose cheerful demeanor cast a wide net over the entire assembly. . . .*

"So there you are," said a cheery voice, interrupting my inventory of the guests. "I'd almost given up finding you."

I looked up and saw a woman of about four- or five-and-sixty whose appearance and manner in every way was so becomingly friendly that I knew it must be Jean Bowden.

"Jean!" I said, actually hearing the exclamation point in my voice. "I'm so happy to see you—I mean, meet you. Although I already feel I know you."

Jean laughed. "Well, I've always felt that the bond between those who admire Jane is something special."

And with that observation—a remark I took to mean, rightly or wrongly, that she felt about me as I did about her—I relaxed. In fact, I even ventured an observation of my own: "After looking around this room full of jolly, animated people, I've concluded that the 'Jane Austen world,' as you called it in your e-mail, is made up entirely of outgoing optimists." I omitted the part about feeling left out.

Before Jean could answer, two women—both professors according to their nametags—stopped to greet her and, in doing so, politely included me in their conversation. It was clear that just by being seen with Jean, my standing in the Jane Austen world had gone up a notch or two. By the end of the luncheon I had talked to amiable Austen scholars, amiable Austen professors, and a few amiable guests who claimed to be descended from the Austen family. Or to be more precise, *they* had talked to *me*, not always with a happy result.

"What do you think of the argument that Jane Austen's treatment of psychological realities has none of the monolithic certainty of her social vision?" asked a woman whose nametag identified her as a professor at a British college.

"Well, I don't think much of that argument," I said. Then I quickly filled my mouth with food, making impossible any further scholarly discussion.

And later, during coffee, I deftly parried another such thrust from a librarian who wanted to discuss Jane's rumored marriage proposal in 1802 from a young man Jane had known since childhood. "They say she accepted immediately and then broke the engagement the following morning."

"Oh, yes," I said with conviction, then added lightly, "What was his name again?"

"Harris Bigg-Wither. He was the heir to Manydown Park."

"Oh, yes, Harris Bigg-Wither, the heir to Manydown Park." Then pointing to the hallway I said, somewhat breathlessly, "Look. They seem to be asking us to gather for the announcement." And with that I took my leave, disappearing into the stream of guests moving into the Great Room for a series of presentations and tours.

One of the presenters was the "American lady" I'd been hearing so much about, Sandy Lerner. She was the driving force, both financially and creatively, behind the transformation of Chawton House into the Centre for the Study of Early English Women's Writing. A cofounder of Cisco Systems, a high-tech company, she had subsequently moved on to other ventures, including the establishment with a former colleague of a private charitable foundation. I liked the idea that a woman who made her name and fortune in the world of high tech was restoring part of Jane Austen's world—not only Chawton House but the literary landscape of Jane's time.

Later, as Jean Bowden and I drove from Chawton House to the country cottage where Jane Austen lived for the last eight years of her life, I mentioned how pleasing I found this high-tech-meets-low-tech union of the two women. "Can you imagine them together?" I asked Jean. "The millionaire business entrepreneur in cutting-edge technology and the author who wrote her novels in longhand at a small table in the dining parlor? Ironic, isn't it?"

"Perhaps not so ironic," Jean said as she pulled the car to a stop at Chawton Cottage. "Jane would love high-tech computers, I think. And fast cars, too."

When Jane Austen and her mother and sister came to live at Chawton Cottage in 1809, their plight was not unlike that of the Dashwoods in *Sense and Sensibility*. They were poor relations who, "in need of a dwelling," were given the use of a house by a wealthy relative.

"When Jane's father died, the Austen ladies had no permanent home," Jean said as she guided me through Chawton Cottage. "They moved from place to place or stayed with relatives. It was only when Cassandra told Edward what their lives were really like that he realized how poor the ladies were. He offered them a cottage either on his estate in Kent or in Chawton. They chose Chawton."

"Where did Jane do her writing?" I asked.

Jean led me to the dining parlor where she stopped before a small pedestal table in front of a window overlooking the road. "It was on this small table that Jane would write, often after breakfast. The coaches came right by the dining room—you can imagine the horses and the rumbling—and they came close enough for passengers to see Jane writing at the table by the window."

I stood for a long time looking at the little table—its round top no bigger than a fourteen-inch cake plate—and tried to picture Jane sitting on her stool, writing in her beautiful penmanship, perhaps glancing up at the rumble of a coach or the flight of a bird. What Jane accomplished in the eight years she lived at Chawton Cottage, sitting at this table, pen in hand, was amazing. During that time she wrote or revised all six of her completed novels. I was startled to learn that Jane was thirty-six when *Sense and Sensibility* was published, the first of her books to appear in print. She died at forty-one.

"The years at Chawton were the most productive of Jane's life, perhaps because she was happy to be settled back in the Hampshire countryside," Jean said as she guided me through the cottage. She told me about the daily routines of the family: "Jane was responsible for the morning meal and in charge of the store of sugar and coffee; her sister Cassandra basically did everything else."

When we passed through the bedroom of Mrs. Austen, Jane's mother, I stopped to look at the pictures and documents lining the walls, including one that reminded me of why Jane's novels remain timeless. It was a copy of a page from the Steventon church register in which Jane, as a young girl, had written her name twice, each time as though she were married to a different man. Seeing this I almost laughed out loud, thinking of the hundreds of times as a teenager I'd sat in school writing out "Mrs. Corky Fox" or "Mrs. Richard Eavey," daydreaming of two boys I adored from a distance. It was reassuring to see that the same young girl who wrote a sharp, satirical piece titled "The History of England . . . by a partial, prejudiced & ignorant Historian" shared, perhaps, the same yearnings.

When we came, finally, to the bedroom shared by Jane and Cassandra—a small room with two chairs drawn up before the fireplace—its intimacy made me feel as though I had invaded the sisters' privacy. I half expected to see them enter the room and position themselves in the chairs, Jane with her needlepoint and Cassandra with her sewing. Above the mantelpiece hung a framed lace collar made by Jane, and on a nearby wall was a patchwork bedspread sewn by Jane and her mother and Cassandra. No wonder Jean Bowden, who had walked through the house for the past eighteen years, spoke of the great author as though she were a living, breathing friend. I asked Jean why there were no beds in the room. She explained that their absence was the result of historians being unable to determine the authenticity of the precise bed—or beds—belonging to Jane and Cassandra at Chawton Cottage.

Jean and I arrived back in Winchester just in time to slip into our seats for a special Evensong at the cathedral, one held in honor of Jane Austen. Sitting in the huge, magisterial nave, I listened as the high, sweet voices of the boys' choir—the same voices I'd heard practicing a day earlier—soared to the vaulted ceiling of the cathedral and then, like falling stars, drifted down as if from heaven. The beauty of the moment hung in the air even after the boys' voices were silent. It was a moving tribute, one that made me wonder what Jane would have thought of all this pomp and circumstance being displayed in her honor. And I would have given anything to know what Jane, whose novels appeared anonymously during her lifetime—the only attribution being, "By a Lady"— would have thought about spending eternity surrounded by the tombs of the early English kings.

After a short ceremony near Jane's grave, Jean and I left for the Wessex Hotel to have dinner. I was eager to hear more of her opinions on Jane Austen's life and work, but I was also eager to learn more about her own life.

Before we even sat down to dinner, I learned something about Jean: when offered the choice of eating in the more formal dining room or the bar, she quickly chose the bar. It was my choice too. "I was hoping you'd choose the bar," I said. "I'm not in the mood for a four-course dinner served from side carts and chafing dishes."

Jean laughed. "I'm never really in the mood for that sort of thing."

We ordered wine and after talking a bit about the day, I asked how she came to be curator of Jane's house. "Were you always involved professionally with the Jane Austen world?"

"Oh, no. I was a botanist for thirty-five years at Kew Gardens in London," she said. "My specialty was orchids. But I've loved Jane Austen since I was twelve years old and first read *Pride and Prejudice*. In fact, they called me 'Jane' at home, because I always had a Jane Austen book in my hands."

I asked how she went from being a botanist at Kew Gardens to being the curator of Chawton Cottage.

"I belonged to the Jane Austen Society and in 1984 learned the curator at the cottage wanted to retire. The job was described as offering 'hard work, poor accommodations, poor pay.' That sounded like me." She laughed, and in that laugh I heard the young Jean, the precocious twelve-year-old capable of her own sharp observations about the world.

"But I wanted to get away from London," she continued. "I always wanted to live in the country; I always wanted to run a small museum; and I loved Jane Austen. So I took the job. It was all signed and sealed within seven days. After thirty-five years at the Kew, I gave them two months' notice."

"I'll drink to that," I said, lifting my wineglass. "To making a decision and moving on with your life."

"Well, I have to admit that when I got to the cottage I was a bit horrified to see what shape it was in. It was pretty depressing at first to see what had to be done."

But after sixteen successful years on the job, Jean decided recently to give up the curatorial position to become the archivist of Jane Austen's house. "I'll be seventy years old this year, and I'm giving myself a party," she said, sounding genuinely excited at the prospect.

Jean and I sat for hours at the table, talking, laughing, and exchanging life stories. As the evening wore on, it struck me that if Jane Austen had lived to the age of seventy she would be a lot like the silver-haired woman sitting opposite me: curious, energetic, smart, sharply observant, and not above enjoying a bit of gossip or categorizing the foibles of others.

When I said good-bye to Jean after dinner it was almost like saying good-bye to a girlfriend after spending a Saturday together roaming around downtown Baltimore. The difference was I wouldn't see Jean the next morning. In fact, I was leaving by train for Exeter just after breakfast. Later, while packing my suitcase for the trip I thought of what Jean had said about the "instant friendship" that can spring up between admirers of Jane Austen. Certainly I felt that about Jean. But there was more to it. What Jean awakened in me was the optimistic twelve-year-old girl who still existed in my head, the one who believed nothing was impossible.

Later, however, while going over my notes about the course I'd enrolled in at the University of Exeter, my excitement was blunted with apprehension. I had no illusions that in a course titled "The World of Jane Austen," I would be anything but one of the least informed students. But, I reminded myself, I had managed to survive a roomful of Austen scholars at the Chawton House luncheon. And, I told myself, if I can make it there, I'll make it anywhere. Including, hopefully, the course at Exeter.

"To get to Exeter you have to change trains at Basingstoke," the ticket clerk at the Winchester station told me. "And when you get to Exeter you want to be sure to get off at the Saint David's stop."

I took a seat in the waiting room next to a young couple saying goodbye to one another. An aura of sweet sadness clung to them as they held hands and whispered, heads almost touching. Then a train came and suddenly the young woman was gone.

I thought of the day I'd said good-bye to Naohiro at the airport in Venice. It was early in the morning and a mist hung over the water; Venice shimmered like a mirage in the distance. After a long sabbatical in Europe I was returning home to the United States. He was flying back to his apartment in Paris. It was a tricky time, early in our relationship, when neither of us was certain we'd see the other one again. But just before we parted he handed me a letter, telling me I should not open it until I was in the air. What I remembered most about that moment was the sweet quizzical look in Naohiro's eyes. It was as though he wanted to say something but couldn't. Or wouldn't. But later on the plane, the voice in his letter told me what I wanted to hear: that we were at the beginning, not the ending, of something we both knew to be special.

Now as my train pulled into the Winchester station, I pushed such thoughts out of my head and ran to the platform to board it. It was Saturday and the train was almost empty. That gave me plenty of room to spread out the maps and brochures I wanted to study before arriving at Exeter University. First, I re-read the description of the course: *"We shall be examining Jane Austen's novels against the social developments of her time with particular reference to the author's witty and incisive comments on eighteenth-century gentility. We will also examine her portrayal of character in the context of literary tradition and her distinctive ways of passing judgment on her fictional creations. The discussions will be assisted by guided visits to some of the special places which influenced Jane Austen's life and work, comprising Lyme Regis, Sidmouth, and Bath."*

A background reading list followed, one including such books as Claire Tomalin's *Jane Austen: A Life* and B. C. Southam's *Jane Austen: The Critical Heritage*. It was suggested also that students read or re-read all six of Austen's novels, particularly *Persuasion* and *Northanger Abbey*, the two novels set in the places we would visit. As usual I'd not had the time to do all the reading, but I had managed to read again the two novels to be discussed and a book of Jane's letters.

But even though my background reading was lacking, I had taken the time to jot down examples of Jane's "witty and incisive comments" and "distinctive ways of passing judgment on her fictional creations." At least in any discussion of these aspects of Jane's work I could refer to my list.

On a page I had titled "Witty Remarks," I noted again with much delight Jane's description of a male character in *Sense and Sensibility* as possessing "a person and face, of strong, natural, sterling insignificance." And on another page I titled "Judgmental Jane," I had noted examples of the probing eye Jane cast not only on her fictional characters but on true-life acquaintances as well. In a letter to her sister Cassandra, for instance, Jane describes a new acquaintance, favorably, as someone who "has Sense & some degree of taste." She then goes on to reveal what is, in Jane's eyes, her potential friend's flaw: "She seems to like people rather too easily."

After reading this last observation I quickly opened to the first page of what was to be my class notebook and wrote: "Note to myself: Do not seem to like people in the class rather too easily. Or at the very least, rather too quickly."

"What I would like you to take away from this course," said Hazel Jones, our tutor at Exeter University, "is the understanding a contemporary reader of Jane Austen might have had." To achieve this, she told the class, we would begin our course by concentrating on Jane's family and background.

It was nine-fifteen on a Sunday morning and the twenty-six students enrolled in the course—two men and twenty-four women—were gathered in the small, comfortable amphitheater that would be our classroom. For some reason I was surprised by our tutor's summation of the goal she had in mind for her students. I suppose my expectations ran more along the lines of analyzing why Jane Austen's novels were able to leap over the centuries separating her time from ours. How, I always wondered after reading one of her books, had she found a writing voice capable of transplanting her characters' yearnings directly into the hearts of contemporary readers? But the more I thought about it, the better I liked the idea of reading Jane's books as though I lived in her time. After all, I knew, or thought I knew, what modern readers make of Austen's novels but had little insight as to what her own contemporaries thought of them.

I'd already had the chance to meet my classmates at a welcoming dinner given the night before. Although the majority of those enrolled in the course were English or American, I was pleased to meet women from Canada, Germany, Italy, and Sweden; it would be fun exchanging views of Jane and her novels with such a diverse group. But what I really looked forward to was having Hazel Jones guide us through Jane Austen's world. During a conversation with Hazel at dinner, it seemed as though I'd known her for years. Despite having only just met, we talked easily and openly about our interests and our lives. It was the way I'd felt on meeting Jean Bowden: that this was a woman who combined a keen intelligence with an appealing down-to-earth manner. And from some of Hazel's observations, including a brief mention of her cats and her garden, I suspected she might be a kindred spirit.

Now as I sat listening to Hazel's first lecture, I quickly realized what a good teacher she was. Focused, organized, and possessed of a sly wit, Hazel displayed a knowledge of Jane Austen and her world so intimate that occasionally I forgot the two women hadn't actually grown up next door to one another. Particularly interesting to me was the light Hazel shed on Jane's childhood; it made me realize how shallow my knowledge was of this period in the author's life.

I had not known, for instance, that it was the practice of Jane's mother to breastfeed each of her babies for three months, and then place the child with a local family or wet nurse to be looked after until deemed manageable at home. Jane, the seventh of eight children, was handed over to a wet nurse at about the age of fourteen weeks. Apparently, this was not an unusual approach to child raising at the time.

"In Mrs. Austen's social level of life, it was almost universal," Hazel said. "But the Austens visited their children daily until they were considered old enough to return to the family, which tended to be between the ages of eighteen months and two years. Two was what Mrs. Austen called the age of reason. But as Claire Tomalin writes in her biography, this sending away of the child may have created some psychological problems for Jane. It appears that things did not go so well between Jane and her mother."

Upon hearing this, the class stirred; I could see Tomalin's book being pulled out, followed by the turning of pages. From my seat in the back row of the risers, I saw a woman raise her hand. Hazel nodded in her direction.

"On page eight, Tomalin writes of the lifelong emotional distance between Jane and her mother," the woman said, referring to the open book before her. "And she says it caused Jane to be a defensive adult who avoided intimacy. But you see, I don't agree with that. One need look no further than Jane's intimacy with Cassandra or Elizabeth Bennet's with her sister Jane in *Pride and Prejudice* to see a woman and a writer quite capable of intimacy."

Another voice, this one just as clipped and elegantly British as the first one, chimed in: "Well, I'm wondering if Jane's poor relationship with her biological mother might not account for all the exemplary mother figures in her novels. Certainly Anne Elliott seems to be looking for maternal guidance from her relationship with Lady Russell in *Persuasion*."

"Yes. And she gets bad advice," the first woman replied.

These remarks ignited a flurry of exchanges regarding the relationship between Jane and her mother. It was a theme—mothers and daughters—that seemed to hit a nerve, at least for the twenty-four women in the room. But then most of what Hazel observed throughout the morning session had the effect of seeming immediate and resonant. Particularly when she moved on to how limited the possibilities were for women in Jane Austen's time.

"It was not that interesting a time, particularly for a woman," Hazel said. "A woman had no way to make money unless she became a governess or lady's companion—which many thought of as a form of slavery. In her novels Jane was always highlighting the difference between men's lives and women's. In *Persuasion*, we hear Anne Elliott telling Captain Harville of the different lives men and women live."

Here, Hazel turned to her copy of *Persuasion* and read aloud Anne's words to the Captain: *"We certainly do not forget you, so soon as you forget us. It is, perhaps, our fate rather than our merit. We cannot help ourselves. We live at home, quiet, confined, and our feelings prey upon us. You are forced on exertion. You have always a profession, pursuits, business of some sort or other, to take you back into the world immediately, and continual occupation and change soon weaken impressions."*

As I watched Hazel and listened to her lovely reading of the passage, she seemed to become Anne Elliott. A willowy woman with long, copper-colored hair framing her pale, fine-boned face, Hazel had about her the air of an Austen heroine. It was easy to imagine her dancing at a ball in a simple gown of pale green silk, her thick burnished hair pinned up with tiny white flowers. That image led to another and soon I was creating a character based on Hazel. She would be a young woman, an orphan consigned to living with poor relatives, who earns her keep as a piano teacher. Although of lowly status, she quickly elicits admiration for her beauty and accomplishments. Just as I was about to give her a name, I realized she sounded familiar. Then it hit me: I had re-created, more or less, the character of Jane Fairfax in *Emma*.

Somewhat dashed by the realization that Jane Austen had thought up such a character first, I shifted my focus back to the classroom discussion. I tuned in just in time to catch the end of what seemed to be a bit of a contest between two women, one British, the other American, both of whom really knew their Austen. I heard a mention of a letter from Jane to her favorite niece, Fanny Knight, urging her not to marry too soon. It seemed they were debating, politely, some minor detail having to do with the letter's content, but I missed the point of their exchange.

What I didn't miss, however, was the passion felt by my classmates for Jane Austen and her fictional characters. I thought of Jean Bowden, of how at twelve she had been so hooked by her first encounter with an Austen novel that her family took to calling her "Jane." It wasn't difficult to imagine any one of my classmates at the age of twelve, bent over a copy of *Pride and Prejudice*, immersed in the ambivalent—and sometimes adolescent—feelings between Elizabeth Bennet and the aristocratic Mr. Darcy. After all, it is a truth universally acknowledged that a single girl of twelve—or twelve-and-thirty, for that matter—will become instantly infatuated with the handsome, wealthy, landowning Mr. Darcy despite, or perhaps because of, his high opinion of himself.

The relationships between men and women, the antipathies between mothers and daughters, the role of women in a male-dominated society: with themes like these, was it any wonder that Jane's novels spoke so effortlessly across the centuries to generations of readers? Of course it

didn't hurt that the world within her words was revealed to us through
Jane's keen eyes. Envy, pomposity, seduction, betrayal, love, loss, pride,
prejudice, and, my personal favorite, self-delusion—all these universal
emotions are exposed by Jane in a way that is always insightful and
sometimes makes us laugh. Partly, I think, because we see bits of
ourselves in every character.

We took our dinner that night, as we would all our meals, in the main
dining room at the Saint Luke's Campus of Exeter University. Although
most of my classmates were staying on the campus in university accommodations, I had chosen to take a room in a nearby bed-and-breakfast
called the Edwardian. It was about the same price as the dorm rooms but
offered a little more privacy. I had decided to do this after receiving in
the mail a copy of each day's schedule. Our days, I saw, would be busy:
breakfast at eight, followed by classroom work; lunch at twelve-thirty,
followed by more classroom work; dinner at six-thirty, usually followed
by some sort of Austen-connected event. On other days we would be
taking field trips to places that influenced Jane's life and work. With all
that togetherness—no matter how pleasant the company—I figured a
little privacy might come in handy.

The dinner was very festive. All of us, I think, were more relaxed now
that the first day was over and we had taken the measure of the course
and of one another. And maybe the wine helped a bit too. After dinner
we left the dining hall and crossed the campus to our classroom for a
showing of the film version of *Emma*. As we made our lighthearted way
across the lush grass quadrangle, talking and laughing like a troop of
aging Girl Scouts bound together by an oath of allegiance to Jane
Austen, I breathed in the soft night air and imagined I smelled the sea
that lay half an hour's drive away.

Although I'd already seen *Emma* twice, watching it with a group of
Austen devotees was a totally different experience, one that ratcheted
up the enjoyment level by several notches. By the time the evening was
over, I felt as though I was leaving a *Star Trek* convention. In the end,
Janeites and Trekkies didn't seem all that different; each connected
deeply to the world inhabited by their heroines and heroes. On my way
home from the campus I thought about my conversation with Hazel. It
confirmed my initial impression that she was a kindred spirit, especially
when the talk had turned to our mutual love of cats and gardens.

"I really miss my garden and my cat when I'm traveling," I told Hazel. "When I was in Japan I called home twice to see how he was."

She smiled. "I know. When I'm away I make frequent calls to ask, 'Have you seen my cats? How do they look? And what are my beans doing?'"

"Yes, I've been dying to call home to see if my crape myrtle is blooming."

We both laughed. But the pleasure we felt was not only about discovering our similar over-the-top responses to being separated from our cats and gardens. It was the recognition that in each other we had found a friend.

By the time we set out on our trip to Lyme Regis, the eighteenth-century seaside resort where Jane and her family went on holiday, the class had metamorphosed into something resembling freshman year in a very civilized high school. The usual selection process that occurs when strangers are thrown together in close quarters had already taken place: friendships had emerged, benign cliques formed, and at meal-times, the same people routinely ate together. For some reason this selection process did not split the class into factions, as it often does when perpetrated by ninth-grade girls trying to shape a hierarchy that places them at the top. No, we remained one class, indivisible, under Jane Austen and everything for which she stands.

Actually, it was fun watching such start-up friendships develop—or not develop—during the first few days. Some liaisons were predictable. Others surprised me. None surprised me more than the friendship between Joyce, a refined Englishwoman from a small village in Dorset, and Lynda, a lively spark plug of a woman from a big city in Texas. True, they had some things in common. Both were exceedingly smart— between them they seemed to have read every book mentioned by anyone in any context—and both appeared to know everything knowable about Jane Austen. But sometimes during class discussions I thought I detected a slight friction in their exchanges, one that had the potential to change from sparks to fireworks.

But I was dead wrong. Instead of turning into dueling Janeites, Joyce and Lynda became a pair. I watched with admiration, and a bit of amusement, as their relationship progressed from prickly exchanges in class to arm-in-arm camaraderie. Often I'd see them walking together—the Brit and the Yank, as I thought of them—chatting, pointing out things to one another, talking about who knows what. Perhaps the subject was Lynda's life in Texas with her Chinese physicist husband, a man she'd met through a mutual interest in ballroom dancing. Or perhaps they talked about the small Dorset village where Joyce lived alone in a converted church. Or more likely, the talk was about their favorite subject: books, books, and books.

It was on the bus trip to Lyme Regis that I found out just how vast a reservoir of literature was stored in these two heads. Since I'd grown to enjoy Joyce and Lynda's company, I purposely chose a seat across the aisle from them. Naturally the talk turned to books. Hardy, Eliot, Henry James, Trollope, Forster, Wharton, Graves. It was like a chain reaction as each name reminded the two women of another author, another book. Trying to keep up with the speed of their associations was like watching the trailing light of a meteorite, one that had passed by too quickly to see.

"Have you read *Lark Rise to Candleford* by Flora Thompson?" Lynda asked me.

"I've never heard of it."

"Oh, but you must read it then," Joyce said, her exquisite accent turning the mundane remark into something that sounded almost like poetry. It reminded me of why, as a child, I was so convinced my life would change if only I had an English accent.

The two women then began telling me about the book, so excited that they started finishing each other's sentences, the way twins sometimes do.

"I'll write down the title and the author's name for you," Joyce said, getting out her pen. Even bent over her notebook, Joyce—who was in her seventh decade—had the straight-backed posture of a much younger person.

"There are a lot of used-book stores in Lyme Regis," Lynda said. "I'd like to buy a copy if possible."

As if by mutual consent, the three of us grew quiet. When the two women began to read, I decided to look over some notes from Hazel's lectures on the shared characteristics of Jane Austen's heroines:

> All her heroines have to strive against some sort of difficulty, and the difficulty is usually family-related. Her heroines learn something about themselves in striving. . . . Her heroine needs to know the character of the man before she marries him. . . . All of

Jane Austen's heroines are reading throughout each book. . . . The heroines come from realistic backgrounds and throughout the novel they find out what they feel about things. They are always conscious of their feelings. They talk to themselves so you, the reader, have access to their hearts and minds, a precursor to the stream-of-consciousness novels. . . . All Jane Austen's heroines are looking forward to something; only Anne Elliott in *Persuasion* is looking backward.

Although the list went on, I stopped at the mention of Anne Elliott and *Persuasion*. It was my favorite of Jane's novels. As usually happened when I tried to choose one of Jane's novels over the others, my thinking voice jumped in to challenge this choice. *What about* Emma? *it asked. Isn't that your favorite? Or what about* Pride and Prejudice, *the novel you used to re-read each summer?* I sighed. It was true; I seemed to flit back and forth between Jane's books when trying to decide on a favorite.

Still, putting fickleness aside, *Persuasion* appealed to me not only for its unique "looking backward rather than forward" structure, but because it tackles, like no other book I know, the morally ambiguous nature of persuasion in all its forms. From Anne Elliott, who is persuaded by her snobbish family to spurn a suitor thought to be unsuitable, to the attempts to persuade Anne's father, Sir Walter, to tolerate the designing Mrs. Clay, the novel offers profound insights into the dangers of influencing another person through persuasion.

Of course it doesn't hurt that the novel *Persuasion* also offers a smashing story of love lost and, after years of separation, regained. Or that the lovers, Anne Elliott and Captain Wentworth, are more mellow (read: older) than many of Jane Austen's couples. Like many women my age, I could identify with lost love, bad advice, and relationships deemed by others as "unsuitable."

We arrived in Lyme Regis in the heat of the day. With not a cloud in sight, the sun was brazenly hot; its light penetrated the waters of Lyme Bay, separating it into parfaitlike layers of deep blue, pale blue, emerald green, and silver gray. In our attempts to dress defensively against the predicted heat and sun, most of us looked very un-Austenish.

Betty and Janet, longtime traveling partners from the West Coast of the United States, wore Bermuda shorts and cotton shirts. Carla, an Italian woman with bold Roman features and curly dark hair, was dressed in pressed jeans and a red knit sweater. Marion from New England had on a white straw fedora and long dark jumper. The fashionable Hilda from Germany took a minimalist approach; her crisp khaki pants and white shirt looked perfect. As for Lynda and Joyce, their approach to seaside dressing highlighted the differences between this compatible pair. Lynda wore a smocklike deep pink top over black ankle-length tights, a jaunty straw hat with flowers perched like a bird on her head. Joyce, on the other hand, chose a covered-up look that came closer to what Jane Austen might choose were she to visit Lyme Regis today. Looking cool and unruffled, she wore a billowy cotton skirt that stopped just above her ankles, a long-sleeved white shirt of handkerchief-soft cotton, and, on her head, a handsome straw bonnet that completely shielded her face from the sun. Hazel, who was fair-skinned, had on a pale cotton sleeveless sheath, no hat, and, I hoped, a lot of sunscreen.

When we stepped off the bus in Lyme Regis, it was as though we had stepped into another century. Which, in a way, was true, because little had changed since Jane stayed here. Certainly the sea hadn't changed, nor had the gravelly beach shaped like a half-moon around the shoreline. And the line of cliffs marking the horizon wasn't new; neither were the crooked hilly streets that ran like fingers through the town. In fact, Hazel had given us a map outlining the site of the Assembly Rooms where Jane danced and the building on Broad Street where the Austen family had taken rooms. It was easy to see why the charm and sea and fresh air of Lyme Regis so captivated Jane that she decided to make it the setting, along with Bath and Somersetshire, for *Persuasion*.

But as fine as the buildings and scenery were, they were not what we admirers of *Persuasion* had come to see. No, we wanted to visit the famous stone jetty known as the Cobb. A stone wall that skirts around the bay before jutting out into the water, the Cobb is the setting for a crucial scene in *Persuasion*. It is where the impetuous Louisa Musgrove suffers an injury when, against Captain Wentworth's entreaties, she jumps off a flight of steep steps. The Cobb incident provides the turning point in the relationship between Anne Elliott and Captain Wentworth; it is the moment—one present in all of Jane's novels—when hero and heroine finally recognize each other's virtues.

When Hazel led us to the Cobb and we stood before the stone wall and the steep dangerous steps that had no railing, it was like visiting a historic site. The literary equivalent, I suppose, of standing on the hallowed ground of Gettysburg. Everything was just as Jane described it, making it impossible to believe that Louisa had not just fallen from these steps before our very eyes, shocking everyone present. It made me realize that Jane Austen was not only a novelist capable of creating unforgettable fictional characters, she was also an excellent reporter able to re-create the actual world around her. In fact, Hazel had told us that Jane was known to do research for her novels. "She would write letters to people asking 'Are there hedgerows in Northanger?' " Hazel said. "Or she'd ask, 'Are there two days between Devon and Bath? Are they more than a hundred miles apart?' "

After an hour or so of visiting Austen-related sites with Hazel as our guide, the class scattered so we could explore the town at our own pace. Since this was a group that loved books, most of us were eager to visit as many bookshops as possible. I headed for the Sanctuary Bookshop on Broad Street, a steep road once described by Jane as "almost hurrying into the water." On the way there, I saw several of my classmates striding with great purpose along the narrow streets. We nodded but didn't slow down in our pursuit of hard-to-find secondhand books. We were like wine connoisseurs in search of the last remaining bottle of Château Pétrus 1950.

When I stepped inside the Sanctuary Bookshop, the familiar musty smell of old books welcomed me. I breathed in deeply, then began browsing through the used books. With its knowledgeable staff, reasonable prices, and a selection of books that ranged from rare items to used paperbacks, the Sanctuary was a book lover's dream. Particularly fascinating to me were the inscriptions in the used books; they hinted at whole lives. "To my dear friend Maud, in memory of the olden days," read the inscription in a copy of *Mrs. Miniver.* And in an early edition of E. B. White's *Charlotte's Web* I found this cryptic message: "To the Charlotte in my life, Love, Wilbur."

There were at least a dozen books I wanted to buy. What I ended up with, however, surprised me: three copies of books by Beatrix Potter, the creator of such protagonists as Peter Rabbit, Tom Kitten, and my favorite, Samuel Whiskers. With help from one of the owners, I learned how to tell apart the various editions of Potter's collection. I ended up buying a variety of printings, including a 1944 copy of *The Tale of Samuel Whiskers,* bound in the original red covered boards with a round pastedown illustration on the front. I left feeling almost smug at finding what I considered a real treasure.

But something happened on the return trip to Exeter that rearranged my idea of what constituted a treasure.

"We have something for you," Joyce said, leaning across the aisle between our seats. Then Lynda handed me a small packet neatly wrapped in brown paper.

Inside was a paperback copy of *Lark Rise to Candleford,* the book that Joyce and Lynda had raved about earlier. Their thoughtful and unexpected gift touched me. "Would you write your names inside?" I asked. "It will remind me of a very special day spent in Lyme Regis with two friends."

Later that night I began reading the book, but only after lingering a long while on the two inscriptions on the flyleaf. The sight of the messages signed by the two women made the small worn volume more valuable in my eyes than a first edition of *Persuasion and* a bottle of Château Pétrus 1950 ever could.

In between the two morning sessions with Hazel, it was customary for the class to take tea or coffee in a garden near the faculty house. I always looked forward to this brief interlude, not only for the coffee and home-made tea cakes but also because it offered a chance to learn more about my classmates. Occasionally, when I'd wind up talking to someone I knew only through classroom discussions, our conversation would lead to unexpected revelations. I suppose the talk that surprised me most was with Beatrice, an Englishwoman who possessed the kind of genteel manners displayed by the well-bred Lady Russell in *Persuasion.* Beatrice and I, it turned out, had a lot in common. We discovered this in one of those strange conversational leaps that took us from cats to ex-husbands. What triggered this sharp turn was my answer to her question, "Who's taking care of your cat while you're away?"

"My ex-husband," I said. "That may sound strange, but we have a very close relationship."

"That's wonderful, isn't it? I am devoted to my ex-husband too. I shall be devastated if anything happens to him. We share so much."

It turned out that, in addition to our friendly divorces, Beatrice and I each had two children, and neither of us had any intention of ever remarrying.

"Why marry now?" Beatrice asked. "I've had my marriage."

"My feelings exactly."

"It's almost as if we've lived parallel lives," Beatrice said. "I wonder what Jane Austen might have made of that."

"Plenty," I said. We both laughed.

It was during such coffee breaks that my friendship with Hazel deepened. Often she'd walk through the garden with me, stopping to answer questions about various flowers and plants I couldn't identify. Other times we'd get together over tea and talk of our lives, our families, our favorite books—*Middlemarch* for both of us—our cats, and, in Hazel's case, her fabulous chickens, each of whom had a Jane Austen–related name.

"Let's see," Hazel said, "there's Fanny Price, Madam Lefroy, Lizzie Bennet, Jane, Cassandra, Mrs. Dashwood, Mrs. Croft. . . ."

By this time I was doubled over, laughing at the thought of Hazel calling out at chicken-feeding time, "Here, Madam Lefroy . . . Here, Mrs. Dashwood . . ."

"Well, I'm a country girl," Hazel said, smiling. "I grew up in the Midlands in an eighteenth-century house, and when I wanted excitement I went to Birmingham. I did go away to university in London for three years, but then I came home to the country. But I couldn't have done without those three years; I saw every play in London and visited every gallery."

One evening before dinner with the group, Hazel and her husband, David, invited me to have a drink with them. David, who had children from a first marriage, was a biologist who taught English in nearby Crediton. A smart, witty man with an open face and easy manner, he seemed to bring out the playful side of Hazel. It confirmed my feeling that I was wrong earlier on to have compared Hazel to Jane Fairfax. She was, in fact, more like Elizabeth Bennet: spirited, independent, and quite capable of delivering a tiny barb along with her quick wit.

To get to the small seaside town of Sidmouth, the bus meandered down narrow country roads marked now and then with clusters of houses adjacent to a general store. We were all in particularly high spirits at the thought of visiting this picturesque town where, the story goes, Jane fell in love with a young man while on a family holiday. "It was a mutual attraction," Hazel told us. "Then the next thing she heard was that the young man had died."

The course at Exeter was almost over; Sidmouth was to be our last field trip. Earlier in the week we'd toured Bath, where Jane, the country girl from Hampshire, lived in rented rooms with her family for five years. By many accounts, Jane did not enjoy her time in this fashionable spa town where the wealthy came to see and be seen, and, according to her biographers, she wrote very little while living there. Still, as any reader of *Persuasion* or *Northanger Abbey* knows, the years spent in Bath laid the groundwork for Jane's knowledge of the social mores she so expertly skewers in her novels.

"The whole point of going to Bath was to be noticed," Hazel had told us when we walked through the town. "If you thought you were someone, you would publicize in the newspaper that you were in town. One of the things that attracted people to Bath was that it had pavements. You could go out and walk—even in the rain—without getting your feet dirty. It was unheard of, even in London."

While I found Bath charming and its pristine Georgian architecture stunning, the visit also had its sad aspects. By tracing the Austens' moves from better to worse rented rooms, it was easy to see how far the family's fortunes declined after they left the countryside for fashionable Bath. But however poor the family's living conditions might be, Jane's acute observations stayed intact. It wasn't difficult to picture Jane at a fancy concert, making notes that would shape a scene such as this one from *Persuasion*:

> . . . The whole party was collected, and all that remained, was to marshal themselves, and proceed into the concert room; and be of all the consequence in their power, draw as many eyes, excite as many whispers, and disturb as many people as they could.

Now, as the bus pulled into Sidmouth and stopped near the long boardwalk that curved around Lyme Bay, we listened to Hazel finish a story about Fortfield Terrace, a hotel where the Grand Duchess Helen of Russia stayed in the 1800s, bringing with her hundreds of servants and an orchestra. Once again we were given maps marked with Austen-related sites. Then we were more or less turned loose. We scattered like children on the last day of school—which in a way we were, since most of us planned to leave Exeter the next day.

The day was warm and golden and the water's undulating blue-into-green-into-turquoise color reminded me suddenly of a tie-dyed dress I wore once, in the sixties, to a beach party. As I strolled along the wide boardwalk lined with green-and-white-striped canvas chairs, my mood was like that of a gardener in early spring: optimistic and eager to see what turns up. I imagined myself to be Jane Austen, out for a stroll on a fine day. Straight ahead, off in the distance, was a zigzag line of red limestone cliffs that rose from the water. Sidmouth's stunning geography reminded me of the Amalfi coast, only softer and less spectacular. To my left was the town, a perfect little seaside village where white buildings mixed with an occasional pink stucco house. And to my right, the gravelly beach where a few bathers sat sunning themselves while in the shallow water a mother stood holding on to her child's hand. I suddenly saw myself at the edge of childhood, standing on the beach with Mother as she held my hand and led me into the lapping water of an inlet near the Chesapeake Bay.

For the next hour or two I walked through the town, stopping to explore the antiques shops and look in the windows of butcher shops where meats were as artfully displayed as an exhibition of found objects in a Soho gallery. I visited the peaceful old cemetery, then stopped to enjoy a cappuccino in the tearoom of Fields Department Store, which advertised "Service as it used to be."

On my way back to our meeting place at the Royal Glen Hotel, I tried again to see my surroundings through Jane's eyes, to observe as she might have the character of the town and its inhabitants. It was of course a ridiculously hopeless fantasy, the idea of seeing what Jane Austen saw, but one that I enjoyed nonetheless. After all, who but Jane had that special "glance"—the one able to spot pomposity and self-delusion from a mile off. Sometimes I thought the columnist Maureen Dowd came close. Her observations on the customs and social mores of political life in Washington struck me as a modern-day equivalent to Jane Austen's chronicle of social and familial life in the Hampshire countryside. It wasn't difficult, for instance, to imagine Ms. Dowd describing a politician as someone who possessed "a person and face of strong natural sterling insignificance."

At dinner that night—the last we would share together as a class—I sat next to Hazel. She asked if I had enjoyed Sidmouth.

"I'm already planning a return visit," I said. "Perhaps with a Japanese friend. We might even bring our own orchestra."

Hazel laughed. "I have something for you," she said, handing me a tiny manila envelope containing a small amount of seeds. Written on the outside were the words *"Cerinthe major."*

"It's a border plant for edging," she explained. "Plant it in early spring.

Maybe even February. The spikes are long and narrow, the color of lilac with navy blue at the center. Everyone who sees it always asks me, 'What's that?' "

"I know just the place for it in my garden," I said. "In front of the feathery pink astilbe just below my bedroom window. That way I'll see it first thing every morning and remember you and Jane Austen and Exeter and how much I learned here."

"Perhaps one day we'll write a book together about gardening. In the form of letters to each other. You in America and me in England."

"Yes, and we'll call it, 'The Novice and the Master.' I think you can guess who's who."

That night I fell asleep thinking of my first gardening letter.

Dear Hazel,

I have just had my first sight of *Cerinthe major*. Blue-green leaves spiraling up the stem into a purplish-blue bract that ends in small clusters of navy blue flowers nodding in the wind. Now please write and tell me how to take care of it. I await your instructions.

Havana Dreams

IF IT WERE any other airport in any other city in the world, I would have been alarmed when the electricity shut down, leaving hundreds of travelers in total darkness. But this was Havana, a city that has a way of turning things upside down, of making mishaps seem like adventures. So instead of complaints, out came hundreds of small flashlights, their beams moving like glowworms across the crowd of American and Cuban travelers trying to find their luggage and, if possible, a way out of the terminal.

In the dim light the whole scene took on a playful quality as people tried to avoid bumping into something or someone, an impossible task. The mood was good-natured and so were the exchanges in English and Spanish that accompanied the inevitable collisions. *Sorry. Excuse me. Disculpeme. Was that your foot? Or your suitcase? Either way, pardon.* I could hear little waves of laughter ripple across the terminal as we made our way to what we hoped was the exit. When I bumped into a Cuban man, almost knocking a briefcase out of his hands, he smiled and made a gallant gesture that said, *After you, Señora.* Bumping into people, I decided, could be fun; it reminded me of an adult version of bumper cars without the cars.

I suppose the holiday mood on the plane had set the tone for such a mellow response to this unexpected glitch. The chartered flight from New York took off with forty American tourists and more than a hundred Cubans on board, and the plane buzzed with excitement all the way to Havana. For the Cuban passengers it was a return to home and family. For Americans it was an exciting chance to see Cuba— mysterious, intriguing, forbidden Cuba—with all its contradictions and decaying beauty before the country's inevitable opening up to tourists. Even Winston Churchill had experienced such heightened emotions in 1895 as he approached Havana by sea, writing that he felt "delirious yet tumultuous" at the thought of visiting Havana, "a place where anything might happen." For me the anticipation of Cuba had the effect of turning back time; I felt like a fifteen-year-old on my way to an unsupervised beach vacation.

So, when the electricity went off in the small terminal and the glow-worms came out and I had to find a tour bus waiting somewhere outside, I did what a child might do: I followed my instincts and walked toward the smell of the sea drifting through an open door. Beyond the door I could see hundreds of flashlights lighting up the eager faces of people waiting to meet relatives and friends who, more than likely, were bringing gifts of medicine, soap, paper goods, clothing, and, of course, the scarcest commodity of all: American dollars. Shouts of recognition greeted visitors as they walked through the door. *Hola, el padre!* called out a young woman to an older man; he was immediately surrounded by a gaggle of children and adults. But the crowd remained polite, even seeing to it that a path was left open for other arriving passengers.

Once outside, however, my instincts deserted me; I had no clue as to where to go or what to do. In a way, it didn't matter. What mattered was the way the soft damp sea breeze moved suddenly across my skin like a hand, brushing my hair slyly as it passed. Its touch created a dizzy longing in me, a wish to say *yes* to someone or something. But who? Or what? Before I had time to search for the answer, reality intruded in the form of a quick tap on my shoulder.

"Follow me," said a tall man with broad shoulders, a big head, and an Australian—or was it British?—accent. Since he was wearing a badge that said "Academic Arrangements Abroad," the name of the trip's organizer, I followed him.

"Does this happen a lot?" I asked as we dodged our way through the crowd. "The power going out, I mean."

"All the time," said the guide, one of two non-Cubans who were to assist us during our stay in Havana. "The Cuban government, I was told, is trying to reduce the use of electricity in public places by fifty percent. So

the lights go out—or they're lowered—and there's no air-conditioning. Usually these blackouts happen during peak periods of use, but they can happen anytime."

When we reached the edge of the terminal, my guide pointed out two motor coaches parked at the curb. I hopped onto the nearest one and plunked myself down in the first available seat, next to a woman I could barely see in the dimly lit bus. Immediately she turned to me and said, "Hello, I'm Annie."

"And I'm Alice. Too bad we can't see one another, but at least when the lights come back on I'll recognize you by your nametag." A slightly awkward silence followed this brief introduction, part of the tourist's protocol of waiting to see if another traveler wants to engage or be left alone. I broke the silence. "Are you involved in the arts?" I asked. The question was the first thing that came to mind, since the tour's focus was on Cuba's architecture and art, including the Havana Film Festival.

"Not exactly, though I'm interested in anything that has to do with historic preservation. But I've always wanted to visit Cuba. And since the trip was organized for Vassar graduates it gave me a chance to travel with some of my classmates. How about you? Why did you pick this trip?"

"Well, I'm *not* a Vassar graduate, but when I saw the trip advertised I took a chance and somehow wangled my way into the group. Visiting Cuba's been a dream of mine too. And the idea of meeting Cuban artists appealed to me, although to be honest I'm just as interested in talking to average Cubans. Which probably means I'll spend a lot of time wandering alone through Havana, poking my nose into things."

By the time the bus arrived at our Havana hotel, Annie and I knew much more about each other than just names. In less than an hour we had exchanged the *Reader's Digest* version of our lives, the way travelers often do. Annie, I learned, was from a small town in upstate New York, was divorced, had two young sons, wrote grants for a living, had graduated from Vassar, and loved the theater and music. The music part didn't surprise me. Her throaty voice had a musical quality that suggested she could sing.

As we waited in the hotel lobby for our room assignments, I told Annie of my plan to stay behind in Havana the next morning instead of leaving with the group on a two-day trip into the countryside. When she asked why, I said I wanted to stay in the city and explore Habana Vieja—Old Havana—street by street. "I'll leave Cuba's countryside for another visit. It's *Habana* and the *Habaneros* I've come for on this trip."

Although Annie seemed interested in my change of plan, she said nothing. I took her silence to mean she didn't agree with my decision.

After freshening up in our rooms, the group met for drinks in a glamorous rooftop setting under the stars. Beneath swaying palm trees we drank *mojitos*—the rum-mint julep made famous by Hemingway—while strolling musicians serenaded us. Ordinarily, being set down in a room with more than forty strangers was not my favorite thing. But I had good vibes about my fellow travelers. For one thing, they seemed extraordinarily good-natured; their responses to the blackout at Havana's airport and the long, tiring wait at JFK in New York proved that. And for another, the group was diverse enough to promise many interesting points of view, not only about art and architecture but politics and history as well. At least that's what I expected from a group that included teachers, professors, journalists, social workers, retired businesspeople, a former headmistress of a well-known Manhattan school, a restaurant owner, an actor from a popular network television series, and a family of five traveling together. But the real bond between this disparate group, besides the Vassar College connection, was the deep curiosity each of us had about Cuba and the Cubans.

I was just finishing my first *mojito* when Annie and I spotted each other from opposite sides of the crowded terrace. We motioned to one another to meet at the bar.

"I decided to skip the trip outside of Havana too," Annie said right off, with no explanation. "So I wondered if we could wander around Old Havana together."

"I'd like that," I said, ignoring the selfish part of me that wondered if a companion would change the experience. But I liked Annie, and the very fact she was willing to spontaneously change her plans was a good sign.

We agreed to have breakfast together the next morning before beginning our reconnaissance of Habana Vieja.

Even before we arrived at Calle Obispo, the main street of Old Havana, Annie and I heard the pulsing sound of salsa music coming from half a dozen different directions. At the entrance to the narrow pedestrian street—near El Floridita, the bar Hemingway frequented when he was in the mood for the perfect frozen daiquiri—we stood watching two boys, baseball caps on their heads, dance to the hot beat of a rumba coming from a radio. Then Annie and I began our slow rudderless walk down Calle Obispo, a street where past and present collided at every turn.

Past mom-and-pop bodegas we walked, inhaling the fragrant scent of strong Cuban coffee and grilled Cubano sandwiches. Past breathtaking Spanish colonial buildings—some restored, others almost falling down—and colorful pink stucco souvenir shops that catered to "dollars only" tourists. Past open-air bars where Cubans sat at tables playing dominoes. Past a group of Santería followers beating drums and chanting under the watchful eyes of attractive young policemen. Past bookshops and stores selling bikinis and high-style shoes. Past tourists searching for excitement and Cubans trying to improvise a life. Past all this Annie and I walked.

Annie, it turned out, enjoyed the aimless lingering and looking as much as I did. It was only when the rain started that we stopped walking in the street and moved instead from doorway to doorway, taking shelter briefly in each one. From the tiny covered entrance to a jewelry shop I watched two laughing Cuban women in bright dresses run by in the rain, their colorful reflections running alongside them, mirrored in the wet street. Annie and I stood there for a while listening to the rain bouncing off the shallow jutting roof. Then I heard another sound: the hypnotic driving rhythm of Afro-Cuban music exploding from a bar across the street. Standing outside the bar, swaying toward the open windows, were several Cubans dressed in colorful shorts and T-shirts, dancing in the rain.

I looked at Annie. "Want to get a drink, hear some music, and stay dry in that bar across the street?"

She nodded and started running across the wet steamy street. I followed her, straight through the open door and into a long narrow room. Along one wall was a dark mahogany bar lined with stools; opposite it, in front of a row of windows opening onto the street, were several tables. The place was almost empty—just a few Cubans drinking beer—but the musicians played as though performing before a crowd at Havana's famous Tropicana nightclub. Annie and I boldly took a table right in front of them. A few of the half dozen musicians in the group nodded as we sat down. We nodded back. Then they began to play again.

I don't know if it was the thrill of being in Havana or whether the music really was as exciting as it seemed. Either way, I gave myself up to listening in a way I'd almost forgotten. Not since I was a twenty-year-old jazz addict hanging out at Birdland, grooving to the likes of Charlie Parker and Thelonious Monk, had I felt so connected to the music I was hearing. Annie, I could tell, felt the same way.

The musicians sensed it, too, I thought—our involvement in their high-energy performance. Maybe I imagined it, but after a while they seemed to be playing for us; particularly the soulful-looking trumpeter, whose luminous solo wove in and out of the percussion-driven rhythm the way Ella's voice did when she sang jazz with Count Basie.

When the first set ended, two of the players came to our table and introduced themselves. Octavio, a round-faced, friendly man who played the maracas and seemed to be the lead vocalist, spoke fairly good English. Angel, the guitar-playing leader, spoke very little, which didn't matter since his chiseled face was dominated by cheekbones as sharp as razors and soft brown eyes that had a language all their own. By the end of the second set, we had met everyone in the band, including Jorge, the fabulous man with a horn. They showed us how to play the guiro, a notched gourd whose sound comes from running a stick along the notches, and the claves, two sticks struck together to set the rhythm and keep it steady.

I was surprised a bit by the respectful, almost gallant, attitude of the musicians toward us; I expected them to be more like the pushy hustlers who'd approached me earlier that morning on my pre-breakfast walk. We'd been warned about these street hustlers, the *jineteros* who hang around hotels offering their services to tourists for American dollars. Sure enough, when I stepped beyond the hotel door, they appeared one by one, first to flatter me and then to deliver their sales pitch. By the end of my walk I had their routine down cold. *Hello, are you American? What a beauty! You must have many men friends. Let me teach you salsa dancing, sell you the finest cigars, help you find a paladar with beautiful food, take you on a tour, anything you want for just a few dollars, pretty lady.* What made the *jineteros* harmless was their lack of follow-through; they simply gave up and wandered off when I said no and walked away.

But the musicians we'd met in the bar seemed antithetical to any macho stereotype of Latin men. So when the third set began and Octavio and Angel asked Annie and me to dance, we didn't hesitate. At least Annie didn't. I *might* have paused for a second, but that's all it was, a pause—one that gave me just enough time to ask myself, *Am I going to look like a total fool?* The answer came quickly: *Who cares?* I moved into Angel's arms.

It's funny how dancing to Latin music never failed to free up my body. As I moved to the music my usually dormant hips sprang to life; they seemed suddenly to remember my year of obsession with the hula hoop. It occurred to me that some forms of music are more about dancing than about listening. And with this kind of driving beat, it didn't matter whether you knew the steps. There were no steps, only the unplanned response of your body to the music. Of course it helped that Angel was a great dancer. Long and lean, he was elegant and smooth in his moves and had a way of taking charge that gave me confidence, however imaginary.

Annie and I stayed until the last slow dance, a gorgeous trumpet version of "My Way." I wondered if this very un-Latin music was a concession, perhaps, to the two American *chicas* who'd wandered in out of the rain and stayed most of the afternoon.

We posed for photos with the band before we left and promised to return with some friends. When an old woman walked into the bar, selling roses—*One dollar for one rose,* she called out—I gave her a dollar, then on an impulse presented the rose to Angel. He bowed. I bowed back, forgetting I wasn't in Kyoto.

"You are such a groupie," Annie said as we walked out of the bar.

"And you're not?" I answered. Annie laughed. It was the laugh of a happy child.

Annie saw her before I did, the thin young woman standing on the street, trying to catch our attention. Holding on to her hand was an expressionless boy of about five, dressed neatly in clothes a couple of sizes too small. She approached us and raising one finger asked, "One dollar, *por favor?*" The woman, who was not much taller than a ten-year-old girl, told us she was pregnant and needed to buy milk. Unlike the hustlers, her request for money was straightforward and not surprising. We were forewarned that since Cuba lost its Soviet patron, along with millions of dollars in subsidies, many Cubans were forced to supplement their meager incomes by asking tourists for American dollars. Most Americans didn't seem to mind helping out such Cubans, who seemed in a different category than the hustling *jineteros.*

Certainly Annie and I didn't; we each handed the woman a dollar bill for milk. She paused. Then in halting English she asked if we would buy the milk for her since Cubans were not always welcome in state-owned "dollar stores." Annie agreed and went off with her to get the milk.

The rain had stopped and the street was crowded again. Families had come out for a Sunday stroll. Three pretty young women with skin the color of brandy flirted with handsome young policemen. A circle of teenage boys danced to hip-hop music from an old boom box. A little girl dressed in red stood outside a café feeding cake to a caged green parrot. A smiling old woman as spare and elegant as Isak Dinesen sat on a step, holding out a white paper cone with a small flower inside. From a second-story balcony, a woman hanging laundry stopped to wave at someone below.

It all seemed so romantic. I was enchanted.

When we returned to the hotel I asked Annie if she'd like to go with me that night to have a drink at La Maison, an old mansion that before the Revolution was owned by a rich sugar baron. "Now it's become a high-fashion center with nightly runway shows held outside in the garden," I explained. "A journalist friend in New York suggested it. She said it's the only place to see what Cuban fashion designers are doing, and that the whole fashionista scene is fun. Sounds very different from what we saw this morning."

"Where is it?"

"In Miramar, where many of Havana's wealthiest families lived before the Revolution. My friend told me that after the Revolution—when many of the owners left or were forced to leave—they gave their houses as 'gifts' to the Castro government. A lot of them were converted into clinics or divided up into apartments. La Maison, apparently, managed to escape that fate. So what about it? Interested?"

"Definitely," Annie said.

We agreed to have dinner first, then go on to La Maison in time for the ten o'clock show.

"By the way, do you know the name of the bar where we spent most of the day?" I asked as Annie turned to get on the elevator.

"No, I don't."

"La Dichosa," I said. "I asked Octavio as we were leaving. He said it means 'The Lucky One.'"

• • •

Leafy and private, Miramar was still considered one of the most stylish places to live in Havana, although some of the converted mansions we saw from our taxi were crumbling from neglect. La Maison, however, looked as pristine as it must have before Castro and *la Revolución*. It even retained a touch of the "gangster glamour" that Havana was known for in the 1940s and 1950s, when the mobster Meyer Lansky and his Cuban counterparts ruled the city. Of course, the Ray-Ban-wearing *Miami Vice* look-alikes gathered on the pavement outside La Maison were not real mobsters, only pretty imitations.

The interior of the house was also posh, a startling mixture of marble and antiques. After passing through a large sitting room that functioned as a reception area, Annie and I were led outside to our table in a large garden with a flagstone terrace. Tall flame-of-the-woods trees formed interlocking canopies over the tables where people sat eating dinner or having a drink. Just in front of our table, a very professional-looking catwalk had been set up, one that extended right into the audience; it was illuminated by a sophisticated lighting system.

Almost immediately after we were seated, a man with dark eyes and a handsome beak of a nose approached us. His slicked-back hair, black suit, and black silk T-shirt made him resemble one of the chic Armani-clad Italian men who hang out in places like Milan and Manhattan. He introduced himself. "I'm Antonio. We talked on the telephone this morning." I must have looked blank. "You wanted to know something about La Maison, to speak about it in English to someone."

"Oh, yes, of course. But how did you know who I was?"

"It was not so difficult. You are the only tourists here."

I asked him to tell us something about the clothes we would see. "I'm interested in knowing who designed them and who buys such clothes in Cuba."

"The clothes are all the work of one designer. Nancy Pelegrin. She is very well known and has a following." He stopped and pointed to a long table of stylish men sitting just in front of the runway. "They are all fashion designers." Then he pointed at a man in a cream-colored linen suit with a white sweater thrown over his shoulders. "He's the most important."

I asked again who in Cuba could afford such clothes but by this time Antonio's attention had wandered. I could tell he was doing what I called "fake listening"—pretending to be interested while his eyes searched the terrace for important people. "Well, you've been very help-ful, Antonio. Thank you," I said, releasing him to the wild. He bowed slightly, then took off like a free-range chicken.

In the ten minutes or so before the show started, I studied the audi-ence. It appeared to be composed of two distinct groups. As promised, the fashionistas were there: tall, gorgeous women accompanied by nattily dressed older men, young handsome men drinking wine together at tables close to the catwalk, middle-aged women wearing couturier designs accessorized by fresh-faced escorts, all of them out to see and be seen by the right people. What surprised me, though, was finding just as many un-fashionistas at La Maison; regular *Habaneros* seated in groups of four, six, eight, who had come for a steak dinner and stayed to watch the show.

Suddenly the lights came on and loud music filled the terrace. A master of ceremonies holding a microphone strode onto the stage. It was Antonio. The stage changed him into a performer; his voice and gestures became loud and theatrical, Cuba's answer to Bert Parks. After a few opening remarks Antonio vacated the stage and the fashion show began. Almost immediately I had to revise my expectations, or to put it bluntly, my prejudices.

The truth is I had come prepared to see second-rate models wearing poorly designed clothes. I was wrong on both counts, particularly in the case of the models. They were, without exception, spectacularly beau-tiful women who had mastered the Naomi Campbell hip-swaying runway slink, including her famous pigeon-toed, crossover walk. Confi-dent, graceful, and tall—some topped out at six feet—these were women who, with a few tweaks, could make it in the big-time world of high fashion. Although every designer garment in the show was white, an element of color was added by the amazing variety of the models' skin tones, ranging from pale honey to gleaming black.

One by one, over the next hour, the women strutted their stuff. Occasionally, the fashionistas in the crowd would let go with a cheer of approval at the sight of a certain model. Particularly lively was the table presided over by the man whom Antonio had identified as the "most important" designer in the crowd. Mr. Big, as I now thought of him, seemed to be a magnet for complimentary bottles of iced champagne and beautiful women who stopped to plant kisses in the air on each side of his face.

At first it was entertaining. But when I lost the ability to tell one white outfit from another, I began surveying the scene beyond the illuminated runway. A vast sea of stars moved above and shafts of moonlight fell through the tree branches like streamers of pale yellow silk. And in the dim periphery of the terrace I saw a different kind of show unfold, one provided by various nocturnal animals. Sleek cats moved with feral grace beneath the tables, searching for scraps of chicken and lobster. A dark bat glided silently over the length of the terrace, as furtive as a stealth bomber over enemy terrain. Two small green lizards zigzagged across a path and disappeared into a bush. I found this uninvited audience fascinating and wondered whether Yves Saint Laurent or Giorgio Armani might be persuaded to add animals to their fashion events.

When the fashion show ended and the models took their final walk, Annie and I prepared to leave, thinking the evening had ended. Far from it. A band was wheeled out, dancers leaped onto the stage, and a Las Vegas–style cabaret show began. When it started drizzling no one left—except Annie and me. Not because of the rain, but because after the fifth dance number, we had been delighted long enough.

As our taxi pulled away, it began to pour. Driving along the wet street I imagined the scene on the runway at La Maison: the models drenched by the rain, dancers slipping on the stage, the band trying to play water-soaked instruments. And most of all I imagined Mr. Big, soaked to the skin, his cream linen suit and white sweater as limp and bedraggled as the cats huddled beneath his table. Perhaps the power had gone out, leaving everyone in the dark. Except the bat, of course. So beguiling was this imagined scene that I almost regretted our premature exit.

The next morning Annie and I decided to hang out at the Hotel Nacional, an old luxury hotel that in its heyday attracted such movie stars as Betty Grable, George Raft, and Frank Sinatra, along with mobsters attending summits, such as the one famously depicted in *The Godfather*. For the next week, the Nacional would cater to a similar clientele, minus the mobsters: it was the official headquarters for the crowd of actors, directors, producers, and fans in town for the opening of the annual International Festival of New Latin American Cinema.

On the advice of the hotel staff, Annie and I took a taxi to the hotel. The fifteen-minute trip took us along the Malecón, a six-lane seaside boulevard and promenade. On one side the Malecón curves past a low stone seawall overlooking the blue waters of Havana Bay; on the other side, past miles of century-old pastel-colored mansions, once occupied by Havana's millionaires. Now many of these fading palaces are tenements, some on the verge of falling down. Sun, seawater, humidity, and more than forty years of neglect have not been kind to Havana's buildings. Still, if one looks with a painter's eye it is possible to see unexpected beauty everywhere. In the pastel paint shedding itself in layers, like a reverse pentimento. In the soft, crumbling stone balconies where laundry swings in the hot sea breeze. In the fading wall signs where colors blur with words into a pastiche, summoning up Monet's paintings of Rouen Cathedral.

Finally, our taxi turned off the Malecón into a long driveway lined with palm trees. Perched atop a small cliff overlooking the waterfront was the Nacional, a majestic Spanish-style hotel that still commands respect.

It seemed relatively peaceful outside the hotel, but inside it was swarming with film aficionados of all ages and from several continents. Serious-looking men dressed dramatically in army fatigues and Gucci shoes jostled with dark-haired beauties in miniskirts and halter-tops. Important-looking men in tailored suits and dark glasses sat smoking thick Cohiba Esplendidos and drinking little cups of Cuban coffee served by waiters in tuxedos. Three troubadours in flared white pants and linen shirts gamely serenaded hundreds of inattentive people lined up to collect their credentials for the opening ceremonies at the Karl Marx Theater. Bored-looking photographers wearing sleeveless vests open to the waist wandered around on the patio outside listlessly taking shots of strutting peacocks fanning their tails. The whole scene, without edits, could easily have been inserted into a film parody of a film festival.

By noon Annie and I agreed we had pretty much seen what we'd come to see. When I asked if she'd like to visit some of the peso department stores we had passed earlier, Annie took a rain check, saying she wanted to explore the Vedado neighborhood surrounding the hotel.

"Okay," I said. "See you tonight when we rendezvous with the group for dinner and the film festival. Hope they had as good a time as we did."

"We'll see, won't we?" Annie said, smiling.

I headed back to San Rafael, a street not far from Parque Central, a lovely green park around which many of the best tourists' hotels, including mine, were located. Although reaching San Rafael meant walking only a block or two west from the park, once I left Old Havana and entered Centro Havana, I found myself in a different city. This was the part of town where poor Cubans lived in run-down buildings carved up into tiny tenementlike apartments known as *ciudadelas*. In Cuba's parallel economy where only dollars are valuable, inhabitants of the Centro neighborhood have access only to jobs that pay nearly worthless pesos. And unlike the restored picturesque area to the east, the Centro barrio attracted few tourists.

Yet, as I walked through the narrow streets alive with playing children and dogs, with pushcarts and men riding beat-up bikes, with music pouring out of open windows and voices calling down from balconies, the Centro neighborhood seemed as lively a part of Havana as any I'd seen. At one corner I stopped to watch a striped green couch being raised by a rope to an upper floor, a task accompanied by a lot of good-natured advice from passersby on the street. At another I watched a fresh-faced young woman fry plantains on a makeshift grill. "Only one peso," she called out to me cheerfully. "The best money can buy." Nearby at a street cart, a little man who looked like a sprightly elf urged me to buy some *guarapo*, a local soft drink made from sugarcane juice.

Now, this is the real Havana, I thought, with all the unearned insight of the casual tourist.

In its heyday before 1959, San Rafael was one of Havana's most important commercial streets, home to the city's major department stores. Now as I wandered through the cavernous stores turned peso shops, I was shocked by how few goods were displayed on the almost-empty counters. In the years since the Soviet Union withdrew its financial support, shortages in Cuba had grown worse and worse.

In one peso store, the merchandise I saw consisted of a few rolls of toilet paper, some old drainpipes, rusting bolts, several bags of boiled candy, and one or two items of secondhand baby clothes. In the bodega next door, where lines of Cubans holding blue ration books waited patiently for their basic monthly food supplies, it was the same: almost-empty shelves. I watched one pretty young woman carefully place a tin of milk and some rice in her plastic shopping bag. As she left, she smiled at me. Her toothless grin was like a sudden slap in the face, one that shook loose the image in my head of romantic Old Havana, replacing it, temporarily at least, with the crumbling reality beneath the seductive face.

Outside on the street, near a fruit stall that sold bruised mangoes for three pesos, or about seventeen cents, I saw one Cuban's answer to supplementing her income. At the entrance to a public lavatory a wizened old woman wearing a threadbare brown dress, black ankle socks, and men's shoes sold toilet paper, sheet by sheet. Although I didn't plan to use the lavatory I stopped to buy four sheets. "Two pesos, please," she said, handing me the paper. When I gave her two dollars instead of two pesos, or ten cents, she shook her head, thinking I had misunderstood. "No, two *pesos*," she said with great dignity.

"But I'm leaving today and I have no pesos," I lied. "Only dollars. So please do me a favor and take them. *Por favor.*" I pressed the folded dollars into her gnarled hand, which, for just a second, became Grand-mother's hand, the one I held on to long ago in big department stores where it was easy to get lost.

She thanked me and then in perfect English said, "I hope you are enjoying your stay in Havana. Please come back. I will be right here." She smiled. And in that smile I saw the faint shadow of a once hand-some woman.

As I walked back to the hotel I marveled at the way Cubans managed to stay so cheerful. All around me I saw people who spent every day searching for food, clothing, medicine, housing and then, if lucky enough to find such necessities, searching for the money to pay for them. Yet despite all the shortages, life went on. A couch was lifted into an apartment. An old woman got up each morning and sold toilet paper. Children played and dogs barked. Some rice, a tin of milk, and noodles seemed treasures to Cubans, well worth the long wait in line.

I thought of Calle Obispo with its restored Spanish colonial build-ings and pastel-painted shops and bars and wondered if the Cubans who lived here in Centro—where, without warning, buildings simply fell down, leaving behind piles of rubble that often were left untouched—resented tourists like me. How could they not? Here I was, an American "rich" enough to stay in a fancy, air-conditioned hotel where each morn-ing a breakfast buffet was laid out with enough food to feed a Cuban family for months. But against all reason I found myself feeling that not only did the Cubans not resent Americans, they actually liked us.

• • •

By eight-thirty that night the street outside the Karl Marx Theater—located, rather amusingly, I thought, in the swank Miramar district—was backed up with people waiting to show their tickets to officials manning the doors. When Annie and I arrived with the rest of our now-reunited group, who were just back from their trip to Trinidad and Cienfuegos, the five-thousand-seat theater was filled almost to capacity. Only a few empty places remained, and they were scattered throughout the dank, cavernous building.

"It's every man for himself," said Jaime, one of the Cuban guides accompanying us. His words set into motion a mad scramble, sending forty more Americans into the mix of people speeding up and down the aisles looking for a seat. Every time I spotted an empty place—usually a seat in the middle of a long row—I was waved off by someone who told me, *This seat is not empty, Señora; it is saved for someone.* Finally, I climbed the two flights of steps to the balcony but ran into the same situation there: *Sorry, but this seat is saved for someone—you see, here is his overcoat.* Just as I was about to give up and walk back to the main floor, a woman near the aisle called out to me: "Here, Miss. Here is a seat." She patted the chair next to her.

It was a very good seat, three in from the aisle and close to the front of the balcony; I couldn't believe my luck. "Thank you so much," I said, squeezing my way past an older woman on the aisle and then past my benefactor. Once seated, I had a chance to look around. Although the building itself was truly ugly—a shoddy-looking concrete structure with stained green carpeting, walls painted a horrible bright blue, and seats covered with rose-colored plastic—the appearance of the audience more than made up for it. Clearly, the Cubans saw the festival as a chance to express their own creativity and imagination. Glamorous women dressed in evening gowns, their hair swept up in Bette Davis style, mingled with young girls in tight jeans and long, loose hair à la Rita Hayworth. The men also telegraphed their self-image by wearing everything from T-shirts and jeans to dark, formal suits or white *Miami Vice* jackets with the sleeves pushed up to their elbows.

I looked at my watch. It was close to nine-fifteen, already forty-five minutes behind schedule. The woman next to me—the one who'd offered me a seat—must have noticed me glancing at my watch. "Things are always late in Cuba," she said, smiling. "And tonight there is a rumor that Fidel will make an appearance, as he usually does. So we wait with our cameras." She motioned to an older woman sitting on her other side. "See, my mother has brought her camera along." The woman, who had a gentle face and tired eyes, nodded to me.

"Have you been to the festival before?" I asked.

"Oh, many times. We Cubans love the movies. You will see this week during the festival the people lined up to see the movies in theaters all over the city. Often, the people from Havana plan their vacations around the week of the festival."

"What about Hollywood movies? Do you get to see many of those?"

"Oh, yes. Two or three times a week we see Hollywood movies on television. They have Spanish subtitles, and many Cubans have learned English from those movies. *Titanic* is my mother's favorite." The woman paused. "May I introduce myself? I am Natalia Cortez. And this is my mother, Maria Ramos. We are pleased to meet you." The two women, neatly dressed in black suits and pearls, bowed their heads in my direction. It was clear from Natalia's elegant use of the English language that she was an educated woman.

"And I am pleased to meet you," I said, introducing myself. "I am an American tourist here. From Baltimore, a city near Washington, D.C."

"Ah, yes, the capital of the United States," Natalia said. "I am a teacher here in Havana and hope one day to go to Washington, D.C., to learn more about your government. Have you come for a special reason to Cuba?"

I told her about coming with a group to meet some of Cuba's artists and to learn more about Havana's history and architecture. "But I also have come hoping to meet people like you and your mother—Cubans I can talk to about art and life here." For the next fifteen minutes, until the program finally started—an hour and a half late—Natalia and I talked. About her uncle who lived in Miami, about my sons, one in Tokyo and one in Princeton, about Kevin Costner, her favorite Hollywood star, and about Ernest Hemingway's connection to Cuba. Just when I felt comfortable enough to ask about Cuba's school system, the program started.

Natalia leaned toward me and whispered, "If you like, we would be happy to have you visit us in our home one afternoon this week. There we can talk longer."

"How kind of you. I would like that." We agreed on a date and I wrote down my name, along with the hotel's phone number. As I handed the card to her the theater lights dimmed. Was it a power outage? I wondered. My question was answered by the appearance onstage of a glamorous woman. A movie star, perhaps? Before I could ask Natalia, the glamorous woman introduced a man in the cordoned-off section of the balcony. As the crowd applauded, the man stood and, as cameras rolled, proceeded to give a twenty-minute talk. Unfortunately, the combination of my poor Spanish and a bad sound system left me completely clueless as to what he said.

After more official speeches there was a long musical interlude featuring an Italian composer who played and sang, à la Burt Bacharach, music he had written for films by Fellini and Benigni. By the time the evening's featured movie, a Chilean film, began, I was praying that Benigni might appear to reprise his hilarious Oscar presentation to, as he put it, "Hilarity Swank for the film *Boys, They Don't Cry.*" Almost immediately, the sound track of the Chilean film failed, leaving those who could not read the English subtitles completely in the dark, so to speak. The audience expressed its displeasure by whistling and hooting until the movie was stopped and the rest of the evening canceled.

Getting out of the theater took even longer than getting in. As I moved slowly toward the exits I asked Natalia if such glitches happened often.

"Things break down in Cuba," she said good-naturedly. "We are used to it. So I can't really say if it happens often. But I enjoyed the evening until it ended."

I told her I had too, particularly because it allowed me to meet her and her mother. "I look forward to seeing you later in the week," I said.

"Yes. At your hotel at one o'clock. But I must ask you a favor. That you meet me outside the entrance to your hotel, please."

Although puzzled by her reluctance to meet me in the lobby, I agreed.

It was still hot and humid when I returned to the hotel, so I went for a short swim in the rooftop pool. After a lap or two I turned on my back and floated under the stars, thinking of Natalia and her mother, who never got to snap a picture of the no-show Fidel. I smiled, thinking of my own mother, who had managed, after several attempts, to snap a picture of the Prince of Wales when he visited her hometown in Scotland. Till the day she died she cherished that picture, always telling me the story of how she and her two sisters had played hooky from school that day. On the back of the picture, which I keep in my bedroom, she had written "Snapped by the Dundas Sisters in Glasgow."

For some reason, thinking of my mother led to thoughts of my older son, Andy. How he would love Havana. The ingenuity of the Cubans, the music, the sun and sea, the pulsing sense of excitement that hung in the air, the faded grandeur of the buildings—I knew all these things would appeal to him as they did to me. Even more, perhaps, since he had an adventurous nature that far exceeded mine. I could imagine him windsurfing in the bay or scuba diving with the Blue Dive Club in Miramar or even fishing for marlin, as Hemingway did, near the village of Cojimar.

As I floated in the water a sliver of moon caught my eye and I thought of Naohiro, of how on his last night in Kyoto we sat near the river, viewing the moon. Would he like Havana? I wondered. Was he too contemplative to enjoy the city's salsa-paced atmosphere? As if to answer my question, I suddenly imagined him with me at La Dichosa, dancing, talking to the band, drinking beer, having a wonderful time. When I began to imagine him floating beside me in the water, the tropical air all around us, I decided it was time to go.

On the way back to my room I noticed through the elevator door that each floor was decorated with a small, elaborately trimmed Christmas tree. It surprised me since I was under the impression that Christmas had been abolished in Cuba. As I passed the tree on my landing I touched it. Artificial, just as I thought. Next to it, however, on a table was a live, exquisitely pruned bonsai tree. Another reminder, I thought, of the collision between reality and artifice that seemed to define so many aspects of Cuban life and culture.

If, as Philip Johnson observed, practicing architecture is akin to wandering through history at will, then Havana is a historian's paradise. On a tour through Old Havana the next morning with our Cuban guides Jaime and Nestor, we walked along streets where Spanish colonial structures coexisted with the baroque and neoclassical, and Florentine Renaissance–style buildings looked down amicably on restored art nouveau and art deco designs. Indeed, the architecture of Havana occasionally reminded me of Florence in that the narrow streets in both cities were designed to offer shade to pedestrians. Havana's sun and heat, we were told, were the driving force behind much of Cuban colonial design; they dictated the basic need to provide the maximum amount of shade, ventilation, and light.

Heat and humidity—along with Cuba's turbulent history—had not been kind to the buildings in Habana Vieja. In every neighborhood there were signs of severe neglect and deterioration. But there were signs also of an ambitious restoration effort under way.

"In 1982, the United Nations named Habana Vieja a UNESCO World Heritage Site," Nestor told us. "More than two hundred build-ings with historical importance are being restored by this project. The budget is small because the government makes part of the investment. But UNESCO protects us. It means no one can arrive here and build a tower or skyscraper." Still, Nestor added a note of caution: "The word 'restored' can mean many things," he said. "Sometimes it means doing just the façade. You will see many people living in buildings where the inside is in very bad shape."

Although Nestor was right about the restoration project preventing the appearance of skyscrapers in Old Havana, I did notice a tiny crack in the neighborhood's historical purity: a Benetton store in the Plaza de San Francisco, the only nod to global commercialism I'd seen in Cuba. *If Benetton comes,* I wondered, *can McDonald's be far behind?* My heart sank at the thought of the golden arches replacing the mom-and-pop bodegas that served home-cooked food and the cool dark bars where one could escape the heat of the day with an ice-cold beer.

On our way back from our tour of Old Havana we passed La Dichosa, the bar where Annie and I spent most of our first day. I stopped to peek inside. No musicians to be seen. Too early for them, I guessed. Only a few men lounged at the bar, smoking, talking, and drinking a cold beer before heading out into the hot sun again. How different La Dichosa seemed today. I wondered if Annie and I would be disap-pointed when we returned later in the week. Perhaps the exhilaration we initially felt would turn out to be similar to love at first sight: a fever-ish infatuation that would be cured, alas, by second sight.

At lunch I had a chance to talk to Nestor, whom I judged to be in his late thirties. A well-educated man who possessed a natural dignity, as many Cubans do, Nestor seemed knowledgeable about Cuban history, past and present. Although I wanted to know about such things as wages, working conditions, politics, and education, my first question had to do with the Christmas trees at my hotel. "Didn't the revolution-aries abolish Christmas in Cuba?" I asked.

"It was abolished. But since the pope's visit to Cuba in 1998, Christ-mas can be officially celebrated again as a national holiday. Before that it was only celebrated privately in homes."

Nestor considered himself lucky because he earns dollars from his job in the tourist industry. He said the reality of life for Cubans came down to whether a worker earned dollars or pesos.

"On one side, people who earn dollars are doing well. On the other side, people who work for the state get just a basic salary in pesos. The average salary is about two hundred pesos a month, less than ten dollars. Everyone gets a stipend from the government, with the highest stipend going to a doctor—the peso equivalent of about thirty or forty dollars a month. Everyone supplements his income. I know a gynecologist making thirty dollars a month who also makes jewelry at home to sell. Poorer people supplement by begging. They ask for soap and medicine and clothes from tourists, then sell it for dollars. Some people do pretty well in the underground economy. That's why hotels have only one bar of soap in the bathroom."

I told Nestor of my shock at seeing how little food was available in the peso markets. "How do Cubans survive with so little food?"

"People are not starving. But we have to spend a fortune on food. And some people do not have the money. Yes, there are a lot of hardships, but Cuba has survived. Cubans have learned how to get by. They improvise. We are very good at improvisation," Nestor said, his voice edged with something approaching pride.

His remarks on the improvisational abilities of Cubans reminded me of something Wilfredo, a smart young Cuban artist, had told us at a morning lecture. "Fidel stated early in the Revolution that artists would have the freedom to do what they want to do; that the Cuban Revolution would never impose any style on them. However what Fidel was really saying was: you can choose the technique but the content is just Revolution." Wilfredo smiled. "But Cuban artists are very smart. Everything you can say in art, they have found a way to do it."

But they haven't found a way to sell their art in Cuba, Wilfredo said. "There is no art market system here. The market for Cuban art is not a domestic market. The Americans and Europeans come to buy. So, in a way, Cuban artists have been influenced to please the tastes of foreign markets."

Sandra Ramos, a successful thirty-two-year-old artist, clearly had found a way to express herself through her art. A woman with fair skin, short brown hair, and penetrating eyes behind dark-rimmed glasses, Ramos greeted us at the door to her newly renovated house in Vedado, a sprawling city neighborhood that has been described as "Havana at its middle-class best." Standing next to her were a translator from a Cuban arts organization and a skittish but elegant Italian greyhound. Ramos's home, which contained her studio, was located on a quiet, tree-lined street and, like the other houses on the block, had a front balcony where plants grew against a backdrop of palm trees. Once known for its casinos, powerful Mafia figures, and pricey mansions, the Vedado—about a ten-minute drive from Old Havana—now seemed a quiet neighborhood of well-kept houses. The inside of the artist's tile-floored house was charming: French windows and doors that opened onto an outdoor circular staircase leading to the floor above and painted white walls that served as a gallery for her work.

After about twenty of us had squeezed into Ramos's small studio, she showed us several series of prints she had done, commenting on them through her translator. *In this series I used a portrait of myself as a child to make comments about my ideas on insularity, isolation, Cuba, the island. . . . In this series I used immersions and burials as existential reflections, not only on Cuban society but on what we are and where we go after we die. . . . For this series called "My Daily Vocation of Suicide," I invented a cartoon character.*

Although I found the political and intellectual themes of her prints challenging, Ramos's sharp wit and whimsical imagination delivered her message in a strikingly original way. The title of one of her pieces, *All Life Cannot Fit into One Suitcase,* immediately made me think of Cuban exiles forced to leave in a hurry when Fidel took over—a simplistic reading, perhaps, but it worked for me.

We were told that Ramos's work, which sold in the range of six hundred to eight hundred dollars, had been exhibited in Japan, England, Mexico, Romania, Spain, and the United States, where she has lectured as well. I wanted to ask Ramos if she was familiar with the work of Lynda Barry, an inspired American cartoonist whose storytelling voice is just as strong as her drawing grammar. Although the subtext of their art might be different, the two women seemed to draw on similar sensibilities to illuminate their ideas and memories.

As I was about to pose this question, a visitor asked the artist, "Were you influenced by Cindy Sherman's work? Is she someone you admire?"

The translator relayed the question to Ramos, whose eyes narrowed to dangerous slits as she listened to the question about Cindy Sherman, a successful New York artist who assumes different personalities in her photographic self-portraits. "She says she doesn't really think of Cindy

Sherman," the translator told us finally. "If anyone influenced her, it might be Frida Kahlo."

Close call, I thought, happy not to have mentioned Lynda Barry.

It was about a ten-minute trip to the Vedado house of another very successful Cuban artist, thirty-one-year-old Esterio Segura. An imposing man with muscular arms, Segura, like Sandra Ramos, has exhibited and traveled extensively outside of Cuba and is represented by a New York gallery in Soho. His sculptures, we were told, appeared in the groundbreaking Cuban film *Strawberry and Chocolate*, nominated in 1995 for an Oscar.

"Esterio is an important artist abroad," said the translator from the arts organization. "Cuban artists are not as well known in their own country as they are abroad. For one thing they don't have access to the media, that great publicity machine that makes celebrities of artists in other countries. For the common Cuban, it is hard to know this kind of art exists," she says, gesturing in a sweeping motion at the display of art in Esterio's house.

Esterio Segura, however, seemed to be quite adept at self-promotion. A charismatic, likable man, he came across as an intelligent and savvy presenter of himself and his art—work that I thought was equally intelligent and savvy. The artist described his work as art that stressed the "themes of Cuban isolation," pointing to one of his life-size figures, a caged man trying to shout through a large megaphone. But the piece that seemed to inspire the most questions from his visitors was a work called *Typewriter Space Occupied by a Dream*. Part of an installation piece, it depicted a life-size plaster man wearing blue jeans asleep on bundled newspapers, dreaming of typewriters, the dream content revealed by the twenty or so typewriters affixed to the wall behind him.

"For many reasons, people get an obsession with something," Esterio explained, his English excellent. "They become obsessed with music or with the wish to be a great writer. An idea about obsession is like a dream. Most of my work is really political, but not in images you can recognize. Sometimes it is a feeling of someone like myself who has lived thirty years in the Cuban culture, filtered through the artist's feelings."

Someone asked what seemed to be the mandatory question put to Cuban artists: "Have you been influenced by American artists?"

"Not really," he said. "The way I make my work is very eclectic. From Michelangelo and Rodin—artists I studied in school—to conceptual artists like Joseph Beuys."

Then someone else asked him: "How can an artist afford to live in a house like this?"

He explained that while it's illegal in Cuba to buy and sell homes, it is legal to trade or exchange homes. "I traded my old house with an old lady who was living alone here. 'Give me your apartment and some money,' she said. And I was doing well enough to do it."

Later, as we waited for the bus with Nestor, someone commented on the contrast between the nicely renovated interior and the run-down exterior of Segura's house.

"Yes, it is true that the outside of the house is not in very good condition," Nestor said. "But most Cubans don't want it to be noticeably nice on the outside. You have to live in secret if you're doing well. There are some bad people in the community. So if you keep the outside of your house a little neglected, it protects you from the 'evil eye.'" It's the reason why, he says, Cubans hide their satellite dishes.

Dear Naohiro,

For three days now I've been worrying about returning to La Dichosa, the bar I told you about, the one where Annie and I danced away our first day in Havana. I couldn't shake the feeling that a second visit could only end in disappointment, that it could never live up to the perfection of that first day. It's funny, but writing this I remember feeling the same way when you and I agreed to meet for the first time after I left Paris. Did I ever tell you how nervous I was when we met for lunch that day in London? All week long I'd worried about whether we'd still feel the way we did in Paris, or whether seeing each other again would just be a colossal disappointment. But walking toward you in the restaurant, then standing face-to-face. . . . Well, you know the rest.

It was just the same tonight at La Dichosa. The minute I entered the bar and saw the band, it was as though I'd never left. Annie and I went with two friends from the group, Ed and Gin, and they, like us, immediately connected to the music, the band, the bar, and everyone in it. We were the only tourists there; everyone else was Cuban. The place was almost filled. Old men sat at the bar while younger men and women were scattered at tables along the wall. One table consisted of a whole family, including a boy about nine, a slightly younger girl, and a toddler.

The four of us sat right in front of the band, drinking beer and eating cheese sandwiches. In between sets, Angel and Octavio and some of the other musicians, who had introduced themselves to Ed and Gin earlier, would drift over to our table. I'm not sure when the impromptu dancing started. But pretty soon everyone in the bar was dancing. Even the toddler, who, like his brother and sister, turned out to have all the right moves. Then something happened that startled us. An old man—a very thin old man—sitting alone at the bar, hunched over a shot glass of whiskey, jumped suddenly to his feet and began dancing. He was spectacular, better than anyone in the bar, and his moves even included the kind of hip-hop spinning that kids do. Everyone was stunned. It was like discovering your cat secretly reads Proust between catnaps. When the old man finished we applauded. I fell in love again.

You would have loved the evening, too. All of it. The people, the music, the dancing, the cheese sandwiches, and, I hope, me.

I was a little early for my meeting with Natalia, so I lingered in the hotel lobby, checking out the tour groups arriving. Tourism is big in Cuba these days and growing bigger. But most visitors come under the auspices of an educational group, as I did. As discreetly as possible, I tried to read the luggage tags that identified the sponsoring organizations. There seemed to be a tour offered for everyone: architects, preservationists, city planners, film buffs, photographers, journalists, environmentalists.

As I read the tags I glanced through the lobby door and saw Natalia crossing the street. A small erect figure with perfect posture, she looked, in the light of day, even more sophisticated than I remembered, her dark hair pulled back into a small knot. I rushed outside to meet her, happy to see she had kept her promise. We exchanged greetings. Then abruptly, she asked me to meet her on the other side of the street, away from the hotel. Natalia began to walk and I followed, curious but willing to believe she had her reasons. She did.

"Some of the hotels frown on Cubans mingling with Americans," she explained. "In many, we're not allowed to enter the lobby. They watch

for us. So I feel more comfortable if I don't put myself in that situation."
I told her I understood. "Do you mind walking?" she asked. "My apartment is about fifteen minutes away. In Centro."

I was surprised to hear she lived in Centro. For some reason I imag-
ined her living in a less run-down neighborhood, one more like Vedado.
As we walked along the Prado, a wide avenue lined with laurel trees and
Spanish mansions whose fading beauty still startled the eye, I told
Natalia about my visit to the peso department stores on San Rafael and
my sadness at seeing such shortages.

"Yes, now they are empty," she said. "But I have good memories of
visiting them with my mother when I was a little girl. So many nice
things to buy then. Once I remember my mother bought me a straw hat
with blue ribbons. It blew off my head the next day, into the bay near
the seawall." She laughed. And so did I, happy to know she had such
memories.

Natalia was twelve when Castro's revolutionary forces took control
of Havana in 1959—old enough, she said, to have memories of life
before the Revolution. "But none of my students have such memories,"
she said. "And neither do some of their parents." A short silence
followed. I thought I heard her sigh. "I can imagine a time when only
the very old will remember that Cuba."

As she talked, I remembered the young Cuban artists I'd met. All
were born post-Revolution, yet in their work they sometimes seemed to
be creating imaginary memories of a time they knew only at second
hand.

On our way to Natalia's apartment—which was in a different section
of Centro than the peso department stores—we passed a movie house
with a renovated art deco façade and several houses with restored
façades that, Natalia said, hid the decaying interiors behind them. We
turned a few more corners, then came to the moderately run-down
three-story building where Natalia and her mother lived. She told me
her mother, now retired, had also been a teacher and received a
pension. "Since she lives with me, her pension is about seventy-five
pesos a month. That's about four dollars. If she lived alone she would
get almost twice that, but it's not enough to live on. So most older
Cubans live with their families."

Even though it was early afternoon, Natalia's building was dark
inside. "Watch your step," Natalia cautioned, leading me to a wide staircase. After I followed her up three long flights of stairs, we reached the

top floor where Natalia's mother waited, dressed in the same black dress she'd worn a few nights earlier to the film festival.

"Come in," she said, taking my hand. The first thing I saw in the small neat room—which looked as though it had been carved out of a larger room—was a small Christmas tree perched on top of an enameled kitchen table. Beneath it were two presents wrapped in white paper and tied with green string.

"It is our first Christmas tree in many years," Natalia said, inviting me to sit on a small plush sofa that was straight out of the 1950s. She took a seat opposite me in a chair that matched the sofa. Almost immediately her mother left the room and then reappeared with three tiny white cups. Instantly the room was filled with the heavenly aroma of *café Cubano*, strong coffee heavily sweetened with sugar. Another trip to the kitchen produced a plate of three biscuits. "These are called *galletas*," Natalia's mother said, putting one on a napkin next to my cup.

It broke my heart to think of how much of their food budget was invested in this small repast. But I already knew these two women valued manners and civility as much as food. So I pushed aside any feelings of guilt and allowed myself to genuinely enjoy their hospitality. It was the best way, I thought, to repay them for their kindness.

Since Natalia was a teacher, as her mother had been before retiring, I asked them to tell me about Cuba's educational system. "School is compulsory through the ninth grade," Natalia said. "At fifteen, the children enter a year of evaluation. Some will go on to three more years of pre-university studies or technical schools." I asked if she would mind telling me the salary of a Cuban teacher. "A teacher with a degree in education starts out at 180 pesos a month, about nine dollars. Without the degree it's less. But my mother and I are lucky. We have an uncle living in Miami who sends us dollars. Otherwise we could not live as well as we do." Natalia anticipated my next question: "It is legal to send up to twelve hundred dollars a year through Western Union."

We talked, the three of us, for another hour or so. When it was time to leave I opened up my bag and lifted out some small gifts I'd brought for them: fresh fruit bought at a farmer's market, some chocolate purchased in the hotel gift shop, and a bar of soap wrapped so exquisitely that I was embarrassed. In a country where paper was so scarce, the Japanese rice paper wrapping seemed decadent. The truth is, I'd been mystified as to why I'd even packed the fancy soap in my suitcase, along with the pencils, aspirins, toothpaste, and bars of regular soap meant to be given as gifts. Now I knew why. "In Japan, gift wrapping is considered an art form," I said, handing over the small presents.

The women gracefully accepted them, taking time to examine in detail the dark blue Japanese rice paper printed with geometric designs and tied with red silk cord. "It is very beautiful," said Natalia's mother. After Natalia placed the elegant bright package beneath the tree, she stood looking at it, a reminder perhaps of an earlier life when little girls wore straw hats with blue ribbons.

It was pouring when we set out for the U.S. Interests Section, America's faux embassy on the Havana waterfront. Since tourist buses were not permitted near the building, a fleet of taxis—all classic American cars from the forties and fifties—waited near our hotel, ready to transport our gang of forty. It was startling to see lined up the heavily chromed, neon-colored cars of my youth, looking just as they did at the local milk bar where, as a teenager, I hung out on weekend nights. Nowhere in Havana had I seen a better example of the Cuban genius for improvisation than in these fifty-year-old American cars, kept running by their owners' mechanical ingenuity and the cannibalization of parts from Russian Ladas and Volgas. Havana is known for its recycling of these classic American cars that, unlike their Russian counterparts, have lasted for half a century. For many Cubans, who drive them as taxicabs or offer tours to visitors, these cars offer a good source of income; a driver can take in up to fifty dollars a day, a fortune by Cuban standards. Traditionally, the skills and resources necessary to maintain such a car are considered a family secret, one that is passed down through the generations from father to son. And, as one might expect, some of these recycled cars are in better condition than others.

I watched as my fellow tourists climbed into a '48 Plymouth DeLuxe with a green body and white roof, then an aquamarine '51 Pontiac Chieftain, followed by a neon-pink '57 Ford with chrome tail fins. When my turn came round, four of us squeezed into a two-tone lime-green '55 Chevy, three in the backseat and one—me—in the front, next to the driver. He turned the key in the ignition, and to everyone's surprise the engine started instantly. But it took only a few minutes to realize that mechanical ingenuity and cannibalization could go only so far. As we roared down the busy Malecón, through walls of rain so intense that everything outside was just a blur of moving colors, I gently asked the driver about the possibility of turning on the windshield wipers.

He laughed, not unkindly, and said, "The windshield wipers are retired. Have been for years."

Between the tailgating, the lack of seat belts, and the inability to see the road, it was a scary ride. When the windows began to fog up on the inside I knew better than to ask if there was a defroster; instead I whipped out a wad of tissues and started to wipe the glass down every two minutes. To my surprise, the driver thanked me, explaining in his understated way, "I couldn't see very well." And he was sympathetic when a stream of water leaked through the roof directly onto my head. "Classic car," he said, shrugging his shoulders.

My mood lifted, though, when we passed Annie and two others riding in a 1958 red-and-white Mercury convertible, top down, all of them drenched to the skin but laughing. When I saw their driver had covered his head with a small washcloth, I laughed too.

After nearly an hour's "briefing" by a senior staff member at the U.S. Interests Section—which is housed in the former U.S. Embassy building, now officially the Swiss embassy—we stood outside in the still-pouring rain waiting for our taxis to return. I was determined this time to find a taxi with working windshield wipers.

"There's one," said Emma, one of the women who'd shared the first taxi with me. We jumped in and the taxi took off. Alas, we quickly learned that the only taxi window with glass was the front one; the rest were open to the elements. We drove back through a stinging rain that, driven by the wind, nipped our faces like tiny knives. Then Emma, a woman I'd grown to like a lot, had a bright idea. "Let's put up our umbrellas and use them as a shield," she said. It worked. Sort of. That is, if you didn't mind being poked in the eyes by umbrella tips. Still, it was Cuba, where mishaps became adventures. Emma, an elegant woman always perfectly put together—who now, like me, resembled a pile of wet laundry—looked at me and started laughing. I returned the favor, and we laughed all the way back to the hotel.

Later, while drying off in my room, I read over the seventeen-page, single-spaced document handed out by the Public Affairs Office of the U.S. Interests Section. It explained, among other things, that the U.S. government's policy toward Cuba "is to promote a peaceful transition to democracy in Cuba through a combination of pressure on the Cuban government and outreach to the Cuban people. The U.S. embargo and diplomatic isolation of Cuba are tools we use to deny resources to the authoritarian Cuban government."

In my own notes, I found underlined some remarks by the official who briefed us. "Many people who come on programs like this," he said, referring to tours such as mine, "are not particularly fans of our policy. We think that's great. It supports our point. It shows Cuban people that Americans have diversity."

As I read this I thought of how, more than anything else, my visit to Cuba had shown me the same thing, in reverse: the diversity of Cuban people. Cubans, at least the ones I met, were not reluctant to express their opinions; all you have to do is ask them. If I were ambassador to Cuba, I decided, it would be mandatory that all my staff members at the U.S. Interests Section spend a night, maybe two, at La Dichosa.

From the rooftop terrace of the stone fortress the clouds were still visible, although twilight was beginning to etch the trees below into lines of delicate tracery. We had gathered for cocktails after a tour of the Ceramics Museum—imaginatively housed in the sixteenth-century Castillo de la Real Fuerza overlooking Havana Bay—and a performance of baroque music by several charming young singers. But when the humid breeze from Havana Bay became heavy with the threat of rain, we left quickly, hoping to reach the Café del Oriente before the downpour.

As we crossed the moat surrounding the fortress-museum and began walking to the café, I fell into step alongside Nestor. I told him of my amazement at the number of museums in Cuba.

"There are museums for everything," I said. "From classical and contemporary art to museums that tell the history of Cuba—like that wonderful decorative arts museum in Vedado. My favorite, though, was the restored convent you took us to see, the one with the beautiful art and covered walkways around a garden. I can't recall the name. But it reminded me of a small fourteenth-century church in Florence that has a spectacular Perugino fresco, and cloisters built around a lovely courtyard. What was the name of the convent you took us to earlier this week?"

"You're thinking of the San Francisco de Asis convent in Old Havana," Nestor said. "When we were there, did you see the classroom with the children in it? We think it is important to show our children their history, so in every museum there is a classroom. The children move through each museum, staying fifteen days in one classroom, then fifteen in another. We want them to learn the importance of preserving buildings and our history in neighborhoods."

I told Nestor how impressed I was by the schoolchildren I talked to. "Not only do they speak English, but most are so friendly and eager to know about America." I hesitated. "Nestor, there's something I've been wanting to ask you. What do Cubans hope will happen when Fidel dies or loses power?"

"It depends on the group. Some people want little change; others a great deal of change." Now it was Nestor's turn to hesitate. Then he said: "I myself want big change."

"What about the fifty families who live crowded together in the kind of house you showed us yesterday, the one that fell down with no warning the night before. What does a group like that want?"

"They will be sad when Castro dies. They get their stipends from the government and don't work. Even though living conditions are bad, they are not unhappy. Some people exist to buy a beer. They wouldn't like change. One of our biggest challenges is to teach discipline to young people so they learn to work for a salary, rather than just receiving money for nothing."

It was our last night in Cuba and we were all looking forward to dinner at La Guarida, a private restaurant with a reputation as the "hippest" place to eat in Havana. It certainly qualified as the most famous of Havana's *paladares*—the name for restaurants run in private homes— since its interior rooms were used as the setting for the Cuban film *Strawberry and Chocolate*. And in a city not known for good food, La Guarida was said to be better than average. But what made La Guarida "hip," I decided, might have more to do with its location than its fame or food.

Unlike many of the *paladares* recommended to tourists, La Guarida was not housed in a restored Vedado or Miramar mansion with private gardens. Instead, this small family-run restaurant was located in the decaying Centro neighborhood on a narrow street lined with tenements—the kind of street, in other words, not seen "up close and personal" by most tourists who, like me, visit Cuba as part of a culture tour. It was startling—and exhilarating, too—to drive on a hot Friday night through streets alive with Cubans out doing their thing.

From my perch in the backseat of a tiny Coco taxi—a three-wheeled vehicle partially covered by a hemisphere of yellow fiberglass and powered by a motorcycle—it was easy to sink into the street life I saw around me. Mothers sat on stoops talking as children played under the streetlamps. Young couples held hands as they strolled past decaying buildings, some on the verge of collapsing, their faded paint hanging in shreds from the façades. Once these were grand buildings, four stories tall, with wide fronts and deep interiors; now they are separated by vacant lots scattered with debris, giving a gap-toothed look to what was a beautiful, symmetric block of houses. Men grilled food in bodegas, calling out through open doors to passersby. Teenagers flirted as they walked along the sidewalk, the boys tagging behind the girls. In Cuba, I now knew, life was lived on the street. I thought of Nestor telling me one day about how important the idea of neighborhood was to Cubans. "I love to say hello to my neighbors when I'm out walking," Nestor said. "I love to be among people who are my neighbors."

Now, as our line of twenty Coco taxis stopped in front of a ramshackle eighteenth-century building in the middle of a run-down block, the Cubans good-naturedly made room for us on the narrow street. Although there was nothing about the dilapidated entrance that hinted at a *paladar* inside, we had arrived at our destination. We followed our guides into the poorly lighted building and up three wide flights of sweeping stairs that, in their time, must have been spectacular. At the top was La Guarida, a three-room restaurant in a converted apartment with thirty-foot ceilings and carved cornices above shuttered windows. As many tables as possible were squeezed into each small room so that the restaurant could accommodate perhaps as many as fifty people. The air inside La Guarida was hot and still, so when I spotted a table next to a window opening onto a balcony, I headed straight for it.

The food turned out to be good enough but nothing special. Still, that wasn't what we'd come for: we'd come to experience the ambience of Havana as it was in its glory days, the Havana of our fantasies. Near the end of the meal, while waiting for dessert and coffee, I left the table and walked down the steps to the floor below. All around the spacious landing, rooms had been gerrymandered to fit in as many tenants as possible. The sound of a disco version of the theme from *Star Wars* boomed out from one room, and in the dim light, I saw through a shuttered opening a man watching television. On a table next to his chair was a small Christmas tree. Then, suddenly, out of the dark hall a young girl appeared.

"Please. One dollar," she said, smiling and clasping her hands together as if praying.

Since it was my last night in Cuba and I had brought dollars to give away, I gave it to her. As soon as I did, three other children, who had caught the scent of an American, gathered around pleading *one dollar, one dollar.* I gave each of them a dollar. "Merry Christmas," I said.

"Merry Christmas," they chanted back, disappearing into the dark hall as quickly as they had appeared.

When I went back to La Guarida, I stepped outside on the balcony. Across the street, on a similar balcony, a man stood playing the trumpet. I listened as the mellow sounds rose and fell in the thick warm air. Leaning over the balustrade, I studied the scene below, the street pulsing with life, with children, with families, with neighbors, all mingling and enjoying themselves. And for the first time I understood the importance of the balcony to Cubans, to men playing music and women hanging laundry, to lovers sitting side by side and children doing their homework. In some primal way, the view from the balcony connected them to their world, past and present.

When the man with the trumpet stopped playing, I waved to him across the narrow street. "Merry Christmas," I shouted.

He waved back. Then, softly, I heard the music drift across the street. And as he played the familiar song, he added a delicate salsa beat. I sang the words to myself, my feet and hips moving to the newly minted rhythm of "White Christmas." Although I'd never heard "White Christmas" played with a salsa beat, somehow it seemed just right.

The Secret Gardens

Halfway down the escalator to the platform of the high-speed train that would take me from Paris to Avignon, I heard the conductor call out the French version of "All aboard!" Immediately, some of the travelers behind me pushed their way past like thirsty hyenas looking for a waterhole, ignoring the fact that in order to do so, they had to roll their luggage over my left foot. I tried to insert myself into the flow of running passengers, but it was like trying to change lanes on a busy highway: no one had the decency to let me in. The only strategy left was to hope the train would wait and that I would be able to hobble toward it quickly enough to get on board.

The train did wait. And despite my limp, I was able to drag my suitcase onto the first-class car, the only ticketing available on the sold-out TGV, as the French fast train is known. After stowing my luggage, I settled back into the plush contours of my assigned seat. I sat for a few minutes basking in the satisfied glow that comes from any successful completion of the most unpredictable and often the most unpleasant aspect of travel: the transportation part, whether by land or sea or air. But after five minutes of such basking, my glow turned into impatience. What, I wondered, had happened to the "All aboard" urgency that greeted me ten minutes earlier?

I looked around, trying to spot a conductor who might answer my question about the delay. Instead, I saw an exquisitely dressed older

woman appear at the entrance to the car; she was wearing a lambskin coat and fur hat, no doubt to ward off the chill of an early April morning. Escorted to her seat by a young man who carefully placed her vintage Vuitton luggage on the overhead rack, she was a woman whose appearance and manner commanded attention. Then the young man bowed—I couldn't help but think of Naohiro—and took his leave, saying, *Bon voyage, Madame Dupré.*

As soon as he departed the train started to move. I wondered: was Madame Dupré the reason for the delay? In any event, she was worth waiting for. From my seat opposite her, I furtively studied everything about her; it was not unlike the way I used to study interesting passengers on the streetcar in my Nancy Drew days. I noted that everything about Madame D. was vintage. The tartan suit and pleated white silk blouse that were revealed when she removed her coat were chic couturier reminders of the 1940s; the Hermès handbag, polished and gleaming the way only fine old leather can; the elegant kidskin gloves that she removed finger by finger. And like a vintage wine, it appeared that the woman herself—I guessed her to be in her eighties—had aged into a subtle, complex distillation of all the years that came before.

I watched, fascinated, as she removed her hat and patted her thick silver hair into place, first one side, then the other. Her lightly tanned skin had clearly seen some sun in its day, but the electric blue eyes made you forget about wrinkles. They were the eyes of a thoroughly engaged woman, eyes that still looked out at the world expecting to see new and interesting things. She was, I decided, the woman I wanted to be at that age, if luck was on my side. Suddenly I wondered if in her travels Madame Dupré ever spotted a younger woman across a train aisle and thought: *That was me, thirty years ago.*

About forty-five minutes into the three-hour trip to Avignon, the sun broke through the damp mist. Like a giant lightbulb being turned on, it illuminated the rooftops of a small village nestled into the side of a hill. I imagined how pleasant the sun's warmth must feel on the backs of the brown-and-white cows reclining in a field, their legs folded beneath them. At that moment a steward came by offering refreshments. In a rich throaty voice I heard Madame Dupré ask for *"un café noir, s'il vous plaît."*

"I'll have the same, please," I said in English, not wanting Madame D. to hear my poor French accent.

"Ah, I see you are American," she said speaking English, her husky

French-accented voice turning the few words into a sound worthy of Jeanne Moreau in *The Bride Wore Black*. "Allow me to introduce myself. I am Fabian Dupré."

Her friendly, forthright manner startled me. Not because she was French—the myth of French aloofness, in my opinion, is way overblown—but because it was so unexpected. Although I often introduce myself to strangers when I'm traveling, this gesture from an older, distinguished-looking woman was a welcome surprise. I introduced myself, then upped the ante by asking, "Are you going through to Avignon?"

"Yes, but not to stay. I go from there by car to my home in Saignon."

"Saigon?" I blurted out, puzzled as to why one would travel through Provence to get to Vietnam.

"No, no," she said. "Not *Saigon*, my dear. Saignon. It's a village in the Luberon." She looked amused at my mistake, but not in a condescending way. What I saw was a woman on the verge of laughing out loud at what was, in fact, a comical misunderstanding. We both started to laugh at the same time.

Our connection felt so natural that it gave me the courage to ask her to explain where exactly "the Luberon" was. "I'm very confused about how Provence, Vaucluse, and the Luberon all fit together."

"It is confusing to many people who do not know the area," she said, explaining that Provence spreads across five territorial *départements* of France, one of which is the Vaucluse *département*. "The Luberon is just a small area in the heart of the Vaucluse region of Provence." Madame Dupré paused. "Now, may I inquire as to the purpose of your visit to Avignon?"

"Actually, I'm going to visit a number of gardens in the countryside around Saint-Rémy and the Luberon. And Avignon seemed the best choice because it's central to all of Provence. It's also a convenient place to meet up with Louisa Jones, the woman who has agreed to show me some of the area's most private gardens. I'm told she knows as much about Provençal gardening as anyone in the area, so I'm excited to have her as my guide." I asked Madame Dupré if she gardened.

"No, my dear, that is something I leave to others. But I admire many of the gardens I have seen in Provence. And what about you? Do you garden? Is that why you've come to visit our gardens?"

I laughed. "Well, I'm what you might call a lapsed gardener. When I was a little girl I spent hours planting and pruning in my grandmother's garden. It's still one of the most vivid memories I have: the two of us in the garden, choosing spots for a new plant, mourning the loss of an old one. I'm told when I was very young that if a plant died I would hold a little funeral for it. But when I hit the age of ten or so, gardening just took a backseat in my life—until a few years ago, anyway, when I finally had the time to take it up again. Now I've become my grandmother, right down to the rubber shoes and big floppy sun hat."

Madame Dupré smiled. "And where do you stay in Avignon?"

"At a hotel called La Mirande. Do you know it?"

"I certainly do. Although I have never stayed there, I have visited friends at the hotel. It is exquisite, one of the most beautiful and well-managed hotels in Europe, I think."

We spent the rest of the time talking about Paris, a city that after many years of snooping was slowly beginning to reveal itself to me.

"Ah, but you will never finish learning new things about Paris," said Madame Dupré. "Even after a lifetime in Paris I find new things and *old* new things, sometimes on a street I walk along every day."

When we parted two and a half hours later at the Avignon train station—she to ride in her chauffeured car to Saignon and I in my taxi to my hotel—Madame Dupré seemed like an old friend. When we exchanged cards, she said that she had to come into Avignon on business later in the week and would call me.

"I would love that," I said, wondering if she really would call or if, as happens often in these chance encounters, I would never hear from her again.

As planned, Louisa Jones and I had coffee early the next morning in La Mirande's charming, glassed-in courtyard. Even though we'd never met I recognized her immediately. The pleasant, open face, high forehead, smooth healthy skin, and soft brown eyes behind large eyeglasses were familiar to me from the photos I'd seen on Louisa's website and on the dust jackets of the many books she's written on gardens in Provence. By the time we finished our coffee, Louisa's down-to-earth personality confirmed what I had gleaned from our pre-trip communications: that she would make a good traveling companion. In one of her e-mails she wrote: "I will bring rain gear in the car, just in case, including boots (size nine, bring socks if your feet are much smaller). I'll also bring bottled water, mints, snacks, books, a regular expedition. But you will have to be indulgent about the car. . . . it will have a few bread crumbs. I will vacuum it but still, when I buy bread in the village I can't resist breaking off a piece on the way home and the crumbs are hard to get up."

From the hotel we walked to Louisa's car, parked a few blocks away in a garage beneath her Avignon apartment, a pied-à-terre she and her husband used when not living at their old restored farmhouse on the northern edge of Provence. Then we took the road south from Avignon to our destination near the village of Saint-Rémy-de-Provence. For about forty-five minutes we drove on narrow roads that wound their way through flat fields bordered by rose-pink Judas trees and fragrant apple orchards. We were on our way, Louisa and I, to visit the private gardens of Dominique Lafourcade, one of Provence's most imaginative garden designers. But first we had to find the unmarked road that would lead us to Dominique's restored farmhouse near the hills of Les Alpilles.

"The gardens of Provence are the most private in France," Louisa explained as she craned her neck looking for the turnoff from the main road. "Most people who come here want to get away from publicity. They want privacy. Usually they don't socialize. . . ." Suddenly Louisa stopped in mid-sentence, pulled the car to the side, and then made a U-turn.

It seemed we had passed right by the small dirt road to Dominique's gardens, an oversight that illustrated just how private these gardens are. After all, if Louisa Jones, a respected authority and historian on all things Provençal, could miss a road she's traveled many times before, what chance did the casual visitor have of penetrating this alluring secret world? But despite her momentary lapse, Louisa Jones knows in a way few others do where such secret gardens are, and she knows their history and their owners. Born in Canada, she has lived in Provence with her French husband for more than thirty years, and during that time has become one of the most respected figures in Provence's garden culture.

Now, as Louisa turned the car off the main road and headed in the right direction, she relaxed and began my education, the equivalent of a crash-course version of Provence 101. First came a brief history lesson.

"This area was laid out by Romans," she told me. "They really created the countryside of Provence—the style we see today of alternating cultivated land with wild scrubland. And it was the Romans who were the first gardeners in Provence. They brought with them the art of pruning evergreen shrubbery into formal shapes, and their predominantly green gardens combined elegance and productivity, like their gardens in Tuscany." Of course, Louisa said, the weather and topography also helped shape the surrounding countryside. "This is relatively flat land for Provence. The wind sweeps through here. All the cypress hedging you see in this part of Provence was designed by the Romans as a sort of climate control—a form of protection from the north wind. You will see a good example of that in Dominique's gardens."

By the time we arrived at our destination, I also had gotten an impor-tant tip from Louisa about local real estate: châteaux were out and farm-houses in. "People are not interested in buying a château in Provence," she said. "They don't want anything pompous or prestigious. They want earthiness and elegance so they look for a local *mas*. A farmstead." And she added that while the region's famous lavender was still very much in evidence, it was not considered by Provençals to be the number-one plant: "The most known and adaptable plant in Provence is laurustinus," she said.

As I scribbled down this last bit of startling information—Provence, in my fantasy, was inseparable from fields of fragrant lavender—I added: *Note to myself: Must look for picture of laurustinus in my plant dictionary back at the hotel. Is it a shrub? A flower? A groundcover? Also: when considering a move to Provence, do not even think of purchasing a château. Just tell the realtor: Show me the mas!*

Finally, Louisa gave me a quick sketch of Dominique Lafourcade, and explained why her gardens are imitated all over the world.

"Dominique was born in Avignon and it is very important for her to live here. She comes from a bourgeois family that has a history of both painting and gardening. Her mother was a great gardener. But Dominique was a painter first, before she became a professional garden designer. She's designed more than three dozen gardens in the area and is known for transforming the traditional Provençal green garden into a very playful, whimsical idiom. That's a big trend today. And Dominique was one of the first people to do it in this area."

Although I wasn't sure what "whimsical idiom" meant in terms of garden design, I decided to see Dominique's garden before asking for an explanation.

The Lafourcade property, Louisa went on to say, was set on more than twenty acres of land, about a tenth of which had been transformed into a garden. "But not a garden that is merely decorative. This is a garden where a good deal of eating and drinking and living goes on.

There are several places for outdoor dining, offering a choice depending on the weather and time of day."

As Louisa said this, a long house with a yellow-ocher façade loomed up alongside the road. We had arrived. After pulling the car into a parking spot near the front door, Louisa pointed out the line of ancient oak trees that stood at intervals like giant centurions guarding the house from the fierce mistral wind. The oak trees, she said, were what first drew Dominique and her husband, Bruno, an architect, to the house.

Although the restored farmhouse was lovely and the trees spectacular, I was in fact a bit disappointed. Its situation on the road was not as private as I had imagined and the planting at the front, while attractive, was not as extensive as I expected. After retrieving our cameras and notebooks from the car, Louisa and I walked alongside a plain fence until we came to a small wooden door. Whatever was on the other side of the fence and door was completely hidden. Louisa opened the door. We stepped inside.

The secret garden! I thought, feeling as surprised and delighted as young Mary Lennox did upon seeing for the first time the walled, locked garden in Frances Hodgson Burnett's classic children's book. But unlike the neglected secret garden that Mary discovered, the one I stood in was perfect. Warm and welcoming, it was a paradise of cool elegant greenery, purple-and-white wisteria-covered arbors, water shimmering in pools and ponds, and mysterious paths disappearing into little garden rooms hidden behind tall hedges clipped into walls.

Just as I spotted a long narrow water canal, lined on either side with young olive trees planted in huge terra-cotta pots—a spectacular sight—a woman as sleek as a Thoroughbred racehorse, with the pale coloring and fine-boned face of Vivien Leigh, approached Louisa and me. She was dressed simply in a gray sweater, boots, and jeans; a wide blue band held back her shoulder-length dark hair. Two golden-haired dogs trotted along beside her, although one of them wandered off to examine the ducks floating in the canal. The total effect—of both the gardener and her garden—was one of rustic elegance come by naturally, without calculation.

"This is Dominique Lafourcade," Louisa said, introducing me to the garden's owner.

After we exchanged greetings, I told Dominique that her garden was one of the most remarkable I'd ever seen. "It must take quite a lot of help to keep a garden looking like this," I said.

She smiled, held up a finger, then pointed to herself. "One gardener and me," she said.

"Dominique does all the clipping herself, with hand shears," Louisa added. "She thinks of it as a form of sculpture. Clipping is important—it's a way of catching the light and the dark."

Given the scope of clipped greenery in Dominique's garden, I was amazed to hear that she was the sole pruner. At home I managed with difficulty to keep two small hedges and a row of cypress trees clipped into a very basic shape. But here there were hundreds of shrubs and trees, each one manicured into the shape that best fit its own character and the garden's design. I looked out at the horizon across a sea of obelisks, towers, cylinders, squares, spheres, some close to the ground, others forming dense walls of green that sheltered a series of smaller gardens. The Blue Garden. The Rose Garden. The Round Garden. The Boule Garden, a whimsical homage to the sphere using both stone and greenery. But it was in the Portuguese Garden that I understood fully the playful quality Dominique brought to gardening.

I came across the Portuguese Garden by following an intriguing path paved with pebbles selected by Dominique from the nearby Durance River. Along the way I passed several secluded places for outdoor dining and a green "room"—an outside space walled in by tall green hedges—containing two upholstered rose-pink easy chairs, the kind you'd expect to see in someone's living room. Casually placed outside on the grass near some flowering yellow plants, the chairs beckoned to me. *Come and sit here, where the smell of grass is sweet and time stands as still as the stone frogs perched at the edge of the small pool.*

Although it was difficult I ignored the siren call of the chairs and walked ahead to a little house near a small pool. Inside the one-room structure was a single bed, some inlaid wooden chests, a massive glazed green pot, a fireplace, and many books. Along with its whitewashed walls, sheer curtains, and brick flooring, the room gave the effect of an oasis. Given that I'd arrived in France only twenty-four hours earlier and was suffering from jet lag, the only thing that prevented me from taking a catnap on the oh-so-beckoning bed was the sudden appearance of Louisa.

"So you found the Portuguese Garden," she said. "It was designed to be a quiet place for rest and relaxation, for a siesta after a private dip in the pool." A few steps behind Louisa was Dominique, clippers in one hand, a piece of greenery in the other. And a few steps behind her trotted a very independent-looking dog, one I hadn't seen before.

"Some kid threw out this dog," Louisa said of the happy-looking mutt. "The gardener recovered him from the garbage pail. An Easter present." Dominique touched the dog's head gently, then smiled slightly in the direction of her four-legged companion.

It seemed that Dominique had a penchant for rescuing things, plants and trees as well as animals. Many of the plants in her garden, she said, were gathered from the wild or rescued after being discarded by neighbors or friends. "It is just basic local vegetation. Nothing rare or exotic."

As Dominique and Louisa discussed the garden I saw Louisa's eyes taking in whatever was being explained to her with a gaze as steady and observant as that of a cat stalking a bird. Or to put it another way, Louisa had the kind of sharp vision and focused eye that all true critics possess, whether they are assessing Renaissance art or Provençal gardens.

I left the two women talking and wandered through the garden. The sight of a family of ducks—once pests but now pets—sunning themselves near the water canal, coupled with the sound of a small nation of vocalizing frogs, made me think of something Grandmother told me one spring as we planted her boldly colored flower garden. *You can tell a lot about a person by looking at their garden,* she'd say while sprinkling seeds from small hardware-store packets, each with a picture on the front of a bright red or yellow or purple flower. *And sometimes after looking at their garden, you'll see that person in surprising new ways.*

What Grandmother said—or at least my memory of what she said— was true. After an hour in the garden Dominique had created, I saw her in a different light. In contrast to her cool elegant exterior, the garden reflected the sensibility of a playful, creative woman with a reverence for nature and its sentient creatures. It was a garden that paid homage, however fancifully, to nature and to life.

"The weather is as changeable as a teenager trying to pick an outfit for a first date," a friend had told me about April in Provence. Louisa had backed up that appraisal. In an e-mail answer to my questions about what kind of weather to expect during my trip—hot, cold, rainy?—and what to pack, she wrote: "When it does rain, it rains hard. . . . Temperatures: cool morning and evening and can be very warm mid-afternoon, so, layers. You know all about layers, I'm sure." What Louisa didn't mention was how windy it could be in early spring. I thought of this as we drove to the next garden through winds that blew rows of tall pencil-thin cypress trees back and forth like tuning forks searching for the right pitch.

The garden we were about to see, one created for an American family by the English designer Tim Rees, would offer a good contrast to Dominique's design approach, Louisa said, as we turned off the main road onto a smaller lane. "Tim Rees designs very much for the cosmopolitan set that has come to Provence. He specializes in wild grass and perennial plantings. But this garden has many parts. One of the main features is a vast meadow of wildflowers situated between the house and the mountains. It's a huge estate. The couple own all the land from the road into the mountains. They bought a small forest from a nursery going out of business and used the trees to cut the north wind, which blows all year round.

"By contrast, Dominique—who is one of the top three designers of big gardens in this area—is very Provençal in her approach. She takes her inspiration from the old-fashioned green gardens that essentially were designed for family living rather than for show. It's a more regional style where foliage shape and color dominate floral elements. Tim Rees's approach is more meadow-style and more formal. But both these gardens were created around old farmhouses."

I asked Louisa to what extent Provençal garden design was influenced by the English garden style, as propagated by Vita Sackville-West in her famous Sissinghurst garden and Gertrude Jekyll in her seminal garden at Munstead Wood. "The English style is what many Americans use as a model for their gardens," I said, thinking of my own mixed borders filled with flowering perennials and grassy plants.

"The English garden used to be the predominant model in Provence. And many people still prefer it, or some version of it. But now there are more gardens of every style and size all over the region. And the old-style Provençal garden has been transformed in ways that build on the past."

I wanted to ask Louisa more about the differences between the gardens preferred by the "cosmopolitan set" and those favored by native Provençals, but there wasn't time. We had arrived at our destination, a 160-acre property situated dramatically at the foot of the Alpilles mountain range. Waiting for us at the end of an avenue of majestic plane trees were Dominique and her sister, both invited by Louisa to join us. Dominique had never seen this relatively new garden and was eager to see what designer Tim Rees had done with it. Checking out the competition, it seemed, was a sensibility not confined to France's superstar chefs; it existed even in the rarefied air of Provence's gardening world.

We walked to the front of the vine-covered house where the view was, as promised, spectacular. From a terrace shaded by soaring plane trees—some more than four hundred years old—I looked across a wild-flower meadow and lavender fields to the rugged silvery mountains. On one side of the house was a formal topiary garden, its Dutch boxwood, yews, and holly clipped into immaculate, original shapes. A lush green carpet of grass stopped just short of the terrace. Terra-cotta pots filled with masses of white pansies and full-blown pink and apricot-colored tulips sat between the pillars on the front veranda. It was all quite fabulous but definitely not the image my brain retrieved upon hearing the word *farmhouse*. It struck me as the equivalent of using the word *dungarees* to describe five-hundred-dollar designer jeans.

Since the owners of the house were away, an attractive, ruddy-faced man who seemed to be part of the house-and-garden staff came out to greet us. After Louisa introduced us, she fell into what seemed an intense conversation with the man. Since they spoke in rapid French that was beyond my comprehension I decided to stroll around the huge estate, a task that, if done properly, could take half the day.

I started by following a long, secluded grass path carved out between a lily pond and a line of tall trees. The wind blowing through the trees created a sibilant swishing sound, one that reminded me of the soft voice of Ouka, my Japanese dancing instructor in Kyoto. It was such an idyllic setting that I sat down on one of the wooden garden benches overlooking the lily pond and listened for a while to the wind in the trees and the *plop plop plopping* of frogs leaping through the water. When I was ready to move on, I spotted a woodland path that disappeared into what seemed a forest.

Is this the forest bought by the owners? I wondered as I walked through the dense shrubbery and flowering plants lining the path beneath the trees. All along the way, paths converged, each one leading off in a different direction. Never mind that I hadn't a clue which path to follow or whether, to echo Robert Frost, the one I took would make all the difference. The truth is, I'd bailed out of the right choice–wrong choice mentality a long time ago. It seemed so clear to me—once I'd wised up to the idea that life is not a straight road with no exit ramps—that life presented opportunities all along the way for a person to change directions. Besides, over the last ten years, I'd grown to like the idea of not knowing where a choice might lead me.

Now, as I approached an open space outside the woodland path, I saw that my random choice had led me to a place I liked very much: to a weathered iron gate, one that might have sprung straight from a Nancy Drew book. Beyond the gate I could see a garden with steps leading down to an allée of olive trees surrounded by extensive gardens of clipped greenery and flowers. I pushed the gate open and saw to my right, at the end of the olive tree walk, a large pool pavilion, its columns and terra-cotta roof reflected in the long rectangular swimming pool. The open veranda of the pavilion held large pots of flowers and chairs arranged to catch the sun. It looked very inviting.

Five minutes later I found myself sitting in one of those chairs. It was not a calculated move on my part; I simply arrived at a chair and sat down. The view from the pool house was spectacular; I could see through the olive trees with their silvery gray gnarled trunks, up the steps and past the stone pillars and tall plane trees to huge pots of pansies on the back terrace of the main house. This is a perfect spot, I thought, as I sat in the warm sun feeling as contented as a petunia on a sunny window ledge. It was hard to believe that just thirty-six hours earlier I was sitting in a drafty airline terminal at Dulles Airport waiting for the night flight to Paris. Even harder to believe was the twist of events that led me to this private tour with Louisa Jones.

I had hooked up with Louisa after my initial arrangement to visit the gardens of Provence fell through at the last minute. The trip, organized by a horticultural group, was described in its brochure as "designed by internationally acclaimed author Louisa Jones who will personally guide and interpret the gardens for us." It sounded perfect, a small group led by a knowledgeable guide with access to many private gardens. The sudden cancellation was a big disappointment. I'd almost decided to bag the whole idea when a lightbulb went off over my head: *Since the trip was canceled, maybe Louisa Jones still has those dates free! Maybe she might be open to showing me some gardens!*

Although it seemed a long shot, I decided to contact Louisa Jones and tell her of my disappointment at the trip's cancellation. Two days after sending off a fax to her in France, I received her reply. Yes, she wrote, she was free for those dates and would be willing to help me with my project of learning about gardening in Provence. A few faxes later, we had agreed on a fee and a tentative schedule. By the time I arrived in Avignon, my knowledge of gardening and Provence had progressed— thanks to Louisa's helpful e-mails and articles—from almost nothing to an advanced beginner's level.

Now, as I sat in the pool house surveying the gardens around me, I wondered: Would an allée of large old olive trees surrounded by lavender look good along the walk to my front door? Before I could decide, Louisa appeared in the distance, near the back terrace of the main house. She appeared to be looking for someone. Then I realized she was looking for me. Reluctantly I left the pool house and made my way up to the terrace.

Louisa met me at the halfway point between terrace and olive trees. As we walked back to the front of the house, she filled me in on some of the garden's high points and a few of the owners' idiosyncrasies. *Some of the large trees are transplanted seventeenth-century plane trees. It shocks a lot of people that it's even possible to buy seventeenth-century plane trees. . . . Every tree has its own character. You see it with these ancient olive trees. Each was chosen for its sculptural qualities. . . . The park and gardens are set on thirty-five acres of land. . . . In the rose garden, they wanted shorter roses—so all the original roses were removed. . . . The gardens are a mixture of grasses, shrubs, and flowers carefully arranged in different heights and volumes. . . . The house was a shell when the owners bought it. They practically tore everything down. . . . Four fountains on the property were removed because they made too much noise when the family ate on the terrace. . . . A hill was built and planted with eighty-foot trees to hide an unsightly pylon supporting electric wires. . . . There are five grounds people to take care of the property. . . .*

As we walked, the wind blew away the sun's warmth. Reflexively, Louisa pulled on her dark windbreaker, and I struggled back into my jacket. Ahead, we saw Dominique, her sister, and two or three others being ushered into a striking, perfectly proportioned building near the main house. It was the *orangerie*, Louisa explained, as we followed the others inside. Once a barn, the building now had a classical façade. Used for entertaining, the large open space inside the *orangerie* had three skylights, a beamed ceiling, and heated stone floors. Furnished with antiques, the building had its own wine cellar and bathrooms. It also had a large kitchen, from which we were served warm praline cookies and hot or cold beverages. I thought everything about it was spectacular.

After consuming as many cookies as possible without drawing attention to myself, I moved to a corner and made a sketch in my notebook of the building's interior design: the skylights, placement of door, beamed ceiling, et cetera. What I had in mind was the possibility—remember, I said *possibility*—of converting my garage at home into an *orangerie*. Of course my *orangerie*—a word I never tired of pronouncing *en français*—would be a smaller version of the original *orangerie*. But as the great architect Mies van der Rohe and I often observed: Less is more. Although, on second thought, I suppose one could make the opposite case: that more is less.

It was late afternoon when Louisa dropped me off back in Avignon at La Mirande. Although still jet-lagged I wanted to take a walk through the area around the hotel, to see something of the city and to get my bearings. All I really knew about Avignon was that each summer it hosted the popular Festival d'Avignon, a top French arts festival, and that it was home to the Palais des Papes, a massive fourteenth-century stone building that rose up from the ground like a range of Alpine mountain peaks.

Now as I walked from La Mirande past those stone walls, through the narrow winding alleys that led to the center of town, I remembered a description of the city given me by a writer who has lived in Provence for many years. "Avignon is okay. A bit scruffy, but there are some good restaurants, the bridge, and a well-worn papal palace." When I emerged from the warren of medieval cobbled alleyways onto the town's large central square, place de l'Horloge, what I found was a noisy, crowded collection of pizza places, cafés, bars, souvenir shops, and an ancient gilded carousel. Although not yet ready to agree with the description of Avignon as "a bit scruffy," I had little desire to hang around the place de l'Horloge.

After walking around the neighborhood a bit more I returned to the hotel and, still fighting my jet lag and in desperate need of a *café noir*, headed immediately for the winter garden. With its country French furniture, glowing Oriental rugs on old stone floors, tables stacked with the latest newspapers and magazines, and the soft, transparent Provençal light turning the room into a luminous jewel, the glass-enclosed courtyard was the perfect place to relax. But then any place you might choose to sit down in La Mirande was a perfect place to relax.

As I sipped my *café* it occurred to me that gardening and choosing a hotel have a lot in common. Just as planting a garden is an act of faith, so too is choosing a place to stay in an unknown city. For each carefully selected perennial that has failed in my garden, there is a corresponding hotel in London or San Francisco or Rome that turned out to be a really bad choice. But once in a while a hotel comes along that surpasses not only your expectations but your wildest fantasies as well. La Mirande in Avignon was such a hotel.

From the moment I stepped into its serene, flower-filled reception area I felt at home. Not because my home is anything like La Mirande, which was built as a cardinal's palace in the thirteenth century, converted into a private residence in the seventeenth century, and, in the late 1980s, restored to perfection and converted into a small deluxe hotel. Far from it. In my home, for example, there is no exquisite Salon Chinois with eighteenth-century chinoiserie wallpaper or comfortable sofas and chairs upholstered with exquisite fabrics from Paris. Nor do the windows in my home feature hand-blown glass. And I won't even bother to compare my dining room to La Mirande's superb restaurant with its painted Renaissance ceiling, or my staircase with the circular stone stairway that swirled its way through the ceiling to the floor above. But despite its elegant perfection—a style that often can be cold and intimidating—La Mirande envelops its visitors in warmth, charm, and comfort.

Later, as I sat in my jewel box of a room going over notes I'd taken during the day, I decided that La Mirande really should be named Le Mirage. Tucked away behind the majestic Palais des Papes, the hotel's honey-colored stone façade rises like a dream from a maze of medieval alleyways. From my window I could almost lean out and touch the fortresslike palace walls that Clement VI had built six hundred years earlier for the Roman Catholic popes after the papacy's move from Rome to Avignon. With such history calling out to me, it was hard to concentrate on studying.

Still, I gave it a shot, turning to the page in my notebook headed, Bold Colors vs. Muted Colors. Beneath it I had written: *Louisa says there are two schools of thought regarding color in the Provençal flower garden. The Van Gogh style, which tends toward intense, bright, warm colors, and the school of muted color where pales and pastels are preferred. . . .*

I stopped reading. Through my open window the sound of a church bell tolling reminded me of where I was: in Avignon, the city described by Rabelais as *l'isle sonnante*—"the ringing island"—because of the incessant tolling of the bells. I rather liked the sound, I thought, as I dozed off into a peaceful sleep.

If she had to name one person who helped shape the most famous gardens in Provence, Louisa told me, it would be master pruner Marco Nucera. "He has had a hand—two hands—in all the most famous gardens of the region. But owners and designers rarely get round to mentioning his contribution."

We were on our way to meet this "silent partner," as Louisa called Marco. He was to show us his own garden before taking us to visit a large property he had worked on in collaboration with one of the region's leading designers, the late Alain Idoux. To hear Louisa tell it, Marco's pruning skills made him the arboricultural equivalent of the sculptor Jean Arp. "He has a natural talent for seeing the shapes in trees and bushes," she said. "There is a poetic quality to his work as well as a theoretical one. Both are equally important."

After a short drive southeast from Avignon, Louisa parked the car near the edge of a small town, one whose streets were too narrow to accommodate cars. Almost immediately a young man with striking good looks approached us. After Louisa introduced me to twenty-nine-year-old Marco Nucera, the three of us walked through the curving maze of cobbled lanes to his house.

"Marco was born in this town and his roots are still here," Louisa said. "He knows everyone. Old ladies gave him candy when he was growing up."

Marco smiled as Louisa said this. It was a slow, appealing smile that, combined with his deep blue eyes and dark hair, no doubt had many young ladies giving him candy now.

We stopped in front of a house with a little courtyard. "It was an old barn originally," Louisa said. "Marco did all the work on it himself."

Marco opened the door and we stepped inside. What I saw surprised me. Marco had created a living space that was as sophisticated and stylish as an expensive loft in Tribeca. The large room had timbered ceilings and a line of windows along the back wall that overlooked a small garden; a stone wall framed one side of a fireplace. It was a cold morning and a small glowing fire filled the room with warmth and the fragrant scent of well-seasoned wood—apple wood, perhaps. The hand of an artist was apparent in even the smallest details: in the three yellow roses placed in a brown-and-cream earthenware pitcher, in the small plants Marco grows in pots set in their own mini-landscape. The artist's touch was visible even in the arrangement of his books and photographs.

One photograph particularly intrigued me. It showed Marco hanging in a huge tree, pruning. The position of his wiry but muscular body made it look as though he were flying; it also suggested the difficulties of working on such a large tree. I asked Marco what he was trying to accomplish when he pruned that particular tree.

"I wanted to keep the natural shape of the tree, but bring out its line," he explained. "Trees each have their own strong character. Landscape pruning is like being a sculptor of trees." Marco stopped to roll a cigarette, expertly sprinkling just the right amount of tobacco into the thin paper, then added, "The day after I prune a big tree I am exhausted."

Marco received his original training at a landscaping school near Avignon that prepares people to work in parks. Following that he took a course that specialized in the maintenance of large trees. In 1989 he became a gardener in a private garden and was put in charge of reviving a huge orchard of five-hundred-year-old olive trees, a task he labored on for three years. Now as a freelance pruner in a region known for its garden savvy—and clients wealthy enough to pay for the best—Marco has become a star. He's the guy everyone wants, not only for sculptural pruning, but also for his ability to size up the aesthetic potential of existing trees and envision how a garden will look as it matures. This last was something I was learning the hard way as various small plantings in my four-year-old garden threatened to grow into giants.

None of this acclaim seems to have gone to Marco's head. Perhaps that's because he derives all the satisfaction he needs from knowing he is good at what he does. "His father makes furniture, beautiful furniture," Louisa said, "so Marco's sense of perfectionism and craftsmanship came from his father. And his ability to get pleasure from his work, he also learned from his father."

Sometimes Marco said things that one might expect to hear from a French poet or intellectual. Things like: "Almond trees have their own strong character and often become the major actor in a landscape." Or: "Sincerity comes from depth and inhibits pretending."

Marco's lack of inhibition and pretense seemed to extend to his everyday life, as I found out when I needed to use *la toilette* and searched in vain for a door to close. There was none. But the openness of the bathroom added to its spare beauty, so much so that I made a mental note to reexamine the use of such doors in my own home.

On our way to see the large garden designed by the late Alain Idoux—with trees and shrubs shaped by Marco—the three of us stopped at a garden owned by Marco himself. A small piece of grassland not too far from his home, it was an unusual garden, nothing like the others I'd visited in Provence. Louisa called it a "garden-turned-gallery," a reference to the way artwork created by Marco's friends was displayed throughout.

As I stood looking at the stone circle built by Marco as a focal point, the image of another garden popped into my head: the dry rock "waterfall" I'd seen at the sixteenth-century garden of Daisen-in in Kyoto. Naohiro had taken me there, telling me it was a favorite of his. "It is very important to understand the garden is an allegory," Naohiro told me. "In this garden, the gardener is telling the story of life by carefully choosing the perfect rocks, gravel, and pruned plants."

To tell the truth, neither the gardening approach used at Daisen-in nor Marco's land art gallery appealed to me. Why, I wasn't sure. Too intellectual? Maybe. Not enough flowers? Perhaps. Or maybe I simply missed that primal sense of connection with nature and the earth that I remembered from Grandmother's garden. But just as I hadn't shared such lukewarm feelings with Naohiro at Daisen-in for fear of disappointing him, I said nothing to Louisa about my response to Marco's land art garden. Especially since she and Marco seemed to share a similar sensibility, one that included, among other things, a highly refined approach to gardening, one that combined nature with artistry.

As I accompanied them through the garden, it was clear from listening to the two of them that Marco and Louisa respected and understood one another. Their personalities even struck me as being similar. Beneath their composed, calm attitudes, a fierce critical intelligence burned in both of them, a mutual trait that seemed to inspire confidence in their judgments. I suspected that Louisa, who had spent decades observing and researching every aspect of the Provençal garden, and Marco, who pruned his gardening philosophy as masterfully as his trees, had added a gravitas to what some might see as simply an avocation for the wealthy.

"The garden we're going to see is about five or six years old and belongs to a French film producer," Louisa said as we drove up and down a country road looking for the lane into the property that Marco had helped shape. "It was designed for them by Alain Idoux, who died in 1997 of Lou Gehrig's disease. The family has three children and they come down from Paris for vacations."

She stopped, then backed up to a long driveway lined with ancient olive trees and was just turning into it when a car coming from the house pulled alongside us. The woman driving rolled down her window and began talking to Louisa in French. She nodded pleasantly to me and then drove off.

"That was the wife of the owner," Louisa said as we continued up the stunning allée of huge olive trees, their silvery gray trunks sculpted by nature over a few hundred years or so. At the end of the drive was a pale stone, three-story house with blue shutters framing the French windows. A large gravel space edged with greenery led to a pair of winding stone steps, one on each side of what I assumed was the main entrance. It would be the perfect setting, I thought, for a bedroom farce, one of those comedies like *La Ronde* where lovers who are married to someone else continually enter and exit bedrooms. Why this occurred to me, I wasn't sure. But I made a note of it, just in case I ran into the French film producer whose house it was.

One of the many pleasures of visiting the gardens of Provence was the element of surprise: surprise at what one might find at the end of hidden allées of ancient trees, behind walls of living greenery. I suppose what surprised me most about these secret gardens was the extent to which each garden had its own distinct character—even though the raw materials used were basically the same. What Louisa would call the "bones" of a Provençal garden usually consisted of imaginatively pruned olive and cypress trees combined with clipped evergreen shrubs and hedges of box, laurel, rosemary, myrtle, juniper, evergreen oak, acanthus, and laurustinus. Thanks to my trusty little plant dictionary I now recognized the formerly mysterious laurustinus as "*Viburnum tinus*, a hardy evergreen shrub with leaves resembling those of bay laurel; its pink buds open into white flowers in early spring." I planned to bring it up a lot when talking to my gardening friends after I returned home.

Now, as I walked with Marco and Louisa through the French film producer's parklike estate, I understood how Marco's unique abilities to envision the larger picture—and project it into the future—played a pivotal role in shaping a landscape, particularly one as sweeping as this. I could see also how his softer style of pruning resulted in a more natural, less formal effect. Louisa confirmed what I was thinking.

"Every garden has its own requirements," she said, "so you can't apply the same style to all of them. This is always a very important point for Marco. When working in larger gardens like this, he takes into account each of the natural forms and tries to make the style as natural as possible. With this house, he needed to find a solution between the foreground and the grounds outside the garden. It's very Japanese in that sense."

The garden was also very Japanese, I thought, in its sense of order and serenity. Although there were many separate gardens and paths leading into sylvan areas or open meadow spaces, the prevailing garden aesthetic, to me anyway, was an uncluttered harmony. I found it most appealing. Near the pool—a simple, pristine rectangle of shimmering blue-green water—I entered a little glade where, in a semicircle of large trees, I found a round dining table surrounded by wicker chairs. Outside the line of trees was a large expanse of green grass, beyond which I could see towers of cypress. I imagined sitting there, as though on an ocean liner, looking across a sea of grass to the conning tower of a distant ship.

A voice interrupted my thoughts. It was Louisa. "We've been invited into the house for coffee," she said.

"Sounds good," I replied, thrilled by the thought of getting a look inside, not to mention a cup of hot coffee on a chilly morning. I followed Louisa back to the house where we entered a door on the ground floor, one that led into a large, superbly equipped kitchen. At one end of the massive wooden kitchen table a uniformed cook was preparing food for the midday meal. Sitting at the other end was an attractive, casually dressed woman, who seemed to be having breakfast. She rose to greet us.

"Hello, I'm Valerie Perrero," she said, inviting us to join her at the table. Immediately, Cook presented us with steaming dark coffee and slivers of cake. Valerie explained she was a houseguest down from Paris, the mention of which prompted a conversation about the glories of Paris, a topic I never tired of.

"Where in Paris do you live?" I asked Valerie after we'd talked for a while.

"I live on a houseboat."

"Really? I've seen a number of them docked along the river and always wondered what life on a houseboat in the Seine would be like. Would you recommend it?"

"Very much," she said delving into some of the mundane details involved. "But if you would really like to know, why don't you come and visit me?" She rose to get a pen and wrote down in my notebook her Paris telephone numbers and e-mail address. Immediately I memorized the e-mail address, just in case I lost the notebook.

"It's a date then," I said, trying to sound casual.

Cook interrupted her apple-slicing to discuss, in French, the luncheon menu with Valerie. I wouldn't swear to it but the menu seemed to feature some sort of duck salad, puréed vegetable soup, and apple tarts. Or maybe it was vegetable salad and duck soup, a sly tribute perhaps to the Marx Brothers.

If Louisa Jones were a garden, she would be the garden of the Martin-Ragets. I decided this after Louisa and I had lunch one day at the home of Monsieur and Madame Jacques Martin-Raget, a couple I liked right away. The garden, like its owners, seemed authentic, straightforward, and unpretentious. Louisa struck me that way too: she was an authentic person who had not lost contact with her roots. Once when we were talking about the old farmhouse on the northern edge of Provence where she and her husband lived quietly with their cats, she told me in a wry voice how disappointed people were when they saw her simple garden and her house with its unmade bed. And although she moved among people who led privileged lives, Louisa exhibited neither awe nor envy of their social or financial status. But she did admire many of the people who opened their houses and gardens to her, including the Martin-Ragets, whom she spoke of with great respect and affection.

"They are a lovely couple, both in their mid-seventies," Louisa told me as we drove on a cool sunny day to our luncheon engagement at their charming old house near the western Alpilles, about an hour's drive southwest from Avignon. "A truly Provençal couple who have Roman profiles still. He is a retired solicitor who comes from a very old Arlesian family. She grew up in the Camargue where her whole family went riding the wild horses at Christmas. This property belonged to his family and had been rented out to a farmer. But when their children were grown, they moved into the house and began to make a garden piecemeal, bit by bit. They both continue to work five or six hours a day in the garden."

When we arrived at the Martin-Raget's, the couple stood waiting on the sunny terrace of their vine-covered farmhouse. In her bright red tartan skirt, navy sweater, dark opaque stockings, and flat shoes, Madame Martin-Raget looked like a lively silver-haired schoolgirl. As for Monsieur Martin-Raget, he could have been sent over from central casting to fill the role of a retired French solicitor. An imposing man with white hair and a tanned face that telegraphed warmth and good humor, he wore a soft green V-neck sweater over a stylish tattersall shirt filled in at the neck with a red foulard scarf. And true to Louisa's description of the couple, both did have Roman profiles. Still.

As we stood exchanging greetings on the sunlit terrace overlooking an orchard of silvery, gray-green olive trees, I felt instantly at home. Why, I didn't know. Perhaps it was the warmth of the greeting I received or the tantalizing aromas from the kitchen that promised a brilliant midday meal. Or perhaps it was just the inexplicable sense of well-being I felt in the presence of the Martin-Ragets. My comfort level, in fact, was so high that in my mind they quickly became "Jacques and Nicole." Not that I'd ever address them in such an intimate way with my speaking voice; it was only my thinking voice that I allowed to take such liberties.

It was decided that we would take a quick tour around the grounds before sitting down to eat. From the house we walked along garden paths that led to a grove of olive trees. "The old tenant farmer who now lives in one end of the house prunes those trees," Louisa explained. "But Jacques still carries his olives to the mill to be made into oil. It's the same mill his grandfather used."

On one side of the property, the land rose into a hill. It had been planted with shrubs and trees and featured a long narrow series of steps over which water flowed down from the top—a clever way of providing irrigation as well as a form of land art. Farther away from the house was a pond stocked with fish and planted with water lilies. In the middle of the pond was a little island, and as we approached I watched four startled frogs leap single file, like lemmings, into the water. We stepped into a nearby greenhouse filled with the scent of orange blossoms. I inhaled the warm fragrance as though it were an elixir that would keep me eternally young. Nicole explained that the greenhouse served as a winter garden for citrus trees and bird-of-paradise plants.

On our walk back to the house I saw wood smoke rising from the chimney, its pungent aroma spreading across the garden like pale scented fog. Although the temperature was in the sixties, the old stone houses in Provence, I was told, can remain cold inside until late spring. The sharp smell reminded me of a long-ago time when Grandmother set the winter breakfast table in front of a crackling fire; it was a Scotswoman's answer to gas heating costs that were "far too dear."

We entered the house through a French door that opened into a light-filled room near the kitchen. Immediately Nicole excused herself, stopping just long enough to put on a long white chef's apron before disappearing into the kitchen. As Jacques and Louisa talked in rapid French, my eyes roamed around the room like a camera, stopping every few minutes to take snapshots that could be stored in memory and retrieved at will in years to come:

Click. A shot of the long rectangular table covered with soft pink and white linen, perfect china, and gleaming silver. *Click.* A round lapis-blue bowl filled with pink gladiolus and white hyacinths glowing at one end of the table. *Click.* Straw hats hanging from wooden pegs and garden boots standing on the terra-cotta floor next to the kitchen door. *Click.* Hanging baskets of full-blown flowers backlit by the sun streaming through glass doors. *Click.* Logs glowing as they burned in a large old fireplace. *Click.* Pictures everywhere of children and grandchildren, of Jacques's grandfather on the farm, of a young Nicole on horseback in the Camargue, a region to the south that is famous for its pink flamingos and for the white horses and wild bulls that still wander freely in the rugged countryside.

When Nicole appeared, sans apron, we sat down to lunch. Fresh asparagus bought from a nearby market garden was arranged on a striking ceramic serving plate, next to a bowl of lemony hollandaise sauce. Olive oil glowed like liquid gold in its glass container. A pork roast appeared accompanied by a platter of *petits pois*—shelled by Nicole—and bits of ham. In the center of the peas was a circle of artichokes and tiny, thinly sliced carrots. A bowl of browned juices from the roast pork, with onions added, was passed around the table. Wine was poured into long-stemmed glasses as thin as paper. And as we ate and drank, time stole silently away, leaving in its place something rare, at least for me: a feeling of contentment.

Eventually, pots of chocolate mousse flavored with bits of orange rind appeared, accompanied by a big bowl of ripe juicy strawberries coated with sugar. I ate everything placed before me, my appetite whetted not only by the superb food but by the company as well. This was a house of many appetites: for books and music and art and flowers and conversation and, of course, food. It was a house that had been nurtured by hardy, elegant people whose lives, like the olive trees surrounding them, had put down deep roots here. And it was a house from which I would take away many good memories. But one memory in particular, I suspected, would become a regular visitor when thoughts of Provence danced in my head.

As we were finishing dessert, Jacques turned to me and asked if I would like a second pot of chocolate mousse.

"Oh, thank you, but no," I said. "I loved it, but one was enough."

Jacques leaned toward me, his large well-shaped head almost brushing mine. "When you love something, you don't count," he said, smiling as though he had someone or something special in mind.

I found this philosophy quite endearing if not always true. Particularly since the waistband of my slacks was telling me to say no, no, no. Instead, I gave myself up to the pleasure of the moment and said: Yes, yes, yes.

Late one afternoon upon returning to La Mirande, a receptionist waved me over to the desk. "Madame Steinbach, I have someone on the line for you," she said, handing me the telephone.

"Bonjour, Madame Steinbach," said the caller, a woman whose accent telegraphed even to me that she was a Parisian. "This is Fabian Dupré. We met last week on the TGV from Paris to Avignon and exchanged cards at the train station."

"Ah, yes," I said. "We had such a nice talk about Paris and about your home in the Luberon. I hope you are well, Madame Dupré."

"Very well, thank you. I am in Avignon presently and am calling to ask if you would meet me for tea before I drive back to Saignon. I could be at the Mirande in twenty minutes. Are you available?"

Her call had caught me off guard and so had her last-minute invitation, coming as it did on the heels of a very tiring day. But I had thoroughly enjoyed Madame Dupré's company on the train and was eager to see her again. We agreed to meet in La Mirande's courtyard. After hanging up, I dashed upstairs to my room to change clothes and freshen up. For some reason Madame Dupré made me want to look my best. So, after some deliberation, I put on what I considered my nicest outfit: a white handkerchief-linen blouse edged in red silk braid and a two-tiered black linen skirt that buttoned up the back. Then I slipped on a pair of black espadrilles bought the day before in a shop on rue Joseph-Vernet, an elegant shopping street that was Avignon's answer to the rue du Faubourg-St.-Honoré in Paris. As I sat wrapping the espadrille laces around my ankles, preparing to meet her for tea, I wondered if the chemistry between us would still be there.

My question was answered the instant I saw Madame Dupré. She looked just as fabulous as she had on the train, although her style was less Parisian and more Provençal. She wore a simple blue sweater and skirt, the exact color of her eyes, and a strand of coral beads. Her silver hair added a third color. For some reason, I thought of Matisse's paintings of Moorish women dressed in colorful robes.

I decided to take a chance. "Ah, yes, Madame Dupré, the lady from Saigon," I said, hoping she remembered the incident. If not, I was sunk, doomed to be remembered, if remembered at all, as a foolish American who babbled on about nothing.

"*C'est moi,*" she said. "The very same lady you speak of, who has come for tea from her home in Vietnam." We both laughed. *Okay,* I thought, *it's still there. I didn't dream it. She is a kindred spirit.*

After ordering our tea and exchanging pleasantries I asked Madame Dupré to tell me about the Luberon, an area that is now known as "Peter Mayle country," thanks to the author's bestselling books about his expatriate lifestyle.

"The Luberon takes its name from the Luberon Mountains," she told me. "And it is the place where many tourists come to see the quaint *villages perchés.* The perched hilltop villages like Bonnieux and Gordes that seem to grow out of the rock beneath them. In the north there are other villages with mountain streams that rush through red cliffs into large springs. Some who live there call it Le Petit Colorado."

"And your village of Saignon? How did you come to live there?"

"The house in Saignon was left many years ago to my sister and me by a relative. When we were younger we came often and stayed for much of the summer. Now we come perhaps four times a year for a week or two." Madame Dupré smiled. "It is the perfect antidote to the hectic life in Paris. Many who write about the Luberon say it has become too fashionable, that it is just an extension of the Saint-Germain-des-Prés crowd. This is so and not so. It is a place where one can choose to socialize or choose to be solitary. Or both, as one wishes."

Saignon, she told me, was a hill town that had escaped much of the gentrification found in many of the surrounding villages. "Yes, we have a few boutiques and restaurants but Saignon still maintains its landscape. It is still a place almost as unspoiled as it was before the Luberon became so desirable a place to have a vacation house."

I asked Madame Dupré if she'd read any of Peter Mayle's books. "Oh, yes. Several. My sister and I enjoy them very much. But I understand he has moved from the village of Ménerbes to another village."

We stayed over tea for a long while, talking about Provence and Paris. I told her I would be venturing into the Luberon in a day or two to see several famous gardens there. She asked if I planned to go to Bonnieux to see the famous garden created by Nicole de Vesian, a legendary designer who was head of fashion at Hermès for many years.

"Yes, that is on the agenda," I said, realizing I was starting to speak with the same formality as Madame Dupré. "Is it true that each morning Madame de Vesian went through her garden clipping bushes with nail scissors?" I asked, pleased to seem knowledgeable about even such a tiny piece of Luberon gossip.

Madame Dupré smiled. "Although I knew Nicole de Vesian—we met many years ago in Paris and remained friendly—I cannot say about the nail scissors. When she came to Bonnieux in the late 1980s she had just turned seventy and knew nothing about gardening. I thought that astounding."

"Astounding and optimistic," I said, thinking of my own garden, of how I crossed off my list any tree that would take more than five years to reach maturity.

"Well, perhaps you will visit me in Saigon," Madame Dupré said, deliberately mispronouncing the name of her village. "I leave this weekend for Nice to visit a relative but will return the week following. Perhaps that would be a possibility."

My heart sank. I was dying to see her house. But I was leaving Provence just about the time she returned from Nice. When I explained this to her, she expressed her regrets. "If your plans change," she said, writing something on a card, "I would welcome you to my house at your convenience. Here is my phone number."

"You are very kind, and I hope to see you either in Provence or Paris," I told her as we walked to the hotel door. What I didn't tell her about were the fast-and-furious computations taking place in my head as I tried to figure out how to stay in the area for that extra week.

On a fine morning under a pale lilac-colored sky, Louisa and I were headed south to Saint-Rémy to visit a garden so celebrated that I knew of it even before coming to Provence: the Theo garden. Its owner, Pierre Berge, who for decades was the business mastermind behind the fashion house of Yves Saint Laurent, named the Saint-Rémy property after the brother of Vincent Van Gogh. The artist had lived for a year at a nearby asylum in Saint-Rémy.

Created in 1992, the garden resulted from a wildly successful collaboration between Berge, an educated and experienced gardener, and

Michel Semini, a sought-after landscape architect among whose clients were numbered many Parisian fashion and film people. After seeing Semini's personal garden in a nearby medieval village, the story goes, Pierre Berge wanted a garden just like it. And Berge, a busy executive used to getting things done quickly, wanted the project completed in six months. The contract was signed in January 1992. By July 31 of the same year, the landscape designer and his forty workmen met their deadline, completing the gardens for the house and pool areas.

"Michel has made a specialty of creating the near-instant garden," Louisa said as we drove through the charming town of Saint-Rémy.

"What does that mean? A near-instant garden?" I asked.

"It means nothing must look new. It means old olive trees and large specimen trees. It means everything should look as though it's been there forever. Not easy to do."

"And, I imagine, not inexpensive to do," I said, remembering what I paid for a mature crape myrtle tree, one with gorgeous deep pink blooms and three sinuous trunks.

"Michel thinks this is his best garden," Louisa said of the garden that, per Berge's demand, was finished in time for the summer season. "But I think it's Berge and Michel together who made it so good."

About a minute after turning onto a narrow, drab street, Louisa pulled the car into a small parking area. From there we walked along a little path flanked by a strip of green shrubbery, then past the kitchen door and up a few steps. Just as I began to feel disappointed by this unremarkable entry into what was touted as one of the most remarkable gardens in Provence, we passed through a small arch in the garden wall.

If I was surprised when I first saw the spectacular gardens inside Dominique Lafourcade's property, I was astonished by the lush exotic courtyard gardens assembled by Pierre Berge on this ordinary street of modest houses. It was as though a brilliant exotic parrot had set up shop among a colony of plain brown wrens. "When Michel first saw the property, he was horrified at the number of ugly things he saw here," Louisa said. "So a lot of his planting was designed to hide them. But Berge was said to have wanted a house situated so that he could walk to Saint-Rémy to market every day."

The mood of the Theo garden was unlike any of the gardens I'd visited. Yes, the long, pale pink farmhouse with its pearly gray limestone terrace and wisteria-covered trellis was the epitome of traditional Provençal style. And, yes, the garden courtyards planted with evergreen shrubs, olive trees, and deciduous shade trees were essentially based on the Provence model. But this was Provence with a twist, an exotic twist that conjured up a Moorish paradise. With its overlay of perfectly placed dwarf fan palms, swordlike yuccas, bamboo trees, oleander, tall droopy palms, golden cypress, and a rare chinaberry tree—not to mention the splashing sound of water from fountains—the Theo garden offered tantalizing hints of Morocco, of Granada, of North Africa. It was hard to believe that Michel Semini had taken a property that was not much more than an open field behind an old farmhouse and turned it into this garden of earthy delights.

As we walked from garden to garden, along pathways bordered by flowers planted under a canopy of trees, Louisa added her insights into the fine detailing it took to create such a horticultural masterpiece. "There is no lawn anywhere in this garden," she said. "That's a highly unusual feature even in Provence. Many Parisians want lush areas of green turf mixed in with their lavender and old olive trees. Not a good combination, since grass and ancient olive trees need contradictory growing conditions."

Near a fountain flanked by four golden cypress trees, Louisa stopped to listen to the sound of the trickling water as it overflowed onto the pebble paving around it. "The octagonal basin of this fountain was measured by laser beams so that its water spills over equally on all sides." She also pointed out one of many playful touches in the garden: the door-sized mirrors that seemed to lead into another part of the garden. But when I approached the seemingly open space, my own reflection stopped me from entering it.

Each part of the garden had its own original charm. A path lined with white Iceberg roses stopped at a colonnaded, ten-sided pool pavilion. At the pool's far end, before an entire field of lavender, was a conservatory that echoed the shape of the pavilion. From there, several paths branched out, inviting the visitor to choose.

Since Louisa always gave me time to experience each garden on my own—a thoughtful gesture I appreciated—I chose a long narrow pathway through rows of olive trees. Stretched out ahead of me on either side I saw masses of blue irises, so many that their dense foliage and blooms almost obliterated the path. Then, without knowing what lay at the end, I stepped into another world, one that Van Gogh—who loved to paint the irises of Provence—might have created. As I walked, gravity fell away; for several minutes I floated in a river of flowers the color of the sky.

I drifted in this manner until I came to an unusual house, one that appeared to have no doors. Surrounded by an olive meadow, the tiny pink house with a tiled Mediterranean-style roof had only an open arch that led through the front wall. I took this no-door policy as an invitation and stepped into a small covered area that had rooms—with doors—on either side. Beyond the covered area was another open arch, one that led to a sumptuous, oasis-like veranda with a splashing blue marble fountain set into a floor of blue and orange tiles. *Of course,* I thought, *it's the Moroccan guesthouse Louisa told me about.*

I proceeded to examine the two guest rooms that opened from either side of the covered breezeway. With their cool tiled floors, warm ocher walls, terra-cotta bathrooms, and wooden latticework designed to allow entry to passing breezes, the rooms had everything a guest could desire—including bookshelves offering a choice of writers from Balzac to Welty. With considerable effort, I restrained myself from having a quick lie-down with the divine Eudora.

Instead I settled myself on the veranda, among a masterly blending of Provençal greenery and exotic Moorish-inspired planting. As I listened to the tranquil sounds of trickling water and daydreamed of caravans in the Atlas Mountains, I allowed myself a moment of discreet self-pity, knowing full well that I'd never be a guest here. Still, it pleased me to be one of the select few who know that there's some corner of a Provençal garden that is forever Morocco.

Dearest N,

It is just before midnight and I sit writing this in my perfect room at La Mirande. The lamps are lit low, the linens on my bed are turned down, and in a minute the bells of the pope's cathedral, Notre-Dame-des-Domes, will toll, ushering in a new day. How I wish they would usher you in as well! Still, your presence travels along with me through each garden I visit.

That was particularly true yesterday when Louisa and I had lunch with Joseph Bayol and his wife, Doudou (I love that name, don't you?), at their charming cottage near Saint-Rémy. He is a painter; she is a gardener. It is a particularly symbiotic relationship since many of his paintings are inspired by his wife's very personal garden. Next door to the house is a small gallery where he exhibits his work, along with that of artist friends. Joseph, a small but strong-looking man with expressive eyes, took me upstairs to the studio to see his work in progress. It reminded me of all the things I enjoy about the artist's world: the sight of his paintbrushes lined up, his easel with its pastiche of colors, the smell of the paint, the thrill of seeing again the way artists turn clutter into beauty.

Doudou, a hardy woman with dark hair and olive-colored eyes, not only helps look after her six grandchildren but also does all the work on her garden. She even dug the pond herself. And unlike some who garden in Provence, Doudou's taste does not run to carefully planned, expensive simplicity. No, her garden is colorful, crowded, exuberant, even a bit wild at the edges. When Doudou began the garden, she simply scattered a packet of mixed flowers, known in France as *gazon japonais*. Since then the garden has grown, but it still remains a storybook fantasy of trailing vines and flower meadows where colors and shapes blur together, the way they do in an Impressionist painting.

Because there was a chill in the air, we ate inside, rather than beneath a grape arbor in the garden. For lunch Doudou had cooked a special rabbit dish, and we sat eating and talking for a long time. You would love the Bayols. They are so warm and friendly and each has the spirit of a true artist. The only thing missing from this enchanting afternoon was you.

Once, during lunch, I caught a glimpse of the whole garden swaying in the breeze as though it were a single flower. Immediately I thought of Monet's garden at Giverny where we first met. I could picture us there: you standing behind me, pointing to a crowd of red poppies, accidentally brushing my hair with your hand. Even now, as I write this, I feel the blood rush to my face, as it did when you made that small accidental gesture in the garden.

I must go now and try to sleep. Tomorrow I meet Michel Semini, a much sought-after landscape designer, and drive with him and Louisa into the Luberon, about an hour's trip by car from Avignon, to see several of his gardens. Then it's off to the hill town of Bonnieux to visit the legendary garden of the late Nicole de Vesian. Louisa says it's the most inspirational garden in the region, and the chance to visit it is exciting. I am happy to hear you dream about "our garden" in Paris. Perhaps we will meet there, as you would say, "in the time of the lily of the valley."

Love, Me

• • •

After lunch at a café in Lourmarin, a fashionable village in the Luberon region with many cafés and boutiques, Louisa and I set out for the garden I most wanted to see: Nicole de Vesian's legendary hillside garden in Bonnieux. For some reason neither of us talked much during the trip to this historic, picturesque "perched village." I didn't mind; it gave me time to make some notes about our garden tour earlier that morning with Michel Semini.

We had arranged to meet Michel at the local *tabac* in the village of Goult and go on from there. As Louisa and I drove southeast from Avignon to Goult, I kept an eye out for a run-down farmhouse that could be bought for next to nothing and restored to its former beauty. With the help of an architectural plastic surgeon I planned to raise a beam here, sandblast a façade there, tighten up the pitch of a roof, and then write a book about it.

Louisa's voice interrupted my thoughts. "The olive trees in that field are three hundred years old and are there just to be sold," she said, pointing to an orchard of trees. "They will cost anywhere from ten to twenty thousand dollars. Plus the added cost of transplanting and pruning and taking care of them. But many garden clients, mostly Parisian and English clients, want these old olive trees with their lawns. For people who grow up here, it hurts to look at olive trees planted in lawns. It's not the character of the place. And lawns will kill olive trees. But Michel Semini developed a system to prevent this."

The system Michel perfected for planting such old, large olive trees, Louisa explained, was based on digging a complex planting hole, then using layers of pebbles and other absorbent material to allow good drainage. This enabled the lawn to be watered as often as necessary without harming the trees. It was not an inexpensive system, she said. "These special planting holes can sometimes cost as much as the trees."

As I tried to calculate the cost of a driveway lined with, say, a dozen old olive trees—$120,000? $150,000?—we arrived at Goult for our meeting with Michel Semini. Although I had no clue as to what the landscape architect looked like, I recognized him immediately upon entering the *tabac*. Who else in this local shop could be the famous Michel Semini but the man who stood at the bar wearing a stylish leather jacket and radiating confidence. With his strong interesting face and dark curly hair cut in the latest fashion, he had the look of a French movie star. After introductions were made and espressos ordered, Louisa and Michel chatted for several moments about the local gardening scene, a sort of update on who was doing what to whose garden. Then it was off in separate cars to see four gardens designed by Michel, all located in the Luberon, an area described by Louisa as having some of the most expensive property in Europe.

"Michel is working on twenty gardens right now," Louisa told me as we drove to the first garden. "He always thinks the old ones are finished, but the owners have a lot of money and start all over again."

Actually, although I didn't say it out loud, the chance to start all over again with your garden is one of the things I like best about gardening. Unlike one's life, a garden can never be botched up past the point of return. At least it is pretty to think so.

The four properties we visited were quite different. First there was the large estate of a widower from Paris. The property had on it an old house, a new house, and houses for each of the owner's three daughters, who usually visited only on holidays. It also had a number of those ancient olive trees that Semini is famous for transplanting.

Then there was the house owned by a French physician, one that had an indoor movie theater. "The garden is small but it was a big project," Semini told us. "We had to bring in so many walls and a lot of earth. We set the stone walls in a pattern that is local to Luberon. With stones set vertically on the top, like a row of teeth. Although it's only two years old it looks like it's always been here." There were white roses and oleander and a lawn in the garden, along with an automatic watering system to keep alive lawns and flowers not meant to exist in such a climate.

The third garden Michel showed us was my favorite. It was a sizable property owned by Parisians who used it as a vacation house. Behind the spacious beautiful house set at the end of a long, long road was the large sloping garden. "Here was a forest," Michel said, standing at the top edge of the spectacular garden. "So we cut everything and built a variety of terraced walls that run like steps. Each layer is planted in a different color. The first is blue, the second, red, the third, yellow, and the fourth, pink and white." I made a note to myself: *Think about turning the backyard into a terraced garden incorporating wherever possible the color theme of navy blue and green.*

The last stop on our tour was a three-hundred-year-old house owned by a French couple who divided their time between Hong Kong and

France. The house had been updated in a very subtle way; the added modern touches turned the old structure into a unique blending of past and present. "The garden is only one year old," Michel said as we walked beneath cherry trees in blossom, walnut trees, and two-hundred-year-old plane trees that had been transplanted to the property. Since this was our last stop with Michel, I decided to ask the question I'd been dying to ask ever since seeing Pierre Berge's "near-instant" garden: "What's the secret to planting a garden that instantly looks as though it's been around forever?" I asked him as we walked to our cars.

His near-instant answer was: "First you must plant dense and very close. Then prune, prune, prune." I wrote it down in my notebook.

"There's Bonnieux," Louisa said as we drove along the spectacular narrow road that winds its way from Lourmarin to this medieval village. I looked up from my notes and saw we had entered a lush valley. Above it, a village tumbled down a steep hillside, its slide stopped only by the huge bedrock formations from which the honey-gold stone houses seemed to grow. Seen from a distance, Bonnieux looked like a Cubist puzzle, with its terra-cotta tiled roofs interlocked into sharply angled geometric patterns. I thought of something Madame Dupré had told me about these *villages perchés*: that they were built a thousand years ago by villagers trying to protect themselves from Barbary Coast pirates.

As usual Louisa began prepping me for our visit. "The garden we are going to see is considered the most inspirational garden and one of the most photographed in this region," she said. "Some people consider it Japanese, others Parisian, others quintessentially Provençal; some think it wild, others formal. There's something for everyone here."

I knew that Louisa admired the late Nicole de Vesian and the garden she created. She had known Nicole and written many fine pieces about this fascinating woman who named her old house "La Louve," after the she-wolf who fed the founders of Rome. The much-photographed garden at La Louve—described by Louisa as "both very simple and very sophisticated"—was admired by gardeners all over the world from Japan to England.

But what interested me most was Nicole's history, the long hard road she traveled to arrive finally at her beloved La Louve. It was a history that included difficult years of making a life for herself and her two young children during World War II, when her husband was a prisoner in Germany. But her story also included a distinguished career in fashion as an innovative stylist who designed everything from the interiors of custom-made cars to the famous Hermès pleated scarves. After her retirement from the fashion world, she moved to Bonnieux and La Louve.

A week before her death in 1996, Nicole—then in her early eighties and hobbled by arthritis and the lingering effects of several automobile accidents—sold the property to an American woman, one who has taken loving care of La Louve.

"When Nicole met the buyer during the negotiations for the sale, she was relieved the garden would be going into good hands," Louisa said as we entered the narrow streets of Bonnieux. Almost immediately she parked the car. "Nicole's garden is on the lower end of the village and this is probably as close as we'll get." We walked down a steep narrow lane and stopped in front of a door that opened directly onto the cobbled alley. Before we could knock, the door opened and La Louve's current owner, a casually dressed, relaxed-looking woman, greeted us warmly. We could see that she had company in the house, so Louisa and I went straight to the gardens that were terraced into the hillside overlooking the valley.

I wanted to write down in my notebook a description of what I saw around me but found I couldn't. As I stood there in Nicole de Vesian's garden, my observing self gave way to my experiencing self. All thoughts of writing or even thinking vanished. All I wanted was to be there, in the moment, walking down the steep steps from one intimate terrace to another, past aromatic domes of greenery and stone walls covered with white lavender, past a river of lavender running through dark green cypress trees. A breeze stirred the evergreens; they responded by releasing their crisp aroma into the air.

I imagined Nicole in this garden; saw her walking, at age eighty, down the steep steps that had no railings, from one terrace to another, stopping now and then to clip a stray bit of greenery. I saw her pausing, just as I did, between cypress columns to stand taking in the view at the edge of a terrace supported by the natural stony hillside beneath it. From the forested hillside across the valley I heard birdsong. The view of the rolling hills covered with trees, rocks, and wild green undergrowth was like a mirror image of a natural, less manicured La Louve.

I was leaving Provence in a few days, and there were more gardens to be visited. But as I stood surrounded by the beauty and originality of this hillside world created by Nicole de Vesian, I knew that La Louve would be the garden I would think of whenever I smelled the lavender in my garden or brushed against the cypress near my front door or saw a stone bench as beautiful as sculpture.

Still, as breathtaking as it was, La Louve would not be my choice if someone offered to transplant to my home in Baltimore any one of the gardens I'd visited. No, the one I'd pick to live with was Doudou Bayol's exuberant, life-affirming garden with its trailing vines and colorful mixed flowers scattered from a packet of *gazon japonais*. Why? Perhaps because it reminded me of Grandmother's garden, of the way she would spill seeds into the wind, letting them root and bloom at random.

Or perhaps it simply comes down to this: if I had Doudou's garden, it would be like having Grandmother back. And of course along with Grandmother would come that little girl who long ago knelt beside her, pushing red and pink petunias into the dark loamy earth, learning with each spade of dirt and transitory flower more than words could tell about the nature of life and death, of loss and renewal.

The Unreliable
Narrator

W HEN THE CHURCH BELL outside my hotel window tolled six times and the morning light pushed its way through the half-open curtains, I decided to get up and hit the streets of Prague. I had learned long ago that the only cure for jet-lag-induced insomnia was to ignore it. Besides, I'd found out that the best time for a traveler to see the "real" city, the one hidden behind its tourist-attraction façade, was between dawn and the first sound of a visitor's foot hitting the street.

I dressed quickly, stopped in the hotel café for an espresso, and then headed for the famous Charles Bridge that spans the Vltava River. From my hotel the route to the bridge led me through historic Old Town Square and along fashionable Parizska Street. At a little before seven, however, the city was almost deserted except for a few pigeons trolling for breakfast along the cobblestone streets. Although tempted to investigate several appealingly mysterious alleys, I didn't stop. My plan was to reconnoiter the area west of the bridge known as Mala Strana, the Little Quarter, a picturesque warren of steep cobblestone lanes located on the slopes below Prague Castle. After nine in the morning, a friend had told me, the climb up to the castle became an obstacle course of wall-to-wall tourists.

As I began my ascent up Castle Hill, however, I realized that crowds were not going to be my problem. No, my problem lay in the streets below me, not the ones above. After an hour of walking on bumpy

cobblestone streets and pavements decorated with mosaics of colored knife like marble, my feet were sending desperate SOS signals to my brain from inside their prisons of so-called walking shoes. I had to sit down. But where? Not much was open yet along this charming, if bumpy, street lined with quaint old buildings right out of Grimm's fairy tales.

I hobbled along for another block or so before spotting an open door; the sign outside read ANTIKVARIAT. Peeking in, I saw a long narrow room lined on each side with bookshelves and displays of lithographs, old postcards, vintage prints. Near the entrance a handsome older man dressed in a tweed jacket, shirt, and tie stood at a desk, making notes on a pad. When he spotted me, he removed his eyeglasses and with a courtly gesture, motioned me in.

"Please," he said, in English. "Come in and look around if you wish." I thanked him and asked where I might find books in English by Czech writers.

"Are you interested in contemporary Czech writers or works by writers like Karel Capek or Jan Neruda? You are standing, by the way, not far from where Neruda was born, on the street now named after him, Nerudova. His father was a grocer nearby."

"To be honest, I don't know what I'm interested in. Besides Kafka, the only Czech writers I'm familiar with are Milan Kundera and Ivan Klima. In fact, I've come to Prague to attend a summer seminar at Charles University that includes a lecture series on Czech literature and culture. So I'm hoping to be educated. But I would really appreciate any suggestions you might have about books that would be helpful to me."

He listened attentively, then nodded and said: "Wait here. I will find something for you." He disappeared into the book stacks.

While he was gone I looked through a number of cardboard boxes set out on a table. They contained stacks of old black-and-white photographs, snapshots of everyday scenes that must have come from various family albums. Children playing in the snow. A smiling young man arm in arm with a woman wearing a dark suit, its lapel pinned with a corsage. Two old women wearing babushkas displaying for the camera what looked like a handmade quilt. Some men in athletic shorts playing a game that resembled soccer. I love old photographs—or snapshots, as I prefer to think of such spontaneous images of a fleeting moment in someone's life.

For some reason, I particularly like snapshots of people I never knew.

The idea of having access to such ordinary yet intimate moments in the lives of strangers appeals to the child in me. She was the person who tirelessly observed through countless streetcar windows such simple things as a family sitting on their front steps or a boy playing with his dog or a woman hanging out the laundry to dry. So when I came across a perfectly preserved black-and-white snapshot of two dark-haired girls dressed in fitted coats with fur collars, dark berets, and gloves—the way girls in their early teens used to dress circa 1940—it was as though I knew them. I thought: *They're sisters on their way to some special event, a birthday party, perhaps, or a holiday dinner with their family.* It was a strong feeling, this sense of connection with the two young Czech girls, but my thoughts were interrupted by the return of the shopkeeper with a book.

"Here is an author you must read," he said, handing me a pristine copy of a book called *Dancing Lessons for the Advanced in Age,* written by someone named Bohumil Hrabal. Although I knew nothing of the author, the title captivated me. "It is all one sentence," the bookshop owner continued.

"*What* is all one sentence?" I asked, confused.

"The *book,*" he said. "The book is all one sentence. Have a look."

On the cover was a quote from Milan Kundera about the author: "What is unique about Hrabal is his capacity for joy. . . . He is our very best writer today." I opened to the first page and began to read. By the end of the second page, I was totally hooked by this one-sentence book where periods had no dominion. *Dancing Lessons for the Advanced in Age,* I thought, would fit right in on one of my bookshelves at home, between *The Aesthetics of the Japanese Lunchbox* by Kenji Ekuan and a collection of essays titled *A Stress Analysis of a Strapless Evening Gown.*

"I would like to take this," I told the shopkeeper, handing him my credit card. "And thank you so much for your help. You've been very kind." Then I remembered the snapshot of the two girls and impulsively pulled it from its cardboard box on the table. "I would also like to have this," I said, getting out my credit card again.

"Please, you may have that," he said. I expressed my gratitude again and hurried out onto the street, eager to find a café where I could begin reading a book by an author whose name included consonants and vowels arranged in a way I suspected I would never be able to pronounce correctly.

· · ·

I finished *Dancing Lessons for the Advanced in Age* just before I went to bed that night. The author's insight and originality amazed me. It also left me feeling, as I often did after reading a particularly brilliant book, that I had no business trying to be a writer and needed to do a reality check on my choice of profession. This time, however, I felt even more vulnerable than usual since my Creative Writing Seminar—a writing workshop that focused on fiction and nonfiction—began the next morning. I'd signed up for the class because I admired the novels and nonfiction travel writing of Mary Morris, the workshop leader, and also because I thought the use of fiction techniques might improve my work as a nonfiction writer. Still, I had misgivings about the "workshop" model, a format described in the brochure as one "wherein individuals present original work which is closely scrutinized and critiqued by the group, led by the workshop leader."

To be honest, the idea of handing over my work to a group of fellow writers for their analysis and criticism intimidated me. On the other hand, such an attitude seemed silly since I'd been doing exactly that for more than twenty years: handing over my work for suggestions and corrections to a group of people known as "editors." Still, the workshop setting struck me as different, a more personal and less professional exchange. In the end, however, my curiosity trumped my fear (one of the sneaky, hidden agendas of curiosity, I believe, is to make you go forward in the face of fear) and I enrolled in the course.

To distract myself from such negative thoughts I began to read a short biography of Bohumil Hrabal, my new favorite Czech writer. I stopped reading when I came to this provocative paragraph: "Though he spoke little English, his favourite poet was Eliot and his favourite prose-writer Joyce. He lived in Prague until 1997, when he died after falling from the fourth floor window of his retirement home while trying to feed pigeons."

Quickly, I did the math. Hrabal died feeding those pigeons—or trying to, anyway—when he was eighty-three. Not a bad way to be remembered, I thought: as a kindly person feeding the birds, rather like Saint Francis of Assisi although, as I recalled it, there was no fourth-floor retirement apartment involved in the Assisi incident. This last long run-on thought made me wonder: Was I starting to think like Hrabal wrote? In any case, falling from a window while trying to feed pigeons struck me as a whole lot better than dying while being pecked to death in a writing workshop.

• • •

It's funny how your mind can go blank when someone asks you to name your favorite book. That's what happened to me the next morning when Mary Morris, our workshop leader, went around the classroom asking each of her eleven students to name a few books and writers they admired. Since I was in the middle of the semicircle of chairs facing Mary, I figured I had a few minutes to think about my answer.

But once again, curiosity won the day. So instead of thinking about my choices, I listened to the fascinating array of names being released like doves into the air, four or five at a time, by my classmates: Michael Chabon, Harper Lee, Dave Eggers, Flannery O'Connor, Michael Cunningham, Margaret Atwood, E. L. Doctorow, Willa Cather, Richard Ford, Alice Munro, Tobias Wolff, Edith Wharton. Suddenly the names stopped and the room grew quiet. Then I realized it was my turn.

"*Victory Over Japan* by Ellen Gilchrist," I blurted out, as though someone had just stabbed me in the back. "And, um, *Because It Is Bitter, and Because It Is My Heart* by Joyce Carol Oates. And anything Mavis Gallant writes." I paused, wondering whether to add Roz Chast and Lynda Barry, two of my favorite narrative writers, who give form to their writing through the use of cartoons. I decided not to. Of course, later when I thought of all the writers I forgot to mention, including heavyweights like Proust and Tolstoy and my beloved E. B. White, I wanted to kick myself or, at the very least, remember to somehow bring up their names in future conversations.

Earlier, Mary had asked the students to talk a bit about themselves and to explain what they hoped to get from the workshop and what they currently were working on. It proved to be a very diverse group in every way, including age, writing goals, and publication status.

There was, for instance, a young Southern woman who was writing a novel that followed the lives of a boy and girl—fourth cousins— from their meeting on a Southern farm to their adult relationship. And at work on his second novel—the first was about to be published— was a young man writing a sophisticated, fast-paced story about the intertwined lives of a group of people, mostly young gay men. Another woman had brought with her a piece she'd been working on for a long time, a true story about her sister who had married a Negro—her word—in the 1950s. As I listened to my classmates talk, it dawned on me that I was not the only one feeling vulnerable and anxious about being on the receiving end of criticism, no matter how constructive.

But that wouldn't happen in this session. No, in this session Mary Morris, an experienced teacher as well as a fabulous writer, eased us into the workshop process by talking first about the writing process.

In a discussion of what goes into writing memoirs and journals, she told us, "There's truth and there's facts and there's authenticity." And on the actual chronology of writing, she said, quoting Rilke: "First of all, you have to experience something. Then grieve its loss. Then you have to forget it. Then you remember it. Then you write." After writing, of course, comes revision. "Revision is one of the most personal parts of writing," Mary told us. "What I do is read my work as though somebody else wrote it. You must read it as though it's not yours. And you must tell a story. Keep asking yourself, 'Am I telling a story people are going to be interested in?'"

Mary told us we should keep a journal while in Prague, a private journal that we would not be asked to read aloud in class. "Keeping this kind of journal is important," she said. I wrote down her advice in a journal I'd already started, one named "Prague Notes," which I now renamed "Not to Be Read Aloud." With its new name, the notebook instantly offered an exhilarating sense of freedom, one that invited me to write down anything inside its covers, no matter how personal or strange.

Then Mary got around to explaining the workshop process to us. Each of us would pass out copies of the work in progress we wanted the class to read and critique. Then on an assigned day, three students would have their work analyzed and discussed. My piece, as it turned out, would be in the last group of submissions, near the end of the workshop. I saw this placement in the last group as having an upside—a postponement of the verdict—and a downside—a postponement of the verdict.

I wrote all this down in a second notebook labeled "Workshop," followed by Mary's instructions on how we should approach the critiquing of another person's work:

1. Think about what a writer is doing well.
2. Think about what's working in the piece and what might be getting in the way.
3. Write down your comments on paper.
4. Listen while your own work is being critiqued.

The first two suggestions struck me as useful insights for an inexperienced critic like me. But the last suggestion seemed redundant. Of course, I'll listen, I thought. That's what "workshopping" (I quickly learned it was okay to use the word *workshop* as a transitive verb) was all about, wasn't it? Still, for some reason, I underlined the part about listening as your own work was discussed, then put a star next to it.

Near the end of the class we were given our writing assignments, to be turned in two days later, at our next session. I wrote it down: "Mary wants a short memory piece. 'I'm looking for a true story,' she said. She also wants a piece that has to do with Prague. She suggests we use various writing styles from straight description to narrative to state of mind at a given moment and that we write two paragraphs for each scene. Then just before she released us, she reminded us that writing is all about advancing the story. 'Remember,' she said, 'the only thing the reader wants to know is: What happened?' "

It was one thing to tell a story so that it left readers furiously turning pages to find out what happened, but first the writer had to *find* a story to tell. And the stories I liked best usually were not just sitting there out in the open, waiting to be picked up like a stone. The stories I liked best were hidden behind things or under things. To find such a story I had learned to look at things from an odd angle or to respond to an involuntary feeling that, despite its random appearance, pointed me in the right direction.

I thought about all this as I left the classroom at Jana Palacha, a massive stone building that was part of Charles University. Near Old Town, the building looked out across the Vltava River to the Cathedral of Saint Vitus with its spiky domes. Each morning I walked from my hotel to Jana Palacha, a fifteen-minute stroll through some of Prague's most historic and picturesque neighborhoods. It was during my first walk to class that I discovered the difficulty of trying to cross the street at any of the major intersections. Instead of a red light–green light system, the Czechs rely on sound to inform the pedestrian when it might be a good time to venture across the street. Or as my guidebook described the process, "When you hear a slow clicking, cars have the right of way. When you hear a fast clicking, you may cross the street somewhat safely." Two things bothered me about this explanation. One, fast and slow are relative terms. And, two, the ominous inclusion of the word *somewhat* before the word *safely*.

It was one o'clock, and if I managed to make it across the street alive, I planned to have lunch at the Kavarna Slavia, a café Mary Morris had recommended we try to visit. She was not the first person to mention it; friends at home and even other visitors at the hotel had raved about the Slavia, a legendary hangout where artists, musicians, and writers have met for more than one hundred years. With its huge picture windows looking out on Prague Castle across the river, the Slavia at first glance seemed to live up to its reputation. Its large airy rooms with a view seemed the perfect setting for a poet to write, as Rainer Maria Rilke once did, or a musician to compose, as Bedrich Smetana had. And it wasn't difficult to imagine the Slavia as a meeting point for Vaclav Havel and other members of the political opposition during the Communist era. But even the most favorable first impressions can give way to disappointment, as mine did of the Slavia.

Still, something positive resulted from my visit: my experience there seemed to fill all the requirements for my first writing assignment. So that night I sat at the desk in my hotel room and began to write:

Why I Love the Slavia

I liked the looks of the Slavia from the moment I walked through the door. If the Slavia were a movie star instead of a café, he'd be Joseph Cotten, or at least the character Joseph Cotten played in *The Third Man*, which, I know, was set not in Prague but Vienna. And while the food at the Slavia was not up to the standards of a man like Joseph Cotten, it was decent enough, except for the salad, unless you like onions and lettuce with a dab of mayonnaise on the side. Prague, let's face it, is not a salad town. But the coffee was not bad and neither was the bread, and the river view was definitely up to Joseph Cotten's sophisticated standards.

Things started to go downhill, however, when I began to choke on a piece of not-so-bad bread. Desperate, I tried to stop the choking by swilling down what was left of my pretty good Joseph Cotten coffee. Still choking, I summoned the waiter—a courtly man of great politeness—to the table.

"Water," I gasped, choking out the word. "I need water."

"Certainly, madam," he said. "Gas or no gas?"

I couldn't speak.

"Sparkling or flat, madam?" he persisted.

I pushed the answer out through a staccato of coughs. "I"—cough—"need"—cough—"water!"

"Vittel or Perrier?" he inquired.

"I need water! And I need it NOW," I shouted, clutching my neck, just as I imagined Liz Taylor must have done during her famous choking-on-a-piece-of-chicken incident.

For whatever reason, the waiter finally understood my dilemma. He turned and ran to the bar, calling out from halfway across the room for a bottle of water, one with "no gas." Within seconds he was back. "Madam," he said, with a slight bow. Then he placed the capped bottle on the marble-top table and waited. For what, I don't know.

All I knew was that whether I lived or died depended entirely on me. Quickly, I uncapped the bottle. I put it to my mouth. I tossed back my head. I drank the water. I lived.

And that is why I love the Slavia.

As I sat reading and revising what I now thought of as "my Slavia piece," I knew it met the criterion of being a "true story." But what of the three assigned writing techniques? Was it straight description? Narrative? And what about state of mind? Shouldn't I have decided on that before writing the story? No, I thought, the story decided on that while I was living, or in this case possibly dying, through it. Fear of choking to death, that's what my state of mind came down to.

One other thing about the style of my Slavia piece. Did I detect a whiff of Hrabal's one-sentence approach hovering around the edges of my prose? Or was I just imagining it? Oh well, time and a few more assignments would tell. And if time didn't spot the Hrabal influence I had no doubt the diligent eyes of my classmates would.

Many of my friends who know both cities well are fond of comparing Prague to Paris—except for the food, of course. Both cities, they liked to point out, have breathtaking architecture, neighborhoods of great character and charm, many undisturbed layers of history, and a river that divides the city and is as much a part of everyday life as the neighborhood café. At first I found the comparison an apt one. But after my fourth day of intense walking through the city, gaping at wall-to-wall art nouveau buildings now restored to their original wedding-cake splendor, and visiting the famous fifteenth-century Astronomical Clock with its Death, Greed, and Vanity sideshow, the comparison grew weaker. With its baroque façades painted in bright blues, yellows, and greens and its splendid art nouveau gems weighed down by perhaps too much decorative icing, Prague, unlike Paris, sometimes made me feel as though I were walking through a giant stage set.

On one such walk I found myself thinking, *If Paris is an opera, then Prague is an operetta.* The analogy didn't quite make sense since Prague is famous for its classical music, particularly its chamber music. There was scarcely a street or alley where classical music didn't spill out from an open window onto the street, meeting and mingling with the sound of a student practicing piano scales or trilling on a flute. It was one of the few cities I'd visited where tourists are besieged not by young men selling knockoffs of Vuitton and Gucci handbags but by university students aggressively handing out programs pushing Mozart and Vivaldi concerts in the city's churches and synagogues. Usually by the time I had walked from my hotel to the Museum of Medieval Torture Instruments in Old Town Square—a stroll of less than ten minutes—my collection of programs hovered at the two dozen mark. Music was the ether of Prague, to be inhaled along with the air.

I breathed particularly deeply when I turned the corner into a small alley and heard the music of a swing orchestra coming from somewhere above. I stopped and listened to the scratchy sounds of one of my favorite pieces of music: an old Duke Ellington recording of "Take the A Train." So many tangled emotions flowed through me as I stood in this unlikely place listening to this unlikely music; too many memories to untangle before the imminent start of the concert I was planning to attend.

A few minutes later, all thoughts of Duke Ellington vanished as I sat in the elegant, unadorned cream-colored nave of Salvator Church listening to a chamber orchestra perform *The Four Seasons.* Although I was familiar enough with Vivaldi's piece to occasionally hum a season or two from memory while walking on my treadmill, it suddenly sounded completely new to me. In one section—"Autumn," I believe, though I wasn't keeping track—I was struck for the first time by its incredible rhythm. It made me want to choreograph a tap dance to it. So much so that I could feel my feet trying to do a miniature time step on the stone floor, an inappropriate response that I channeled into my "Not to be read aloud" journal in the form of choreographic notations. Next to the strange marks, all shaped like tiny feet, I wrote: "Hearing, seeing, feeling familiar things in a new way is part of the glorious alchemy of travel."

Later while reading in bed I wondered—since I was still two scenes short of my class assignment—whether there might be a straight description or a narrative scene in the Vivaldi experience in the church. Instantly I knew I had nothing. Not because nothing happened—a lot happened—but because I was too deeply engaged in the experience to observe it as a writer. It was the writer's classic dilemma, I thought, turning off the light. To let the observing self take charge, or to give the upper hand to the deeper experiencing self: that is the question.

It was Emily Dickinson, I believe, who wrote, "I like the look of agony because I know it's true." Although her observation had nothing to do with the perils of attending a writing workshop, I couldn't get it out of my head as I studied my classmates' faces. Things were just about to get down and dirty in the workshop process and the "look of agony" was starting to make little inroads around the eyes of the three writers waiting to have their works in progress critiqued.

By now, the group was well past its going-around-the-room phase where we read aloud our short, assigned scenes, most of which had been greeted with a positive comment or two, including my Slavia piece, which someone called "nice"—an adjective that, had I died while dining at the Slavia, would be completely inappropriate. During these readings everyone listened politely. But the group's energy, it seemed to me, was being reserved for the trio of writers whose work was on the agenda to be "workshopped," a word my unconscious consistently transposed into "horsewhipped."

What we were about to critique were not quick sketches or scenes but stories by writers who had invested a great deal of time and emotion in creating the private, some might say secret, worlds inside them. And anything said, even in the spirit of constructive criticism, had the power to kneecap an author, even if the story was set in a fictional world.

"Anyone want to volunteer to go first?" Mary asked the three writers scheduled to read their work.

"I'll go first," responded one of the writers without the slightest hesitation. The ice broken, we all settled back in our chairs as he began to read.

After he finished, Mary Morris reminded us of the basic critiquing "rules"—think about what's working in the piece and what's getting in the way—and then turned us loose. A loud silence filled the room. No one seemed to want to go first, or to go at all. My guess was the silence resulted from the combination of not wanting to hurt another writer's feelings and not wanting to set yourself up for retaliation when your turn came. Slowly, though, voices started chiming in with opinions:

"Beautiful writing but no narrative drive."

"The dialogue doesn't work for me. Sounds more like a TV sitcom than a novel."

"The descriptions are beautiful, but there are so many and they're so long that they get in the way of the story."

"Too many points of view. I can't tell who the narrator is."

Up to this point Mary had not added her comments, ostensibly waiting until she heard from the class. But when someone unfavorably compared one writer's style to that of another student, Mary quickly jumped in. "Don't compare stories or styles of one student to another," she said briskly. The minute she said it, I understood the importance of what she was telling us: that a successful workshop experience depended on keeping the critical process free from anything that might be construed as a personal attack.

Of course, it is a truth almost universally acknowledged that all writers are born with an extra gene, one capable of searching out a thorn in even the most flowery praise. As I watched my classmates listen to the group critique their writing, another truth rose to the surface, a "rule" I hadn't understood when Mary first outlined the workshop process. *Listen while your own work is being critiqued*, she had told us at our first meeting. Now, as I looked at the tense faces of the students whose work was being interpreted, or misinterpreted, I understood how hard it was to resist the urge to defend your story, to explain why you did something this way instead of that way.

Only after the group finished scrutinizing each of the pieces did Mary voice her suggestions to each writer:

We can't tell the characters apart physically. We need to know what people look like. . . .

What they look like should not be a police-blotter description. It should be integrated with how they're feeling, what they're doing. . . .

We should be experiencing what the character is experiencing, not what the author is speaking. . . .

Show. Don't tell. What you want to do in fiction or nonfiction is dramatize. Don't tell us a character is beautiful or lonely. You want the reader to see that she is beautiful or lonely. But you have to find the right moment to dramatize it. Give us a scene. Scenes are your story's connective tissue.

Then Mary posed a question to the class: "What is a scene?"

"It's when characters interact and something happens," said a young man whose short story had been critiqued earlier by the class.

"And what is the difference between a scene and an anecdote?"

Silence.

"A scene," Mary told us, "is a moment when there is some form of tension. A scene leads to the next scene. And a causal connection between scenes is what leads you to the story. A scene should be very clearly developed, and when the action is finished, the scene is over. An anecdote is, 'Oh, I missed the train. You'll never believe what happened. . . .' An anecdote leads to nothing."

Before dismissing the class, Mary gave us our next writing assignment, one to be read aloud when we met again. "Pick an emotion," she said, "and write a scene around it." She ticked off a few emotions for our consideration. Anger. Love. Curiosity. Anxiety. Jealousy. Nostalgia. Without thinking, I added one more to my list: Schadenfreude.

"And remember what makes a character," Mary called out as we left the room: "Showing, not telling. Dramatizing. And giving us the backstory on your character."

After class I walked along Siroka Street in the Old Town looking for a café where I might have lunch and write a bit in my journal. Siroka was an interesting street, one that ran across Josefov, the Jewish quarter and former ghetto, into the elegant bustling Parizska Street. It was one of the streets I usually took to get to and from class, and the swift transition from Parizska's shops displaying designs by Yves Saint Laurent and Hermès to the weathered reminders of Josefov's lost history never failed to startle me. I particularly liked walking through the Jewish quarter, a neighborhood redolent of the past. I had tried several times to visit the sixteenth-century Pinkas Synagogue, where the names of the many thousands of Bohemian and Moravian women and men killed in concentration camps are meticulously painted on the walls. But my timing was always off; either the lines of people waiting to get in were too long or my time too short.

But now as I walked along Siroka Street looking for a café, a sign caught my eye. It said: THE FRANZ KAFKA CAFÉ. Although the café didn't look open I peered through the door into a shadowy room that seemed deserted. But as my eyes grew accustomed to the dim light, I saw a few people scattered at tables, some playing chess. It could be interesting to have lunch there, I thought; it might even produce a scene for my workshop class, one using the emotion of angst. But before making up my mind, I decided to walk a few blocks more along Siroka.

Three blocks later I spotted La Dolce Vita, a bright, lively café, where people sat outside in the sun laughing and talking and eating bright-colored roasted vegetables with delicately herbed cheese and crusty bread. In other words, La Dolce Vita was the anti-Kafka café or, in this case, the antipasto-Kafka café. I took a table in the sun and sighed out as much angst as I could. Then I ordered a white-bean-and-tuna salad along with a glass of Orvieto.

It was while waiting for my espresso that I thought of hearing earlier, on the little street off Tyn Square, a recording of Duke Ellington's "Take the A Train." Actually, I didn't *think* of hearing it, I *heard* it again, that syncopated rhythm tapped out on piano keys by the great Duke. And suddenly I was somewhere else, back in the hospital parking lot sitting alone in my car on an icy night, the night before Mother died in the room whose light I could see through the windshield of my car. It was almost midnight, long after visiting hours were over, but I had left my newspaper job six weeks earlier to take care of her, was in fact practically living at the hospital, so much so that the nurses had stopped asking me to leave. Only Mother asked me to leave. Late at night, she would take off her oxygen mask just long enough to say, *You look tired, Alice. Go home and get some rest.* And I *had* left that icy night; left to run out to my car, left Mother's hospital room with its machine dripping toxic medicine into her arm and its Get Well Soon cards pinned to the bulletin board, left so she wouldn't see me weeping, stricken by the thought of what I was losing in that room. But everything changed when I started up the engine and the radio came on, filling the car with sounds of Duke Ellington telling me to take the A train. Suddenly a happy memory ran across the years to greet me. I was a little girl again, sitting outside on the lawn with Mother, listening to the radio, and when the A-train song came on, I tap-danced to it on the grass while Mother snapped her fingers to imitate the crisp *tap tap tap* sounds.

Now, as I thought of that little girl tap dancing on the grass to the sound of her mother's snapping fingers, I smiled. The happy memory had come just in time to rescue me from all the sad ones still crowded around Mother's deathbed. I wondered: Is it ever possible to isolate one emotion from all the others that are out there, just waiting to elbow their way in? And if I were writing this memory—instead of thinking it—what emotion would I be trying to retrieve? Sadness? Nostalgia? Anxiety? Love? Anger?

All of them, I decided. Plus happiness—the happiness of a little girl basking in the glow of her mother's undivided attention.

After lunch I decided to walk back to the school's computer room and type up some thoughts on a longer piece I might submit as my work in progress. The truth is, I had no work in progress to be "workshopped," a word that by now had elbowed its way into my temporary vocabulary. (I planned to hit the "permanently delete" key on it once the workshop was over.) Yes, I'd brought with me a travel piece, but it was an already published freelance piece intentionally written in a stylized manner as part of a newspaper series. The reason for this transgression, I told myself, was that I'd been working hard on another newspaper piece until two days before leaving for Prague. And at that point I had writer's burnout. At least that was my excuse. But I wanted to attend the seminars, so I brought along a piece that had been a work in progress several months earlier.

Now it didn't feel right to me, handing in only my travel piece. So I had decided to spend most of my time over the next week writing a new piece, a memoirlike story about the string of psychoanalysts who ran through my earlier life like a Freudian river. I planned to call it, "Dr. Schadenfreude, I Presume?"—a nod of the head to an emotion teased out by the psychological stress of my impending date with the "work-shopping" squad.

As I retraced my steps along Siroka Street and headed for the computer lab where I hoped to spin my story from straw into gold, I passed again the Pinkas Synagogue. I was surprised to see only a few people waiting in line. Instantly, I changed my plans—my psychoanalysts, I decided, could jolly well wait another fifty minutes or so for their turn with me— and instead bought a ticket to visit the synagogue and the Old Jewish Cemetery adjacent to it.

The Pinkas Synagogue was an airy, open space of natural stone and ash wood that reflected the light. On its pale walls the names of 77,297 Jewish victims from Bohemia and Moravia had been painted in clear unadorned black letters—except for the surnames, which were a deep ruby red. The simplicity of this remembrance of the dead was, like Maya Lin's memorial to Vietnam veterans, both powerful and heartbreaking. It was also intense, and the more names I read, the more intense it got. At some point I began hearing that passage in Samuel Barber's "Adagio for Strings," in which one crescendo follows another and another until, just at the breaking point, it stops and there is silence.

As I moved from wall to wall a sign caught my eye; it directed visitors upstairs to an exhibition of drawings made by children at Terezin, a transit camp for Jews built by the Nazis in an old fortress town north of Prague. It became infamous under its German name, Theresienstadt. I knew of these drawings from a book given me, one that told the story of how an art teacher at the camp, a Viennese artist named Friedl Dicker-Brandejs, managed to save the drawings made by doomed Terezin children.

When I followed the arrow upstairs to several long rooms of paintings and drawings, I found myself surrounded by the voices of lost children and, for the next hour, I listened to them. There was Ruth, who told me she witnessed four nude figures huddled under a shower, fear oozing from their bodies. And Helga, who whispered about having to watch as a woman's head was shaved by a stern man in a white coat. And Ella—oh, what did Ella see, I wondered, that made her draw such a cruel-looking young guard who blithely dangled a child from his right hand?

And then there was Lily. At the end of the room—or was it the beginning?—I saw it, a watercolor so pure in line and perfect in composition that it belonged in an art museum. Mystical and evocative, it was like a glowing illustration from one of the fairy-tale books I devoured as a child. An orange boat with blue sails was poised between a black sea and a night sky hung with a green sliver of a moon and green stars. The boat was sailing straight toward the paper's edge, into a wide band of blackness. When I leaned in to read the artist's signature—Lily Bobaschova—I could see the drawing's title: *Night*.

How to explain it, the impact that Lily's drawing had on me? The rush of excitement at her talent, the feeling of connection with her sensibility, and then the crushing sadness of knowing the reality that produced her art. Without knowing why, I wrote down Lily's name and a description of the drawing, even trying to sketch it in miniature in my notebook. And later, when I found myself in a nearby bookshop on Maiselova Street asking the owner to recommend books on Jewish life in Prague during the late 1930s and early 1940s, I still had no notion of what I was looking for.

It was only when I sat in a café on Tyn Square writing down a list of questions in my notebook—*Where would a twelve-year-old Jewish girl go to school? When were the Jewish children in Prague forbidden to go to school? Where would an educated middle-class Jewish family live in Prague?*—it was only then I realized what I was after: I wanted to imagine Lily's life. Not her life in Terezin; that life was unimaginable to those who had not experienced it. What I was searching for were clues to Lily's life before the deportations began in 1941, before the arrival of the dark night.

In my notebook I wrote: "After seeing Lily's painting today, I thought of something Mavis Gallant observed about the writing process: 'The first flash of fiction arrives without words. It consists of a fixed image, like a slide or a freeze frame. . . .' I think of that now, realizing what rushed through me at the sight of Lily's painting was the 'first flash of fiction.' Even as I write this, something is trying to take shape in my mind. Now I must try to find the words that go with that gathering image."

On the morning my Kyoto travel piece was to be critiqued, the class arrived to find the sign on our classroom, Room 111, had been vandalized. A large X had been drawn over the words FICTION AND CREATIVE NON-FICTION WRITING, THE PRAGUE SUMMER SEMINARS. Above the X, printed in large letters, were the words GO HOME! Of course, no one could say for certain who had posted this suggestion, but several ideas were floated.

"Perhaps it was an American student who wanted to get into this class and couldn't," suggested one classmate.

"I bet it's one of the Czech students here for summer study," said another.

"It could even have been a maintenance person, someone who's annoyed at having to clean up after us," said a third classmate.

Personally, I couldn't imagine who might have done such a thing. But I put the Czechs at the bottom of my list. All of the Czech students I'd met and talked to in the larger seminar on Czech literature and culture were friendly and smart and seemed unlikely suspects. And it didn't make sense to me that an American student would do such a thing. Either way, the incident introduced a minor key into our activities, and for a day or two a slight tension existed in the hallways.

Signs of tension had made their way into the classroom as well. One rumor had it that at an evening get-together, two male classmates, perhaps helped along by some very robust Czech beer, had unofficially critiqued each other's work as "garbage." Naturally, this minor skirmish between the two had attracted supporters on both sides, depending, I supposed, not so much on the personalities involved as on who liked what style of writing. Such a blunt exchange, however, would never happen in the classroom; by this time we understood the need to be cautious when offering up our criticism which, because it was intended to be constructive, would never include the word *garbage*. However, my own feeling was that while constructive criticism might work in theory, more often than not it was nullified by the writer's inability to *listen* to criticism constructively. Which may be why the poet Elizabeth Bishop steadfastly refused to write criticism, explaining, "It is better, given the choice, to have friends."

But then we were not in Prague to make friends. Still, we didn't want to make enemies either. By now we knew there were hidden minefields guarding the soft, sensitive spot inside each writer and so we stepped gingerly—most of the time.

The first work in progress on the day's agenda was a short story by a female graduate student who was about to have a book published on her solo trek into the heart of New Guinea. It was a very polished story about an adventurous woman who finds herself in a dangerous situation in a remote country. It was good enough to be published, I thought, although my short-story tastes run more to Alice Munro, where the danger lies not in foreign locales but in the familiar terrain of everyday relationships.

"Very gripping, although I'd like to see more descriptive passages," said one male writer who was very good at descriptive passages.

"I wasn't sure about the ending, about what was going to happen," said another writer who was fond of closure.

On the whole, the response was quite positive, one of the best receptions so far and a well-earned one, in my opinion.

Next came a memoirlike story from a young, lovely-looking woman who was still in college. It told the story of her mother's thirty-fifth birthday, using the writer's experience of how she, as a child, interpreted the events that led her father, a sailor away at sea, to find a way to celebrate his wife's birthday. Although the story was brief, its simple honesty and moving point of view won over most of the class.

Then it was my turn to be workshopped. After the usual minute of silence during which everyone waited for someone else to speak first, someone finally did.

"You used the word 'alas.' Ugh. You should never use that word," said a woman who, I had thought, liked me.

"Why should we care about this anonymous person who's traveling?" asked a man who, I suspected, didn't like me.

"You made some good observations about culture and food, but I think your piece would be better if you rewrote it in first person," said a woman that I wanted to like me.

Although I thought I was prepared for such an indifferent response to my piece—which to be fair was not really an appropriate candidate for a workshop format and got what it deserved—I wasn't. Criticism, whether of the constructive or deconstructive kind, hurts. Although I hadn't had a stake driven through my heart—criticism-wise—it was no fun being on the receiving end of any wound, however nonfatal, to my ego. Or as Gertrude Stein might have put it if she'd thought of it first: what a writer writes *is* the writer.

The rest of our session was devoted to a discussion of structure in writing a novel. Mary started by posing the question: "What are some of the decisions a novelist needs to make before sitting down to write?" Then she suggested a few questions that might help us in such decision making. "What is the shape of the story? Is it going to be a number of stories interwoven? Or just one? Who are my main characters? How did they get here? Is it going to be third person or first person? Or both? Where do I start? How will I tell the story? In what voice?"

Mary paused, then paraphrased for us what one famous writer had to say about telling a story: "Basically, you tell a story the same way a stripper strips. You don't walk out on the stage naked. You don't take off your clothes too fast. You don't take off your clothes too slowly. It's all in the rhythm."

I thought this metaphor brilliant and helpful and wrote it down in big block letters with a double underline. Perhaps I found it brilliant because it was something I thought I had finally learned to do in my writing.

I also thought of something helpful that I'd read about the Italian poet Umberto Saba. Apparently, after publishing a book of his poems, he wrote a book of criticism about them as though he were a separate writer. It too seemed a brilliant idea, one that given the right circumstances I might copy at some future time.

Later that day while searching through my notebook for the telephone number of the Fred and Ginger building in Prague—so-nicknamed because the modern Frank Gehry design was said to resemble the famous couple dancing—I came across the photograph of two girls in hats and dark, fur-trimmed coats, the snapshot given me by the bookstore owner on my first day in Prague. I'd forgotten all about the old black-and-white photo, but now as I studied it, my heart began to pound. To my surprise I recognized the girl on the right, the one whose face reflected intelligence and trust. It was Lily. The Lily who painted *Night*. The Lily whose life in Prague I was trying to imagine. Now at least I knew what she looked like.

Immediately I postponed my plan to visit Fred and Ginger that afternoon and instead walked over to Precious Legacy, a Jewish tourist center on Maiselova Street near the synagogue where I'd seen Lily's watercolor. A man who worked in the Pinkas Synagogue bookshop had suggested Precious Legacy as a place to go for information on the history of the Jewish community in Prague. By this time my reporter's instincts had kicked in and I carried with me a list of questions that, if answered, might help me in my effort to piece together parts of Lily's life before Terezin. I already had gone around the neighborhood talking to shopkeepers who spoke English and looked old enough to remember those years.

After an hour or so of talking to the staff, going over their printed material and buying a book or two, I left Precious Legacy and, at their suggestion, headed for a nearby shop that specialized in books dealing with Prague and Judaism. It was there, in the bookshop named V RAJI, that I met Hana, a customer who, while looking through the stacks, had heard me questioning the staff about Prague between 1939 and 1942.

"Excuse me for interrupting you," she said, "but I heard you asking about the day the German troops arrived to occupy our city. And if you are interested I can tell you some things. My name is Hana Weiserova and I was ten years old when my family and I watched the armored cars roll through the streets. I remember how the big metal helmets the soldiers wore frightened me."

To say this sudden encounter with Hana surprised me would be an understatement. It was as though Lily—the "fixed image" of the "first flash of fiction," as Mavis Gallant described it—had dissolved into the living, breathing woman standing next to me in a bookshop on Maiselova Street.

"Oh, no, I am thankful for your interruption," I told Hana after introducing myself. "It was very generous of you. And very helpful. You see, I am interested in learning about Jewish life in Prague during that time. Particularly what it might have been like for a young girl from an educated family." I told her of my visits to the synagogues and museums and of the books I was reading.

Hana listened, nodding her head, a gesture that shook loose a few strands of her fine, silvery hair. "May I suggest something?" she asked.

"Yes, of course. I will be grateful for any help you can give."

"If you like I can walk with you through the neighborhood and tell you certain things. And I will answer what questions I can."

And so Hana and I began to walk through the Jewish quarter, stopping frequently as a pleasant memory occurred to her about a kosher delicatessen, or a sad one about how Jewish children, after being barred from playgrounds, were allowed to play only in cemeteries. At one point I asked Hana where she learned to speak such fluent English.

"I learned English in the refugee camp," she said. She offered nothing more about this part of her life and I asked nothing more. When we passed by the Jewish Town Hall on a street lined with elegant houses from the early twentieth century, Hana stopped, pointed to one of the four-story stone buildings and said, "Once I lived there." Again, her spare observation hung in the air without embellishment.

However, when we turned at the Old-New Synagogue and started up beautiful leafy Parizska Street—only a block away from where she had lived—Hana recalled the life that was hers before 1939. "My older sister and I used to walk along this street almost every day, going in and out of the music stores and buying oranges from the fruit vendors or just looking in the shopwindows. But that was a long time past and now it's all so changed," she said, stopping in front of a shop devoted to expensive cosmetics by a Japanese firm named Shiseido. Hana, her face illuminated by the bright lights from the shopwindow, looked tired. I realized then how draining this "tour" of her life must have been and was ashamed that my self-interest had kept me from seeing it before this.

When we reached the edge of Old Town Square, Hana and I said good-bye. "You have been a good teacher," I said, "and I feel I've learned a lot. Thank you so much."

"I hope you have understood more now than before," she said, graciously taking my extended hand. And then without saying good-bye, Hana left, disappearing into the crowd of anonymous tourists waiting for the Astronomical Clock to sound out the hour.

That night I gathered together all my notes, along with my questions and answers, and sat at my desk. It was time to begin writing.

She stands on the curb along Parizska Street on a cold morning in March, the fur collar on her coat turned up to cover her ears. Her sister Ruth looks frightened as the German soldiers march by wearing heavy iron helmets that make them look like fierce pagan gladiators. Her mother weeps. Her father stands upright, his head high, but a tear is collecting in the corner of each eye. At a window across the street Lily sees the outline of faces peering through lace curtains. No one on the street speaks. Only the roar of motorized cars and the pounding of boots on the cobblestones shriek through the silence. The year is 1939. Later, as the family walks back to their apartment on Maiselova, something causes Lily to stop at the street crossing and take her sister's hand. With the other hand, she reaches up and touches first her mother's face, then her father's. Then it is time for the family to cross the street, from one life to another.

By this time, I was in a complete writer's trance. Everywhere I went I saw Lily. It was as though I'd stepped through the looking glass into Lily's Prague.

Six months later, on a golden October afternoon, Lily walks along Parizska Street on her way to an art supply store. Her birthday is only a few days away and she has been promised a new set of sable brushes as a gift. She will be twelve years old. Lily is hoping that the owner of the shop—a friend of her father's—has been able to find the brushes, which now are very scarce. Everything is changing so much. Now her sister Ruth, who is fifteen, has to be tutored by their father, since the Germans have closed Czech high schools. Because they are Jewish, Lily and her sister are forced to carry special identity cards and must observe a curfew of 8 P.M. Hardest of all for the younger girl is the ruling that forbids all Jews to own radios. Lily will miss the evenings she and her family spent together listening to the music of Mozart and Bach. Lately, she has been hoarding paper and charcoal pencils, fearing that those too might soon appear on the list of things forbidden to Jews.

One afternoon after attending a lecture by the great Czech writer Ivan Klima, I walked along the river thinking about this man who, as a Jewish child, had been sent with his parents to Terezin. Unlike Lily, he had survived the camp to become in his adult years a novelist, playwright, and critic of the first rank. But in 1970 a second wave of oppression rolled over Klima—and Czechoslovakia—when Communist authorities suppressed his books, along with those of other Czech writers.

"Our books were removed from shops and libraries, even small secondhand-book shops," Klima had told us. "After two years the cultural department decided it would be better not to mention us at all. We were nonexistent people." Klima, whose passport was confiscated, worked as a street cleaner.

But he and other banned writers continued to write, publishing their work in samizdat editions—books typed on onionskin paper and sold surreptitiously for the price of the copy. "Samizdat books were nonpolitical books," Klima told us, as if to raise the question of why they were banned. "Many of them were stories about relationships between men and women, about some of the 'surprises of marriage.'" Near the end of the talk, he passed around a worn, dog-eared copy of an original 210-page samizdat book. As I fingered the fragile sheets of paper, my thoughts drifted to the plight of the weary typists who may have produced several thousand samizdat books, pounding out each letter on round, old-fashioned typewriter keys.

As I walked toward the Jewish quarter—I was on my way to visit the Old Jewish Cemetery—I thought of something I'd read earlier about the origins of samizdat in Prague. It had developed after Klima began to hold monthly meetings at his home with other banned writers. The group met, read aloud their new work, and discussed it. It suddenly occurred to me that Klima's group readings and critiques sounded a lot like a workshop experience, minus, of course, the Communist oppression.

The Old Jewish Cemetery, which dates back to medieval times, is said to hold perhaps twenty thousand graves. Maybe more than that, since there are many layers of graves in this cemetery, which had to expand downward when it could no longer expand out. Crowded into this space are twelve thousand tombstones; the oldest, marking the grave of Avigdor Karo, dates back to 1439. It is an amazing sight, the thousands of stones leaning against one another, some in dizzying, almost upside-down positions, others arranged by the years like a tilted miniature Stonehenge, all of them appearing to have been heaved from the earth by some spiritual fault line of restless ghosts. I thought I saw Lily there.

She stands in the shady old cemetery looking up through the trees at the sunlight that slants across her cheek. There are dark circles beneath Lily's eyes but brightness still shines from her small intelligent face. In this sheltered corner of the graveyard, two of her friends stand between the tilting tombstones, throwing a red ball back and forth. In another corner, young children play hide-and-seek, disappearing behind, and sometimes beneath, the grave markers of their ancestors. Lily opens her sketchbook and begins to draw the strange sight of these small ghosts playing silently among the dead. She fills page after page of her sketchbook with small charcoal figures of children who have no voices.

On my way, finally, to visit the Fred and Ginger building one afternoon, I heard music coming from a church near Charles Bridge and stepped inside. A silvery-gray light filled the cool damp nave where a few people sat with bowed heads. Immediately my attention was drawn to a statue near the altar. I got as close to it as I could and stood in a side aisle studying the marble, life-size male figure posed in a curved, one-hip-higher-than-the-other stance. What was there about this statue that seemed so familiar? Suddenly I remembered Adrian Hoch, my professor at the British Institute, calling to our attention the prevalence of this posture among the stone statues in the Bargello Museum. The thrill of connection ran through me. I wondered if my excitement about linking together such disparate information was, in a very small way, the same feeling experienced by Richard Feynman when arriving at an elegant proof of some mathematical problem. With very little evidence to support my theory, I decided to accept it as an accurate one.

Out on the street I walked past block after block of gorgeous buildings; their neo-Gothic and art nouveau façades formed a sinuous wave along the river embankment. Finally I came to the corner that displayed the Fred and Ginger building. It is also called the Dancing Building, and its design resulted from a competition in the early 1990s to replace an old building that could not be restored. The winner was Frank Gehry, who collaborated with Vlado Milunic, a Croatian-Czech architect whose name seldom comes up in discussions of the famous building. Not all Czechs, however, expressed admiration for the building's design. A few days earlier I had talked to one such critic, a smart young Czech who worked at the Anagram Bookshop in Tyn Square, one of my hangouts. "My first thought on seeing it was, 'It's amazing,'" she told me. "But after seeing it five or six times, you think it looks out of place. I would rather have re-created it to be exactly the same as the old building. And now they say the construction is turning out to be shoddy."

Now as I approached Fred and Ginger, which functions as an office building, I saw what she meant. Some of the façade was peeling, and it seemed to me, even at first glance, out of place among the neighboring art deco buildings. And once inside the building—although I wasn't allowed to go beyond the reception area—I realized that the Gehry-designed structure possessed none of the joy or élan conveyed by its namesake dancers. The interior was in fact rather gray and cramped-looking. And the much-touted French restaurant on the top floor, the receptionist told me, had closed. A façade is a façade is a façade, I thought, as I left and headed for the nearby National Museum.

When I arrived at the museum, Lily was already there.

She stands beneath the vaulted dome, her head tilted back, studying the painted murals high above her in the recessed walls. Under her arm is a sketch pad; it almost covers the yellow star on her jumper, the one marked JUDE. *It is 1941 and Lily comes often to the museum now that all Jewish children have been barred from attending school. She has walked from the small apartment her family is sharing with her father's sister and their grandmother. Another family has already moved into Lily's old house. Often she stops at the old house to stare at the rooms, the contents of which she has cataloged in her head, and at the garden, where her little dog Mina used to play. Mina is gone now—Jews are not allowed to have pets—and Lily cannot think of her without feeling a fresh sense of loss.*

On her way back from the museum she stops in front of the Maisel Synagogue. Lily thinks of the days—it seems so long ago—when she and her family worshipped there. Now the synagogue is a storage house for furniture confiscated from the homes of deported Jews. She watches as the soldiers unload whole lives: carved desks, mahogany dining tables, children's beds, a bookcase with glass doors, and finally a small Steinway piano. Suddenly Lily recognizes the piano. She has played many duets with her friend Ella on the dark ebony piano. But that was before Ella and her family disappeared two months earlier, in the first deportations of Jews from Prague.

Lily cries silently at the sight of the piano, at the thought of where Ella might be, of what might be happening to her. But then she pulls out her worn-looking sketchbook— there is not much paper left in it—and preserves the memory of Ella's piano, sketching it in a few bold strokes. Lily has been sketching a lot lately; instinctively she knows it is her art that will save her.

The writing seminar continued, with classmates reading their assigned work and presenting rewrites, if they had any. I had started to look forward to the short fragments of memoir written by an interesting young school counselor from upstate New York who as a young girl had lived for two years on an Indian reservation. Her stories revealed a strong resourceful woman behind the quiet, somewhat shy façade she presented in the classroom. I was charmed also by the longer piece being worked on by a gentleman from Tennessee; it related a true story about the movie star Gloria Swanson and her "American Housewife Dress Collection." The very idea of the glamorous 1930s vamp—whom he seemed to have met—having anything to do with endorsing a "housewife dress collection" was both amusing and psychologically fascinating.

But even though I had learned to enjoy certain aspects of the class-room situation, by this time I knew the workshop experience was not for me. For one thing, listening to literature read aloud—poetry being the exception—in no way approximates the experience of reading a writer's work on your own. To become fully engaged in a story, I need to see the words on a page, to see how they fit together, how they shape ideas and meaning, and how they sound as my thinking voice says them. The narration of a book is something quite apart from the book itself, a truth I was painfully aware of whenever it was my turn to read. It didn't matter that I kept thinking *Meryl Streep, Meryl Streep* as I read aloud; what came out seemed more along the lines of Edith Bunker than my idol Meryl. As with so many other things in life, it helped to be from the South in such a situation. Whenever the thick honeyed voice of a young Southern woman reading from her novel filled the air, I was mesmerized. So much so that I forgot to listen to the story.

But the real sticking point for me was this: that the workshopping of a story took place for the most part not between a writer and editor but between a writer and other writers. Of course, our workshop leader Mary Morris always weighed in with her editorial suggestions and was available for longer one-on-one sessions; but the heft of the process seemed to lie in the critical observations of my classmates, who, perhaps, were not as free as a good editor should be of personal likes and dislikes when making literary judgments. Certainly I wasn't.

In fact, in my brief professional stints as an editor I quickly realized editing was not my strong suit—mostly because of my impulse to rewrite everything so it reflected my thoughts and style. Once, in Miss Dennis's ninth-grade creative writing class, I even rewrote Gertrude Stein. I so totally disagreed with Miss Stein's dictum "If it can be done, why do it?" that I shaped her thought a little more to my liking, writing, "If it can be done, why *not* do it?" And even though I described the quote in a footnote as "Gertrude Steinesque," my writing teacher Miss Dennis—who was a huge fan of "Miss G. Stein," as she called the writer—suggested I stick to editing my own stuff. I choose to think Miss Dennis said this not because she disliked my editing but because she admired my writing.

As the day approached when I would read my Lily story, I noticed something strange: I was beginning to appear in Lily's imaginary life as a woman named Ellen.

It is 2001 and an American woman visiting Prague stands before a small water-color, forgetting to breathe. Ellen leans in toward the glass case and reads the title: Night. *The tourists lined up in the gallery move around her, glancing impatiently as they pass the woman who lingers and lingers before the small painting. But Ellen cannot move. She wants to remember every detail of this drawing, of the orange boat with blue sails moving high above the earth, across a sea of indigo sky, under a sliver of green moon, through floating green stars. A look of alarm crosses Ellen's face when she sees that the boat is sailing a fixed course, straight ahead into a starless black night waiting ominously at the paper's edge. In one corner, the young artist has painted a burning candle but its light barely penetrates the darkness. She reads the name of the artist: Lily Bobaschova. Finally, Ellen forces herself to breathe and then moves on.*

After writing this I thought of something Mary had told the class. "Writing is one third what happens to us; one third what's told; one third what we make up," she said. That seemed to describe Lily, who was a composite of something happening, something told, and something made up. Ellen, on the other hand, seemed to spring completely from the "what happens to us" part of the equation.

In a secondhand-book shop on Nerudova Street, Ellen finds an old, perfectly preserved photograph of two girls standing on a street in Prague. The hats and stylish coats with fur collars worn by the girls suggest the late 1930s. Ellen studies their faces, particularly that of the girl in the foreground, the one looking boldly into the camera. She has dark hair and a heart-shaped face dominated by eyes that suggest both curiosity and comprehension. "It's Lily," Ellen thinks. From the bookshop Ellen walks back across Charles Bridge to the Pinkas Synagogue. There she climbs the steps to a gallery of children's drawings and stops before a small watercolor titled Night. *From her handbag she takes out a snapshot of two girls and, for several moments, looks back and forth between the drawing and the photograph. "It's Lily," she thinks. Ellen is sure of it.*

On the evening before I was to read "Lily" to the class I sat at my favorite café—the Ebel Coffee House in Tyn Square—trying to finish a letter to Naohiro I'd started days earlier. Why I was having trouble with this particular letter puzzled me. Usually, writing to Naohiro was like continuing a conversation that had no beginning and no end. Perhaps it was simply that I spent so much of my time in Prague either writing or talking about writing that my word batteries were dangerously low. But to be honest I doubted this was the case. The real reason, I suspected, was perched somewhere on the line that separated what I knew consciously and whatever was waiting to make its way from a deeper place into my consciousness. Without thinking about it, I tore up the unfinished letter and began to write.

Naohiro,

For the last hour I've been sitting in a café trying to figure out why I'm having trouble writing you. I'm still not sure, but something is stirring inside me, something that made me tear up the unfinished letter I've been carrying around and start this one. Where it will lead me I don't know. But as you once told me when I was similarly confused about my feelings, "To learn of the pine, go to the pine." I remember how you laughed when I told you that if the poet who wrote that had substituted the word "unconscious" for "pine," it would describe what a psychoanalyst asks the analysand to do. Funny, but just writing down what you said to me in Kyoto when I expressed uncertainty about our situation reminds me of how nonjudgmental you are. It is one of the things I admire most about you: the ability to close the divide that usually exists between people who are different from one another.

And so I see that this last sentence has led me in the direction of what has been bothering me. Our differences. Yours and mine. Why do I think of this now? Probably because of something I am writing—a fictional re-creation of a Jewish girl named Lily who died in one of the concentration camps. It's a strange association, I know, but every association of one thought to another is strange at first. Perhaps this comes up now because I feel a certain amount of guilt in trying to imagine and write about a girl whose life ulti-mately is unimaginable to me.

We have been shaped by such different cultures, you and I, that I sometimes wonder whether it is possible for us to imagine one another "whole against the sky," as a poet once put it. Suddenly I think of this. Do you remember the day in Paris—we were having lunch at Madame Cedelle's little tearoom on the rue de Beaune—when I told you of my belief that it is our sorrows that shape us, not our joys. And you replied with deep feeling that to be the person of your sorrows was an honorable thing. Then you told me of growing up in Hiroshima after the city was decimated. "I do not forget the person of that sorrow," you said. "I bend still to him with great respect." I shall never forget how startled and moved I was when you said this. Startled because you seldom talked about that part of your past, and moved because at that moment—although you could not see it—my heart bent to you with great respect.

Naohiro, forgive me for rambling on and on. But in allowing my mind to wander down whatever path it desired, I seem to have come to a clearing. I can imagine you now sitting across the table from me, a sleight of mind that is not hard to do. Imagining you, in fact, suddenly seems as natural and real as the chair I sit in, the pen I hold, the paper I write on.

When I read my Lily story in class the next morning, it was not finished. The truth is, it would never be finished. Not by me, anyway. Although I knew how Lily's story ended, the reality of that ending was not something I wanted to make up. In fact, I worried that I'd gone too far already in imagining Lily's life. After all, what did I really know? A few facts gleaned from a brief encounter. A smattering of history from books. The memories told me by a survivor from one of the camps. To be honest, all I really knew about Lily was what her drawing told me.

But it was too late to turn back, so when it was my turn to present my story to the class, I began to read aloud from my notebook:

She stands on the curb along Parizska Street on a cold morning in March, the fur collar on her coat turned up to cover her ears. Her sister Ruth looks frightened as the German soldiers march by wearing heavy iron helmets that make them look like fierce pagan gladiators. . . .

It took less than ten minutes to read aloud what I had written over the last five days and only a minute or two to read the last two paragraphs, written late the night before:

On a bitterly cold night in December of 1941, Lily sits in St. Nicholas Church listening to a string quintet perform Vivaldi's Four Seasons. *She senses it may be the last time she hears such music and listens with the intensity of an animal trying to escape a steel trap. For an hour or so she frees herself from the world narrowing around her and has only one thought: How can drawing a bow over the strings of a violin produce such sublime sounds?*

On her last night in Prague, Ellen sits in St. Nicholas Church listening to a string quintet perform Vivaldi's Four Seasons. *When the music ends, Ellen has only one thought: How can drawing a bow over the strings of a violin produce such sublime sounds? As the audience applauds, Ellen looks across the aisle just in time to see a young girl leaving. It's Lily, she is sure of it. She's thinner than she was in the photo and there are bluish rings of fatigue beneath the curious, lively eyes, but it's definitely Lily. Ellen tries to follow her out onto the street but the girl disappears into the anonymous crowd gathered around the Astronomical Clock in Old Town Square. But it was Lily, Ellen thinks. It definitely was Lily.*

When I finished reading, Mary asked the class for their comments. I waited as though standing before a firing squad, a doomed traitor desperately wishing for a blindfold and a last cigarette. Neither was offered.

"I thought it was too detached," said the female graduate student. "Not soulful enough."

It took a major act of self-control on my part to refrain from answering the charge of "not soulful enough." I wanted to say, *But I meant it to be unemotional on the surface, as though Lily was frozen by trauma. I wanted it to have a Chekhovian air of loss kept in the background, of loss closing in but not yet.* I wanted to say that and much more, but I didn't.

Two people liked the bit about Lily watching the Germans move the piano she had practiced on with her friend Ella. But they had suggestions on ways to improve it.

"The piano should be put on the ground," said a short-story writer. "It would give Lily more time to sketch it and make the scene more believable."

"Yes, and wouldn't it take longer to actually move a piano that size?" said someone else.

I wanted to explain that Lily's sketch was done in short, bold strokes and that a quick sketch of a piano didn't need to have the intricacies of a Leonardo drawing. But I didn't.

"Ellen needs to be developed so that we know her better," said a woman who had been working for years on a long story.

I wanted to respond by saying, *Give me a break. I've only worked on this for five days.* I wanted to point out— *Enough already,* my thinking voice interrupted. *Stop whining about how you didn't have enough time and what you wanted them to feel and trying to explain everything, as though you could do that to your readers. Either a reader gets it or they don't. Grow up!*

Although I did not welcome this intrusion by my know-it-all thinking voice, it was good advice. I took it and said nothing. No, that's not true. I said *almost* nothing until the end of the critiquing. "It's not a finished piece," I said, as though I planned someday to finish it.

Since it was the last day of Mary Morris's two-week workshop— another two-week writing seminar would start the following Monday with a different teacher—the entire class, along with Mary and her husband, the writer Larry O'Connor, headed for lunch at a nearby restaurant. Although I was not staying for the second workshop, most of my classmates were. Still, the lunch had a festive, last-day-of-school gaiety about it, one that seemed to erase any hurt or competitive feelings left over from the workshopping experience.

Now that the pressure was off and the "writer" label temporarily abandoned, I saw a different side to most of my classmates: a less guarded, kinder, gentler side. The two men who had called one another's work "garbage," I was told, more or less apologized for their lack of civility and undiplomatic vocabulary. And I overheard a few revisionist critiques of the favorable type being offered from one writer to another. But the most notable difference, to me anyway, was that we talked about things other than writing and writers. And as we talked, I learned things about my classmates that their writing hadn't necessarily told me. In one long conversation with the college student whose work I'd admired, I discovered how surprisingly similar our early lives had been. And after talking at length to a smart thirtysomething man who was living in Paris—where he was writing a second novel while waiting for the first one to be published—I came away regretting we hadn't connected earlier.

And so we ate and drank and lingered in the big, loud restaurant, snapping pictures of one another, exchanging e-mail addresses, and saying good-bye over and over again, and through it all not a word of criticism was uttered. Quite the opposite, in fact.

"You have such pretty hair," said the woman sitting next to me.

"That's just what I was thinking about you," I said.

And we both laughed.

Lassie, Come Home

SOMEWHERE in the first ten minutes of my initiation into the art of being a shepherd, I found myself about to be charged by ten Scottish Blackface rams. Not Blackface ewes, mind you, but full-grown males who seemed to resent my attempt to redirect their usual movement patterns. Even from a distance I could see their eyes challenging me, the way New York City drivers challenge a cop who has the chutzpah to reroute traffic on Fifth Avenue. *Go ahead, just try it and see what happens* was the message I got from their wide-set eyes.

While the Blackies waited out my next move, I quickly reviewed what I'd been told about these Scottish sheep: that the ewes can be "crafty" while the rams, or tups, as they're called here, are likely to be "aggressive." While outwitting a crafty ewe was something I might attempt, outrunning ten aggressive tups? Forget it. And the worst part—well, maybe the second-worst part, the first being the imminent danger of being trampled to death or impaled on the wire fence—was that I'd brought it on myself. After all, my Border collie sidekick, young Peg, was only responding to my commands and appeared to be as confused by them as I was.

It had all looked so simple when Mark Wylie, my host at his working sheep farm called Hill of Camstraddan, spoke or whistled out his commands to Peg, the ones that told her to move the sheep forward or to the right or the left. Perhaps it was because I lacked a Scots accent or couldn't whistle properly. Or perhaps it was because I was not really communicating commands but just shouting words out in as loud a voice as I could, the way you do in a foreign country when you don't know the language. In any case here I was, facing down ten angry tups that were about to make a move on me.

So I did the only thing I could do. I shouted out to Peg, "Away to me," a command I thought would send the dog racing to the right of the sheep, heading them off, as it did when Mark had issued it. Instead, it sent the tups charging straight toward me while poor confused Peg ran back and forth behind them, trying to figure out what to do. Where, I wondered, was Babe, the champion sheep-pig and movie star, now that I needed him? There was nothing left for me to do but affect a nonthreatening posture toward the charging rams. So I tilted my head and tried to look friendly, or at least relaxed, as though it were just another casual Friday at the office.

It didn't work. They kept coming. But then at the last possible moment, the tups parted like the Red Sea, half of them going to one side of me, the rest to the other. It was a strangely exhilarating experience, this parting of the rams, the way their moving bodies passed by me like big white clouds—close enough to touch me—their black faces blurred while the sound of their pounding hooves rose up from the muddy field like beating hearts. When it was over I looked around for Peg, wondering if she had run by me too, unnoticed in the commotion. She hadn't. I spotted the dog slumped in the grass, a disgusted look on her face, humiliated no doubt at the cartoonish effort in which she'd been forced to participate. After all, Peg was used to working with someone like Mark, someone who knew what he was doing and did it with grace and finesse. So much for making a good first impression with Peg and the other dogs, one of whom was watching through the fence, his muzzle poking beneath the pasture gate with what seemed to be a grin plastered on his face.

Mark, known for his prowess as a sheepdog handler, quickly stepped in to soothe our feelings—Peg's and mine. "Let's try it again," he said. "And this time when you give the commands, remember you don't need to be loud. You have to sound forceful. Almost angry."

We tried again, Peg and I. This time, the rams, emboldened perhaps by their previous victory, became stubborn and refused to move where my commands and Peg's legwork wanted them to move. One particularly defiant ram turned and challenged Peg, standing his ground when the dog tried to move him back to the others.

Mark assessed the situation: "The ram's getting prepared to have a go at Peg. Peg's a young dog and she's still learning. The sheep wouldn't have done that with Spot," he said, referring to the dog watching from the sidelines.

At Mark's suggestion I gave Peg what I thought was the command to stop. "That'll do," I said. But Peg didn't respond.

I issued another command, this one in an angry voice. *"Lie down!"* I said, impersonating an army drill sergeant. Miraculously, Peg lay down. Well, halfway down, anyway, more of a crouch, really, than a lie-down.

"*All* the way down," Mark said firmly.

I said it again, as forcefully as I could. "All the way down!" This time Peg responded instantly.

Mark smiled and said, "Aye, Alice, you'll be takin' that dog home with you."

It was a joke, of course, but Peg obviously had no sense of humor. Upon hearing the news of her impending departure with me, she looked as dejected as I'd ever seen a dog look.

I had come to a Scottish farm about an hour north of Glasgow to learn the rudiments of training Border collies and to attend the dog trials held in the nearby village of Luss on Loch Lomond. The Luss Sheepdog Trial, a rung on the ladder to the National and International Trials, takes place each year on the first Saturday in June. I had arrived a little late. A year late, to be exact.

My plans to stay on a working sheep farm a year earlier had been canceled by the foot-and-mouth outbreak in England and Scotland. It was a terrible, sad event that forced many farmers to either kill their animals or, in an attempt to stop the disease from spreading, quarantine their livestock on closed farms. This led to the cancellation of many events involving animals, including most dog shows and trials in Great Britain. As a result, the owners of the farm where I was to stay—Anne and Bobby Lennox—suggested I postpone my visit. Which I did. But instead of staying with the Lennoxes at Shantron Farm, a five-thousand-acre property with 2,200 Scottish Blackface breeding ewes, I arranged to stay at nearby Hill of Camstraddan Farm with Mark Wylie, a sheep farmer and avid dog trainer.

Anne Lennox, whom I'd gotten to know over the year or so we talked by phone or e-mail, suggested the change. "Since Mark is a keen dog trainer and the trial takes place near his farm, it'll be better for you to be right there where the action is," she told me. "He and his wife Christine offer bed-and-breakfast accommodations, and Mark is happy to work with you and the dogs."

And so on a cloudy spring day I arrived at Hill of Camstraddan Farm, my suitcase packed with rain gear, energy-boosting PowerBars, and a large tube of sunscreen with a SPF of 32—a bizarre last-minute addition made, given Scotland's weather, against all reason. From the road, Mark's farm resembled an illustration from a child's storybook. The neat white house with a glass conservatory was set on a gentle rise that overlooked a dozen or so sheep grazing in the front pasture. Circling the house and its outbuildings was a lush ring of green shrubs and trees that gave way in the rear to a thousand acres of craggy hills, which rose to two thousand feet above sea level. About six hundred Scottish Blackface and hardy Cheviot breeding ewes, according to Mark's brochure, grazed year-round on those rough hills.

Since I had stayed at a lodge on Loch Lomond for a few days before going to the farm, I arranged to have one of the locals drive me from there to nearby Hill of Camstraddan. After meandering along a lovely back road for five minutes we turned onto a highway, then five minutes later turned off the main road and rattled up an unpaved driveway, stopping just behind the house. A fair-skinned, good-looking man wearing the inevitable knee-high rubber Wellies, a windbreaker, and a dark cap printed with the word *Alaska* stopped tinkering with his car's engine and looked up. Whoever he was, the windbreaker-cap-Wellies look suited him; he could have posed, just as he was, for one of those Dewar's ads that show outdoorsy men doing something outdoors. It turned out to be Mark Wylie. After exchanging pleasantries with me, he carried my suitcase into the house and up to a comfortable-looking room on the second floor, one with a large window overlooking the front pasture. He explained a few things—how to turn on the hot water, when breakfast was served, where the house keys were, and so on—and then left me to "settle in."

The first thing I noticed was how quiet it was. Unnervingly quiet. As quiet, I decided, as Proust's cork-lined room must have been. The second thing I noticed was a feeling of claustrophobia seeping in through those similar-to-Proust's sound-suppressing walls. I don't know what I expected life on a sheep farm to be like, but I didn't expect it to be so quiet. I thought I'd hear dogs barking and sheep bleating or boisterous, shouting shepherds bringing in fluffy ewes to be sheared or any of the other sheep-farm images from *The Thorn Birds* that were projecting themselves onto my mind's screen.

I sat on the edge of my bed and hummed "Mary had a little lamb" while tapping my feet on the floor, just loud enough to make some noise as I wondered what to do. I felt I had lost control of my plan, whatever that might be.

Then, without thinking too much, I left the room, raced down the stairs and out the side door to where Mark stood. "Look," I said, "have you had lunch? I haven't and I'm hungry. Could we go somewhere for a bite to eat and talk a little? I mean, if you have chores to do or you've already eaten, I'd understand but. . . ."

Mark cut short my breathless invitation to lunch. "Just let me go and put on a jacket," he said, disappearing into the house. He was back in a few minutes, a tweed jacket substituted for his windbreaker. Then we hopped into his vehicle and left, amid all the lovely noise a twenty-year-old Land Rover is capable of making on a bumpy dirt road.

The Colquhoun Arms Inn takes its name from the Clan Colquhoun (pronounced k'hoon—as I learned the hard way), which for about nine hundred years owned most of the land in and about these parts. Part pub, part inn, the Colquhoun Arms is one of those places that make you feel instantly at home, no matter where your actual home might be. Maybe what made it so cozy was the presence at the next booth of a collie dozing beside his master's feet, his big paws providing a pillow on which to rest his long muzzle. The sight of this hardworking dog at rest in the pub, oddly enough, made me think of his pampered French counterparts, the elaborately groomed poodles who regularly perch beneath tiny café tables in Paris.

Located just on the edge of Luss village, the Colquhoun Arms was Mark's choice and a very good one, too, since its homey atmosphere broke the ice between us. For more than an hour, closer to two, we sat in a booth eating thick homemade leek-and-potato soup and crusty bread spread with slabs of fresh butter, followed by hamburgers and then coffee as we talked, talked, talked. I could see why Mark's neighbors and friends described him as a man of great charm and an irresistible talker. They were right on both counts. Mark was a charmer. What I found most appealing, however, was that he seemed quite unaware of just how attractive and charming he was; he never made a move that seemed unnatural or calculated to impress. Still boyish-looking at forty-two, he had a natural intelligence and quick wit. Not the Oscar Wilde type of jaded wit but one that sprang from growing up close to the land and, of course, close to sheep and sheepdogs.

"My mother's side of the family were all farmers, and I was sent out to gather sheep when I was quite young," Mark told me. "Then I worked my uncle's dogs from about fourteen years old. Sheep, in this terrain, are almost wild animals. Their main aim is to get away from you, and they're nowhere near as afraid of a man as a dog. But hill sheep are smarter than other sheep, always trying to beat the dog and the man."

He became interested in training dogs for trial competitions when he was seventeen. "I started to feel really confident then. Thought I could beat the sheep. But the first trial was a disaster. I had Spot, this big, black beautiful dog—I loved him to bits—but I was too young to be trialing and so was Spot. He was only eighteen months. We came in fourth."

"That sounds pretty good to me," I said.

"Aye, except there were only four dogs in the trial," he said. We both laughed.

I asked Mark to tell me about the dogs he had now at Hill of Camstraddan Farm.

"There's Tan, four years old and a great working dog but not good for trials," he responded enthusiastically, in a voice that that suggested we had arrived at a favorite topic of his. "Sheep are afraid of Tan. He upsets them. They bolt and run, or huddle in a corner. Then there's a bitch called Trim who's eight and a half. By far the best dog I've ever had. She has a tremendous 'engine' in her heart and lungs and she has great stamina. But she's getting to the end of her prime. Trim doesn't do much sheep-gathering anymore. Because of her age I don't work her hard. Sometimes when they get to be ten years old, we retire them off to a small easier farm. After all the work they've done for us, we don't want to give them away to a place where they'll be tied up. These dogs need mental stimulation, even if it's rounding up Frisbees. A friend who was given a working sheepdog quickly gave him back. Said the dog was rounding up people on the street every time they went out."

Mark pauses. "Where was I? Aye, my dogs. Then there's Peg, who's a young one, only fifteen months. And Spot, four years old. When my youngest son Struan was four, he picked out the wee six-week-old pup, and Spot's turned out to be one of the best dogs I ever trained. When Spot sees sheep, it's like watching a switch being turned on."

It was a description that, tweaked a bit, might apply to Mark as well.

When Mark talked about his dogs or anything related to dog trials, his face lit up—just as if a switch had been turned on. Clearly he was a man smitten with Border collie fever, a condition not unusual in this dog-centric part of the world.

"What are the qualities that make a working sheepdog good at working sheep?" I asked Mark, hoping he'd ignore my Gertrude Steinesque syntax. "Is there any way you can tell whether a pup might turn out to be as good as, say, Spot or Trim?"

"Picking a pup is like a lottery," Mark said. "You don't know how they'll turn out. Two pups in my life were duds. They had no interest in sheep. I gave them away as pets. To get a right good dog, you've got to get a hill dog. Hill dogs are sharper than field dogs, and lots of times will do the thinking for themselves, without commands. Stamina is very important. A good hill dog can run a hundred miles a day. Apart from the husky, they can outrun any dog. That's what you want, a dog that will get in there and go. The dogs I like working with are forceful dogs, and they're hard to stop. The 'stop' command is hard for them because it's a killer instinct that you're harnessing. You're expected to kill the sheep and then the both of you will eat them."

The lunch crowd had thinned out and I knew Mark needed to get back to work. But I wanted to ask him another question, one that probably would seem stupid to him. I decided to ask it anyway.

"Do you ever think of your dogs—say, when they're off duty—as pets?"

Mark thought for a bit before answering. "Although I certainly don't think of them as pets, I do think of them as more than a working tool," he said. "They're part of a team—companions you're relying on just as they're relying on you. They have to learn to trust you. You go through a lot of stages with them. At first they're eager to learn. Then they rebel, then they respect the teacher. I hold these dogs in higher esteem than pets. They're like children. You want them to be like you, with character, boldness, toughness, and a bit stubborn." He paused for a moment, then smiled. "They're in a pack. And right now I'm the top dog. They rely on me and the only one they want to see is me."

He stopped for a minute, then said, "But when they're pups we do rear them as pets in the house for nine to ten months. I believe champions are made in the house. The dogs learn manners, the kids play with them, and they learn to be around people. I think it's important they be reared in the house."

"How do young dogs raised in a house for almost a year take it when they're put out?" I asked. "One day they're a pet, the next they're a working dog."

Mark answered my question with one word: "Hard."

When we left the Colquhoun Arms I decided to walk back to the farm. That is, if I could figure out how to get there.

"It's easy," Mark said. "You can go up the path behind the pub and follow it to the A82, then cross over and walk until you see the farm. Or you can take the nature trail."

Since my chances of surviving any attempt to cross the A82, a busy highway linking Glasgow with the West Highlands, were in the slim-to-none range, I opted for the nature trail. Mark's directions, which I wrote down, or tried to, went something like this: You follow the Old Road that runs in front of Colquhoun Arms, cross a little bridge, and then look for a gate on your right. You want to open it and go down the steps that lead to a field. Then you want to walk along a path that will take you along a wee stream and under a bridge. On the other side of the bridge, you'll see a dirt road and soon you ought to see the farm up on your left. When you come to a big gate at the end of our front pasture, open it—but be sure to close it behind you so the sheep don't escape—then cross the pasture to the steps and gate leading to the house.

Although I should have concentrated on Mark's directions—directions are not my strong suit—my mind fixated instead on the part about closing the gate "so the sheep don't escape." This could mean trouble, I thought, as half a dozen scenarios played out in my head. Worst-case scenario? A toss-up between the sheep escaping and trying to cross the A82, or the sheep escaping and chasing *me* across the A82.

After Mark left I poked around the Colquhoun Inn a bit, then set out along the road that would take me back, I hoped, to the farm. It was a beautiful country road, lined with big green trees beyond which were verdant pastures dotted with white sheep with black faces—the same color combination, it suddenly struck me, as that of a Border collie. This was the Old Road, the one used by drivers before the A82 was built; now its pastoral setting was only occasionally disturbed by the sound of a motorcar.

It is lovely in this part of Scotland in late spring. Along with the country's usual rolling, sometimes craggy, beauty, it was lambing season, and the sight of so many newborn lambs trotting alongside their mother ewes was a visible reminder of how life renews itself despite natural disasters and the interference of the human species. I was enjoying myself so much in fact that I must have passed right by the gate Mark had mentioned. This only occurred to me because I suddenly remembered standing on the bridge mentioned in my notes, looking down at the wee rocky stream below. I turned around and retraced my steps, although now all my instructions were backward. Lost already, I thought, as I prepared for the usual lengthy search for the right direction.

Instead I found the gate just where it should be. I walked down the steps and followed the path by the stream to an opening from which I could see Hill of Camstraddan Farm. All that remained was to open the big gate into Mark's front pasture and hightail it across the lengthy field without interference from the rams. As I listened to myself say this, I felt like a sports announcer doing a play-by-play broadcast of a football game.

The rams—the Scottish ones, not the Los Angeles ones—were huddled in a far corner beneath a tree, but they stirred at the appearance of the figure in a bright red windbreaker. I walked slowly, staying close to the fences, hoping that the color red did not have the same effect on rams as it does on bulls in Pamplona. In such a manner I managed to creep forward through the muddy pasture until I saw several steps leading up to a gate that opened onto the front garden of the house. Quickly, I sprinted up the steps, unlatched the gate, and stepped into friendly territory. When I turned to look back at the field I saw that not a creature was stirring, not even a ram.

Mark, who was working outside, greeted me with a wave. Although I suspected he'd seen my pathetic journey across the sheep field, he didn't mention it, asking instead if I'd like to watch him put Spot through his paces with the rams.

"I'd love it," I said.

We walked to a nearby barn where the dogs were kept and Mark opened the door. Immediately upon hearing his voice, the uncaged dogs that had been so silent began barking in a cacophony of happiness, straining at the chains that tethered them. It made me think of Mark's assessment of himself as "the top dog in the pack." He took me around the large room, telling me a little about each dog. As he approached, they strained at their leashes and attempted to jump up and down in a fury of excitement. When we got to Spot, Mark loosened the chain and Spot, watched enviously by the dogs left behind, playfully bolted outside the way any normal dog would after being cooped up.

However, Spot's demeanor changed as soon as he went through the gate and saw the sheep. "See, there it is," Mark said. "What I told you about. Spot's just turned on the switch."

I could see it. The dog's body seemed to pull itself together in an act of intense concentration; his eyes darted about as though he were a short Secret Service man looking for any movement, anything out of the ordinary. Spot, I was told, had the "eye"—a powerful, hypnotic stare that could make sheep move. Gone was the dog who had responded playfully to Mark; in its place was another dog, one who was all business.

Out in the field, Mark explained that the purpose of a command was to get a dog into a given position relative to the sheep. To do this, he said, a handler must know how to get his dog to start, stop, go left, and go right. If the handler uses a whistle, he must learn the different whistles, such as a soft low one to send the dog to the right. If verbal commands are used, well, it would be too simple of course just to say stop, start, left, or right, so a special sheepdog vocabulary has evolved, one familiar to anyone who saw the movie *Babe*. The verbal command "come bye" tells the dog to circle around the sheep to the left, or clockwise. To direct the dog to swing counterclockwise to head off the sheep, the command is the nonsensical "Away to me." If a time-out is needed because the dog is moving too fast or the sheep have gotten out of control, the command is "Lie down!" And when it's time to stop the dog—which Mark says is the most difficult thing to do, especially with a forceful dog like Spot—the handler, strangely enough, uses the polite phrase, "That'll do." Mark uses a combination of verbal commands and whistles.

"The goal is to get your dog to handle sheep in the easiest, quietest way possible," Mark said. "And the hardest thing is to get them to take the sheep away from you. Their natural instinct is to bring something *to* you. Throw a stick and a dog will bring it to you."

For the next fifteen minutes I watched Mark and Spot in the field, engaged in a three-species competition. Mark had his eyes on the sheep and the dog. Spot also had his eyes on the sheep but his ear tuned to

Mark's commands. And the sheep, who had their own agenda, had their eyes on Spot, sizing him up in order to plot their escape. I watched as Spot responded to Mark's string of commands: in just minutes he sent Spot to the left, to the right, slowed him down, stopped him, then delivered a low whistle that sent him "just a wee bit to the left and then back to the right." And as I watched, a pattern emerged. It seemed to hinge on Spot's driving the sheep forward in a straight line by moving behind them and, when necessary, to the side, pushing back into line any animal that spilled out from the rest. It was not unlike the way a baker shapes dough, patting it and smoothing it into a neat, symmetrical loaf of bread.

Looked at that way, it didn't seem so hard. Maybe I could learn to do this after all, I thought—just as I had thought after hearing Ella Fitzgerald sing for the first time.

But my attempt later that afternoon to duplicate Mark's prowess in the field had resulted in the disastrous Peg and the Ten Blackies incident, shattering any such illusion. I found the outcome eerily similar to the dismantling of my earlier Ella fantasies at the Miss Henrietta Freedenberg School of Music in Baltimore.

The next morning while I was having a breakfast of ham, eggs, tomatoes, muffins, marmalade, orange juice, and coffee—all prepared and served by Mark, who ran the B&B since his wife Christine had a full-time job—he suggested Peg and I have another go at it. Since I had spent most of the previous evening reading books on Border collie training from Mark's library and jotting down pages and pages of notes, my confidence apropos Peg and the Ten Blackies was way up. We agreed to meet in the pasture in an hour. This gave Mark time to finish some chores and allowed me to study my notes and plan a strategy.

I poured myself more coffee and began to read a page from my notebook titled: Top Tips about Tups and Pups.

1. The most important command is a dog's name. It can mean half a dozen things. "Come here." "Pay attention." "Off." "Think." "Get up." The meaning depends on how and when it's uttered.
2. The fewer commands you give the dog, the better.
3. First you have to look at things from the sheep's point of view. Then you have to pretend you're a Border collie.

4. Whether using a whistle or voice command, what's important is how you give the order. The arms should not be used much.
5. To be correct, the sheep should be aware of your dog when it pulls up, or stops, behind the sheep before driving them to the handler. It gives the sheep a chance to see the dog. This first impression makes a tremendous difference to your run.

Aha! I thought when I reread this last tip on first impressions. So it's not just me who's eager to make a good first impression. It's true of the dogs as well. Now that I understood this, I vowed not to let either of us—Peg or me—make anything less than a right bonny first impression from now on.

Well, I'd done it again. Spooked both Peg and the Ten Blackies. Only this time, instead of charging me, the tups had retreated to a far corner of the field, where they were huddled behind a tree, up against a fence. Even a novice like me didn't need to be told this was the worst possible position from which to move sheep. Figure it out. What conceivable commands could I give Peg that would accomplish the task at hand? The two flanking commands—to sweep around the sheep clockwise or counterclockwise—were useless here. A sweep of any kind was impossible, given that a tree was in front of the sheep and a fence behind.

In handling Peg I had broken just about every one of the rules memorized from my notes. Instead of few commands, I had Peg starting, stopping, sitting, lying down, standing, going to the right and the left and the right again until she was as confused as I was. As for not using my arms much, well, let's put it this way: I looked like a crossing guard at the intersection of four elementary schools. And forget about the looking at things from the sheep's point of view and then pretending to be a Border collie. This approach did nothing but convince me never to eat lamb again or listen to what other people told me to do unless they could produce a notarized document proving their competency.

And poor Peg. If she had any expectations of our killing the sheep together and then sitting down to eat them, they were long gone. In the end the only command that made any sense, the one I finally gave to Peg, was "That'll do," releasing her from any further responsibility in this fiasco. She crept away after hearing this, not looking at me or Mark or the sheep.

Fortunately I had plans to visit Anne and Bobby Lennox at Shantron Farm that afternoon. Otherwise I would have brooded all day about the Ten Blackies Behind a Tree incident. Although we'd not yet met, I already liked Anne, liked her from the moment I heard her lilting Scots accent on the phone. "Aye, it'd be cheaper to take the train from Glasgow to Helensburgh and rent a car there," Anne had advised me in our first phone conversation, channeling the whole of Scotland right through the long-distance wires. In my head it was Grandmother telling me which streetcar to take to the Pratt Library in downtown Baltimore and where to get off. It was Mother explaining how to set the table and fold napkins. It was Aunt Maisie spinning long stories about growing up in Scotland with her two sisters, Aunt Mabel and my mother. Just the sound of Anne's voice was enough to excavate from its shallow hiding place the vocabulary of my childhood—the one that included such phrases as "I dinna ken it" and "Ach, weel, you canna go doon that way."

I couldn't wait to meet Anne.

Shantron Farm, about four miles from Mark Wylie's place, is possibly the most glorious five thousand acres in all of Scotland. Set among rolling emerald hills that eventually turn into green mini-mountains, the farm offers panoramic views of Loch Lomond's shimmering blue water and the surrounding countryside. It is, in fact, so picturesque that it is used in the filming of *Take the High Road*, a popular Scottish television soap opera. "Aye, that's supposed to be the entrance to Kerr's Kreamery and Farm Shop in the *High Road*," Anne said as we passed a sign on one of the farmhouse doors.

As she showed me around the house and gardens, it occurred to me that Anne was exactly as I'd pictured her. With her fair Scottish skin, wide smile, straight brown hair pulled back from her face in a no-nonsense way, and simple forthright manner, Anne epitomized my idea of a woman who'd grown up close to nature—not only Mother Nature but her own innate disposition. She struck me as a sort of Scottish Jane Austen: a woman capable of spotting anything that fell into the unnatural or phony category.

Just as we were about to go into the house for lunch, a tall, relaxed-looking man with dark hair and matching beard, dressed in a plaid work shirt and jeans, came around the corner of a barn. A sturdy Border collie accompanied him, one that had the most alert-looking ears I'd ever seen. They stood up from the dog's head like twin antennas that, with a few minor adjustments, likely could tune in weather reports from downtown Osaka.

"This is Bobby," Anne said, introducing me to her husband. He smiled and shook my hand, then turned and introduced me to the dog: "This is Lynn." Right away I liked him. Bobby, that is, although I found Lynn appealing too. So I decided to go with my instincts and ask Bobby a dog question right off.

"I've been looking over some of Mark's books on Border collies and can't figure out why they usually have names like Cap or Kep or Mirk or Shep. Is there a formula for picking out a collie's name?"

"It's best when a dog's name is short and ends with a guttural stop, like an 'n' or 'p' or 't,' " Bobby said.

"Like Lynn," I said. "Well, that explains it. I couldn't figure out why none of the dogs had names like Blackie or Whitey or Fluffy."

Anne had cooked a lunch for us, one we shared with Ainslie Marshall, a young intern from a sheep farm in New Zealand who had come to Shantron on a work-abroad program. Lunch was served at the small kitchen table, the plates set down between stacks of books and papers. Bobby, who had to ease his long legs beneath the table, ate his lunch from a plate set down on top of a pile of books. But the whole seating and eating arrangement turned out to be quite pleasant and homey, including the food Anne served: homemade carrot-and-tomato soup, meat rolls and mashed potatoes with gravy, and a big fresh fruit salad. It was a hearty, satisfying meal, fit for either a working sheep farmer or a guest visiting a working sheep farmer.

I asked Ainslie and Bobby to tell me about the differences between New Zealand sheepdogs and their Scottish counterparts.

"The New Zealand huntaway is our version of the Border collie," Ainslie said. "It's a powerful dog that's good at driving sheep forward. But it moves them by barking."

"The kind of dogs we use," Bobby said, "are good 'eye' dogs. And they usually don't bark. They move the sheep by staring them out, controlling them with their 'eye' or a turn of their head."

"That doesn't happen here at Shantron Farm," Anne said, dryly. "Usually there's a good deal of shouting that goes on first."

Anne's riposte drew laughs from Ainslie and me and made Bobby smile.

I liked the streak of irreverence that Anne possessed, or to put it another way, that possessed Anne. A woman of many parts, she was straightforward, confident, and well-informed, with strong opinions and an unlimited supply of raw energy. In addition to running the farm with Bobby, managing the household, and raising three children—a nineteen-year-old daughter and seventeen-year-old twins—Anne also ran a charming B&B in a stone cottage close by the family house. It was clear she had put a lot of thought into decorating the cottage, which could accommodate three sets of guests, and into the gardens surrounding it. To advertise the B&B, Anne had constructed one of the most sophisticated websites I'd found in the search for my Border collie–sheep farm adventure.

The B&B, Anne told me, was a way to supplement the family income, a necessity given the decline in the economic fortunes of sheep farming. Bobby and Anne were worried that a time might come when they could no longer afford to operate Shantron Farm.

"In the mid-1990s we saw the handwriting on the wall," Anne said. "There's no living to be had from running a farm. We told our children, 'Don't even think about it.' I'm fifty years old and trying to make ends meet so we can continue. It's a way of life that's in our heritage, in our bones. But if it went bust, we would just have to walk away."

Anne's comments about advising her children not to become sheep farmers reminded me of something Mark had told me. When I asked him what his three children, who ranged in age from eight to nineteen, wanted in terms of their professional lives, he instantly replied: "Not to be sheep farmers."

Bobby, whose family has lived on the farm as tenants since the 1750s, said life on a sheep farm changed radically in recent years. "It's a good life. But the fun went out of it about four years ago when the subsidy system came in. The paperwork and the red tape that's snowballed since then has made it much more of a business than before. And the value of livestock has plummeted down in recent years."

After lunch, Bobby, who was going off with Lynn to round up some sheep that had strayed off the property, asked me if I'd like to come along. It was just what I had hoped for, a chance to see a working sheep-dog really working. I said yes immediately. But first Bobby wanted Lynn to move a few ewes and lambs from a nearby pasture into a fenced area behind the house.

"She's very biddable, very good with lambs and ewes," he said of Lynn. "She seems to know what you want her to do. Best dog I ever had." Bobby, who never mastered the whistle commands, opened the pasture gate and watched as Lynn shot off like a bullet into the pasture. The ewes, who'd already gotten wind that something was up, began to circle the wagons around their lambs. From the start it was clear that Lynn was a top dog who knew her stuff, but, as Robbie Burns and my grandmother liked to point out, "The best-laid schemes o' mice an' men gang aft agley." Or to put it in modern vernacular: stuff happens and things fall apart no matter what. And it's true of dogs and men as well. As Lynn tried to get one large ewe and her lambs into the gate, the ewe turned and faced the dog.

"The ewe is challenging Lynn," Bobby explained, moving slowly closer to the action. "She's protecting her young." What followed was a pas de deux between dog and ewe that lasted until the lamb broke away and made it through the gate on her own.

"Sit down, Lynn. I'll take it from here," Bobby said, closing the gate behind the ewe and her lamb. "All you're doing when you work with a dog is just controlling the dog's natural instincts to bring the sheep to you and take it away from you. It goes back to their hunting instincts."

That chore finished, we climbed into Bobby's jeep—Lynn lying in the back on some old blankets and me sitting in the front on some jumper cables. As we drove back into the hills, the jeep climbing higher and higher, I could see the countryside around Loch Lomond widen into an astonishing panoramic view. Occasionally the appearance of this strange metal intruder on wheels caused a grazing ewe and her lamb to look up briefly from the sloping pasture.

Finally Bobby parked the car. We had arrived at a place where the strayed sheep apparently had been spotted. It was time for Lynn to take control of the situation. Bobby set her free, and without waiting for any commands, she took off at a dead run, sped down a sloping pasture, and then disappeared into the void of a steep drop in the green topography. Five minutes passed. Bobby, who stood at a distance from me, seemed unconcerned about Lynn's disappearance. I looked at my watch again. Exactly ten minutes since we'd seen Lynn. I started to worry. What if she was hurt? In a ditch somewhere or lying at the bottom of the nearby gorge with a broken leg?

I was about to suggest to Bobby that we search for the dog when suddenly two lambs appeared on the distant ridge, their little black faces parting the grass as they ran forward, the mother ewe close behind. A few more minutes, then another lamb and ewe appeared, and another and another until five lambs and ewes were running up through the pasture to higher ground. And then finally, Lynn came into sight, mouth open to reveal her dark pink tongue, running at full throttle, moving the sheep forward. I could barely restrain myself from cheering. For me it was the equivalent of seeing an old Lassie film where Lassie appears, just in the nick of time, to rescue some child from disaster. My response surprised me: my eyes welled up with tears. Tears of happiness. Something about the whole transaction between man and dog and sheep touched a place deep inside me. It was the same place, probably, that was home to the sleeping child within, the girl who once talked to dogs, telling them stories and whispering secrets into their soft velvety ears.

On the way back to the house, I asked Bobby whether he would be running Lynn or any of his collies in the upcoming Luss trial.

Bobby told me he had no interest in dog trials. "It's too time-consuming when you run a farm like this," he said. "And with shepherds who know how to gather sheep off hills getting scarcer all the time, I depend on my dogs for the work they can do."

As Bobby talked, I could hear Lynn in the back of the car. She was asleep but still panting heavily. Or maybe she was dreaming. I wondered if she dreamed of sheep, of racing the wind through the spring pastures or climbing the rugged snow-covered hills to help pull out a half-buried ewe in winter. On the other hand, if she was anything like the animals I knew well, Lynn was likely dreaming of her next meal.

We drove in silence for a while, through fields dotted with large tufts of whiteness, followed by smaller ones. Along the way Bobby pointed out the house where he was born, the site of an Iron Age fort behind it, and the hundred-foot-deep gorge where a Colquhoun leaped to safety from the MacGregors after the battle of Glen Fruin.

I told Bobby—whose quiet dignity and measured speech suggested a man at peace with himself—that I couldn't imagine him living anywhere else.

"I can imagine it," Bobby said. "But I wouldn't want to be living it."

That evening, as usual, I walked from the farm to the Colquhoun Arms for dinner. It was quite cozy there at night, lively but not rowdy, a place frequented mostly by locals and, of course, their dogs. While I walked I thought about something that happened with Anne before our lunch at Shantron Farm, an incident that rocketed me back to childhood.

On a quick trip to nearby Helensburgh where Anne had her car serviced, we strolled through the small Victorian town's shopping area, home to such establishments as Boots the Chemists and the Washed Up Laundrette. After stopping to admire the luscious display of home-baked sweets in the Criagard Tearoom, we decided to go in for a cup of tea and a sweet. When the waitress appeared, I surprised myself by instantly pointing to a plate of sugary, pale brown squares in the window.

"I'll have one of those," I said, not sure why I was so drawn to the unappealing-looking confection. The answer came when I took a bite of the square. It was Grandmother's strange brown candy! The candy she served in pie-shaped slices straight from the round aluminum cake pan she baked it in. I couldn't believe it. Was it possible that after trying for most of my life to re-create Grandmother's candy, I'd finally stumbled across it? "What is this called?" I asked Anne, trying to conceal my excitement.

"It's called Tablet," she said, sounding a bit puzzled. "It's a wee bit like your American fudge. Do you like it?"

I answered by telling her the whole story. At least the *Reader's Digest* version of the story, concentrating on Grandmother and the aluminum cake pans, leaving out the part about Proust's madeleines and other literary references. I ended by asking Anne if she thought the shop's owner might give me the recipe.

"Aye, but I have the recipe at home. I'd be happy to give it to you."

"Aye, that would be luvely," I said, rolling a piece of the sugary candy around in my mouth the way I used to with Grandmother's pie-shaped fudge. "Tablet," I said aloud, the way a child might when making the connection for the first time between a word and the thing it stood for. I couldn't wait to tell my older, smarter brother Shelby what the name was for the mystery candy from our childhood.

My thoughts of the incident with Anne earlier that morning were interrupted by the waitress at the Colquhoun Arms plunking down my dinner on the table. I dug into the fish-and-chips as though it were, well, a piece of Tablet. As I ate, I could hear a heavy rain pounding down on the cars parked outside. I tried not to think about how difficult the walk home through the fields would be. Anyway, a rain as heavy as this one sounded probably wouldn't last very long.

I was wrong. A half hour later, while I huddled at the pub's front door watching sheets of rain blow across the roads outside, the weather was growing worse. As I wondered what to do, the couple who'd been at the table next to me appeared at the door, seemingly ready to leave.

"Aye, it's still raining, is it?" the man said. "Perhaps we should give it a wee wait."

"Don't be daft," the woman replied. "We're not walking, after all. We have a car."

My ears pricked up at the word *car*. After all, Mark's farm couldn't be that far out of their way, whatever way that was. And given that I had no umbrella and no flashlight to get me down the steps and through the nature trail, why not ask for a lift? On the other hand I'd overheard (read: eavesdropped) a few bits of their conversation at dinner and thought them a wee bit strange. There was something odd about the way they related to one another: the man, talkative, pushy, and too complimentary, was met by constant rebuffs from the woman, who was sedate, English, and fiftyish. But what the heck. I decided to take a chance and dropped a hint—something about hoping I didn't get washed away walking home through the flooded fields. Pleasantries were exchanged and eventually the offer of a ride home was made.

With the woman at the wheel of the car, we headed up the dark, rainy Old Road at about eighty miles an hour. "You should turn here," I said from the backseat when we approached the roundabout to A82. Instead she went straight through, driving like a crazy woman to another back road. The woman didn't react to my cry of alarm. The man just laughed. I was getting very nervous, not only about the white-knuckle ride but also about their unresponsive attitude. Don't panic, I told myself, as we hurtled along the road. Think. What would Nancy Drew do? I started to look for some sharp object in the cluttered back-seat, something I could use as a stabbing device, should it come to that.

Just as I was writing the headline that would appear in the next day's local newspaper—AMERICAN WOMAN KIDNAPPED IN SMALL SCOTTISH VILLAGE. WENT WILLINGLY WITH HER ABDUCTORS. NO RANSOM NOTE YET—the car stopped at the driveway to Hill of Camstraddan Farm.

"Well, here you are, lassie," said the man.

"Aye, have a good sleep," said his accomplice.

"Thanks," I said, grateful for any kind of sleep as long as it wasn't the Big Sleep. Then I jumped out of the car, not bothering to close the door, and ran up the hill toward home.

As the days passed I grew used to the sight outside my window of sheep grazing the front meadow amid an endless vista of hills rising and dipping, with fences shaping the whole landscape into patterns of white dots against a green background. It was the first thing I saw in the morning and the last thing at night.

One evening as I sat in my room reading *The Versatile Border Collie,* I heard soft whistles outside my window. Having quickly ruled out Romeo or Cyrano de Bergerac as the possible source of the sounds, I got up, turned out the lights, and went to the window. There in the fading light was Mark, putting a dog through its paces with the sheep. Since the local dog trials were less than a week away I assumed he was trying to squeeze in some quality practice time with the dog—probably Spot—before the event. The trials were important to Mark. I knew this because he'd told me some of his reasons for competing with other dog handlers in such trials.

"The camaraderie, for one thing," he had told me. "And just to get that bit of respect when you go out there and they're all watching your dog and your dog does well."

Mark's feelings were in sharp contrast to those of Bobby Lennox, who seemed to have no interest in dog trials; who in fact seemed not to need any kind of attention or affirmation for himself or his dogs. To be honest I identified more with Mark than Bobby. Writing, like sheep farming, is a solitary profession. And what I hoped for each time my work was published was pretty much what Mark wanted when he competed in a trial: to get a bit of respect, to be noticed, and to do well.

The workouts with Peg were going better than before. She occasionally did what I commanded her to do. Once when Peg correctly went to the left of the sheep when I said, "Come bye," I suddenly remembered the first time I roller-skated down the steep street in front of our house. I suppose what roller-skating and my slight success with Peg had in common was the thrill of a new accomplishment. Mark even commented on my better handling of Peg. His theory was that I was more relaxed and Peg was growing used to my voice. My theory was that things took a turn for the better after I started to give Peg a little tummy rub after each session. Mark didn't seem to object, although I suspected this was not something I should try with Spot, who regularly watched Peg and me through the fence.

It had become my custom after a session with Peg to walk into the village for lunch at the Coach House Coffee Shop. From the minute I laid eyes on the Coach House, even before I tasted their superb Lomond Latte, I knew it was a place that would have good coffee. Don't ask me how I knew. It's a gift. You either have it or you don't.

Warm and friendly, with very good food and an unexpected dash of sophistication, the Coach House immediately became my hangout. Its owner, Gary Groves, was a burly Scotsman with a wild shock of unnaturally blond hair and an entrepreneurial attitude worthy of a venture capitalist. From the full kilt regalia he wore (he'd even add a shield and sword to the outfit for a photo shoot with tourists) to the well-displayed scrapbook of articles about his shop, Gary knew how to work all the Scots-related angles to his advantage. His strategy, coupled with hard work and good management, had paid off. The Coach House Coffee Shop was a success, probably the most popular place in the village for visiting tourists. Of course, it didn't hurt that the charming village of Luss appeared weekly on the *High Road* television series, an add-on that greatly increased the entire town's tourist appeal.

In addition to taking lunch there, I often walked back to the coffee shop in late afternoon—when most of the tourists had cleared out—to have a second Lomond Latte and to talk to the waitresses. By now, my thinking voice insisted on saying everything in a perfect Scots accent. Things like telling myself: *Aye, Lassie, so ye canna get the wee Peg to bide your commands. Buck up, it'll no do you any good to be dour.* Now and then the accent would break loose, forcing its way into my speaking voice. On one such occasion, when asked by a tourist for directions to the bus that went to Balloch, I heard myself say, *It'll no be near here. Ye must go right round the visitors' center and luke for the bus sign.*

And by now, most of the waitresses knew—as everyone in the village seemed to—that I was "the American lady staying at Mark Wylie's," although there were conflicting stories as to why I was there.

"I hear you're learnin' to ken the sheepdogs," one waitress said to me. "Ach, nae," said another, eyeing the large notebook I scribbled into every day. "Canna ye see the lass is writin' a book?"

Actually, I was doing both: learning what I could about the collies *and* writing a book, a mystery set in a village in the Scottish Highlands. The book's working title was *Tartan Noir*, an homage of sorts to my Scottish heritage and the fact I've always loved the color black. The female protagonist in *Tartan Noir* was a contract shepherd and dog handler named Fiona Eweing MacCheviot—Chevy for short—who in her spare time went around solving mysteries with the help of her Border collie, a bitch named Chick. At first I thought of making my two-legged sleuth a retired gardener who specialized in poisonous plants or a lapsed investment banker now involved in socially responsible investments, but in the end, neither seemed right. When I hit on the idea of Chevy and Chick it was as though a lightbulb went off over my head. *Tartan Noir*—which involved a string of deadly high jinks at a rigged dog trial—was to be the first of a series featuring the two young sleuths.

Since plotting, a major component of mystery writing, is not my strong suit—my tendency is to let the story take me in whatever direction it wants to go—the book required intense concentration interrupted by frequent breaks. Often I'd use these breaks to study a large folding chart I carried with me, one that traced the lineage of champion Border collies from Old Hemp to Old Kep to the great Wiston Cap. Or, alternatively, I read over *The Scottish Farmer*, a newspaper that ran ads featuring collies for sale alongside the occasional singles ad. I was particularly drawn to one personal that read: *"I am a young country lady of 59 years. I refuse to give up hope of finding my kind, tall, gentle, witty young man— 60 plus; to share love and laughter with me; I adore music and animals. Yours forever hopeful, Mary."*

One morning Mark surprised me by asking if I'd like to work with Spot. Instead of jumping at the chance, I hesitated. Me? Work with Spot, the champion? In my mind it was tantamount to being asked to edit Jane Austen.

"Sure, I'd like that," I said breezily, trying to conceal my trepidation.

What followed was weird. For the first time, I managed to move the sheep in the right direction and get the job done. Then I realized it was actually Spot who got the job done. What was odd was the way he did it: by doing the opposite of everything I asked him to do. What was it Mark had told me that first day? Something about how a good hill dog has to do some of the thinking for himself. I guess you could say that on this particular day Spot did *all* of the thinking for himself.

Later when I told Mark—as if he didn't know—that Spot had totally ignored me, his answer was brief. "He's my dog," Mark said. Although from the satisfied sound of his voice, Mark could just as well have said, "I'm his master."

It rained heavily for the two days before the trials. And for the two days before that and the two days before that. Every morning when I turned on the television for the weather report, it was essentially the same. *Scattered showers with sunny spells.* Or, *Sunny spells with scattered showers.* Or the much more intimidating, *Rain with strong winds.* What this last forecast meant was a day of heavy, nonstop rain driven sideways by the wind so that it felt like a hundred needles stabbing you. Umbrellas were of no use in such weather nor was a rain hood.

Fortunately this was not my first visit to Scotland, and I'd packed accordingly. Rain slicker with hood. *Check.* Regular rain boots. *Check.* Rain pants. *Check.* Windbreaker with hood. *Check.* Rain poncho big enough to go over rain slicker with hood. *Check.* Waterproof backpack. *Check.* And the all-important Wellies, the knee-high rubber boots worn on a sheep farm by anyone with any sense. *Check and double check.* Even so, getting around on foot was not easy. The fields were muddy and slippery, and the long wet grass made walking more like snowshoeing in deep snow.

Still, I trained Peg in the rain—or rather she trained me—and commuted as usual back and forth to the village for meals. I even began to like walking in the rain, as long as it wasn't windy. In such rainy, overcast weather, Loch Lomond and the shoreline that surrounded it took on a ghostly magisterial look, erasing the line between shore, water, and sky, blending it all into a silvery gray mist, like a waterscape painted by Turner. Still, in this kind of weather the dog trials would be a disaster, and I worried that they might be canceled. Not just because I had come expecting to see them, but also because of the disappointment it would bring to Mark and the other dog trialists, particularly given the cancellation of the prior year's events.

As Friday, the day of the local trial, grew closer, I asked Mark to explain how the National and International Sheep Dog Trials were decided and how the locals fit into the bigger picture.

"Each country has its own National competition—Ireland, Scotland, Wales, and England," Mark told me. "In order for a dog to compete in a National Championship trial, it has to win an Open trial at the local level—such as the Luss trial coming up. The top-ranked dogs from each National then compete in the International Qualifying Trial with the fifteen highest-ranked dogs, irrespective of country, going forward to the International Supreme Championship trial." Until recently, Mark explained, only these four countries competed, but now there is a separate trial, the World Trial, in which handlers from the United States and Europe compete as well.

"And how are the dogs judged?" I asked. "How does a dog win one of these trials?"

"The dogs get one hundred points to start with, and the judges deduct from that for any fault they see. They can deduct points if a dog rushes the sheep on the outrun, scattering them. Or if a dog, on the fetch, doesn't get the sheep moving in a straight line at a steady pace. A dog that bites sheep is disqualified. If you have a very good dog, the score can be in the high nineties."

I asked Mark which dog he planned to run. Spot?

"Aye, Spot. But also Trim."

His answer surprised me. Trim was eight, an age considered by many dog handlers as past a dog's prime. Surprised or not, I now knew who I'd be rooting for in the trial. I'd be in Trim's corner, rooting for the middle-aged bitch to win.

Dear N,

By now you've probably gotten my very long letter about life on the farm, so this will be a shorter note, one I hope to finish before falling asleep after a long but exciting day. I couldn't wait till morning to share with you my visit this afternoon to one of the most spectacular houses I've ever seen. It's called Hill House and was designed in 1902 by one of your favorite architects, Charles Rennie Mackintosh. Although the phrase *art deco* had yet to be coined when Mackintosh designed the house, its clean, geometric design and sharp angles seem almost to be a harbinger of that style. To find such an architecturally sophisticated house in Helensburgh, a small town about eight miles from the farm, astonished me. Try to imagine stumbling across the fabulous Paris Maison de Verre in the heart of sheep country and you'll see what I mean.

There is, by the way, a staircase in Hill House that reminded me of the one we saw at Maison de Verre. Do you remember it as clearly as I do? The architect who showed us around the Paris house described it as "a 'monumental ladder,' not a staircase." (Perhaps my memory of the staircase is so vivid because of its lack of handrails and risers—a little detail that, as you well know, is quite intimidating to me given my fear of falling.) Although the Hill House staircase is less spectacular, it has the same effect of appearing to float in the air.

I was taken to Hill House by Anne Lennox, a woman I've grown to admire as well as like. She's the woman I told you about, the one who identified the mystery candy made by my grandmother as Scots Tablet—a discovery just as exciting to me as Hill House! (And yes, I will whip up a batch of Tablet for you, although I doubt you'll like it. It's too sweet for a Japanese palate. Too sweet, really, for any palate but that of a sugar-addicted child.) Anne, who epitomizes the down-to-earth openness of a country woman, surprised me with her sophisticated take on the architecture and the architect of Hill House, explaining that the exterior of the house was a perfect example of "rough casting," a process that consists of throwing gravel into the wet mortar. I'd never heard of rough casting. Have you? Anyway, this was a side of Anne—her interest and knowledge of architecture—that would have remained unknown to me had we not gone to Hill House.

I'm counting the days until our meeting in London. Can it be true that in less than a week I will be lucky enough to see you get off the train at Waterloo Station? I have so much to tell you and so much I want you to tell me. I'm eager to hear how the plans are progressing for your daughter's wedding in Tokyo. And also to see photographs of the house you designed for her and Haruo. I must go to sleep now. When I wake up, we will be one day closer to each other.

When I finished the longer-than-intended letter, however, I was no longer sleepy. As usual, thinking only encouraged more thinking and I was wide awake, imagining my meeting in London with Naohiro. I imagined us, after the initial rush of excitement and pleasure, cooking together in his rented apartment at Ovington Place.

First we'd walk from the apartment to Chelsea Green, a charming square with a collection of small, excellent food markets. We'd stroll along Walton Street with its specialty shops and art galleries, stopping in at Naohiro's favorite—a whimsical shop featuring exquisite hand-painted children's furniture—then popping into one of my favorites, a gallery specializing in antique paintings of pets. From Walton Street we'd turn onto tree-lined Sloane Avenue, and when we passed a white limestone building, I'd say *That's where I lived one summer.* Finally we'd make the turn onto Whitehead's Grove and walk the two blocks to Chelsea Green. After stopping at the greengrocer's to buy fruit and vegetables, we'd stand in the fishmonger's shop, bickering like an old married couple about which fish to buy. *If we're going to grill it, I think it should be a flat fish like sole,* I would say. And he'd say, *I think more of a meaty fish, like monkfish, that we could braise.* As usual we'd end up selecting our favorite: fresh salmon straight from Scotland's famous River Dee.

Although it was late and I needed a good night's sleep, I couldn't stop replaying in my head an unruly string of associations. My mind raced from Naohiro to Anne to Mark Wylie to Paris to London, one thought crashing into the next until it resembled the thinking equivalent of a rear-end collision: *Naohiro persuading me to climb the scary staircase at Maison de Verre by turning it into a game, the way a parent might do for a fearful child. . . . Anne telling me that she had met Bobby at a Young Farmer's Club meeting. . . . Naohiro writing that his daughter had met her fiancé at a Cherry Blossom Viewing in Tokyo. . . . My curiosity about how Mark Wylie had met his wife Christine, an attractive woman I'd run into only once, as she was leaving for work, dressed in a crisp suit and pumps. . . . My own first meeting with Naohiro on the train to Giverny. . . . The sudden thought of how random all these meetings seemed. . . . What if Anne had skipped the farmer's club meeting or Naohiro's daughter wasn't in the mood for cherry blossom viewing and stayed at home instead? What if I had taken a later train or if instead of sitting next to me, Naohiro had chosen a seat next to some other stranger? What if. . . ?*

That'll do, said my thinking voice firmly, releasing me—as if I were a Border collie—from all further responsibilities to the task at hand. A few minutes later my mind went blank and I fell asleep.

The next morning I awakened to a strange sight: the sun shining through my window. Although the weather could change drastically before the local trial began at seven P.M., it was a promising start. As I ate breakfast in the little glass conservatory I saw that the sheep were sleeping in the sun, wooly white commas in the brilliant green grass.

"I've never seen them sleep in such an unguarded, open way," I told Mark as he slid a plate of eggs and grilled tomatoes in front of me.

"Aye, they look quite content, don't they?" Mark said.

Content. The word startled me. It seemed to fit exactly what I'd been feeling in the past several days but hadn't put a name to. After all, I wasn't used to being content. What I was used to was always looking ahead to the next thing. Or to be precise, to *proving* I could *do* the next thing. But my stay in Scotland had stirred feelings inside me that had nothing to do with planning for the next thing or proving myself. Whatever bits and pieces of my true self had unraveled over a lifetime as I tried to meet the expectations of others seemed to have knitted themselves back into place. I felt more confident than I had in years. It was a confidence so clear and uncomplicated that, had it been any more ascendant, would have bordered on arrogance.

I was surprised, too, by the increase in my physical strength. But I suppose being outside every day, working with the dogs, climbing hills and walking back and forth to the village and the lake was bound to make my body stronger. And I suppose learning the ins and outs of dealing with Peg and the Blackies could only boost my confidence. I thought of all the things I'd been learning over the last year and a half, of how different the demands and rewards were as I went from one lesson to the next. Yet each of them—from cooking at the Ritz Escoffier School to studying the world of Jane Austen—seemed to have added a new layer of muscle to both mind and body.

The sun's appearance in time for the local trial was the good news. The bad news was that Mark, who planned to run Spot and Trim in the Friday evening trial, would not be able to participate in Saturday's more prestigious competition.

"It will be the first time since I was nineteen that I'll miss running at the Luss Open trial," Mark said of his sudden change of plan. "But I've been talked into going to Islay to perform with the ducks for a charity which was let down at short notice."

The "ducks" Mark spoke of—officially known as the Loch Lomond Ducks—were part of a performance that consisted of Mark, twelve Indian Runner ducks, and a Border collie, usually Trim, putting the wee waddlers, instead of sheep, through their paces. It was quite comical to watch the ducks being herded about in a gentle fashion, and the show was popular with tourists and locals alike. It also turned out to be a lucrative sideline for Mark, who, like most of his fellow farmers, needed the additional income.

I was disappointed to learn he would miss the Luss Open. Disappointed for him and for me. I knew that some of the sport's "dangerous men," as the top handlers are called, were scheduled to compete at the trial. Stuart Davidson, for one, a Supreme International Champion who in one year alone had won five major events, and, for another, the colorful veteran John Angus MacLeod, who had competed at the highest level for fifty years. "John Angus is obsessed by dog trials and spends a fortune on dogs," Mark had told me. "The trial is never over until John's dogs have had their run. And everyone will stop to watch him." Mark was bound to be disappointed at having to miss such a challenging competition. As for me, it meant I wouldn't have the chance to watch Mark and his dogs compete at such a high-level trial.

Earlier I had asked Mark to explain the difference between the local trial and Saturday's Luss Open trial.

"By tradition, and unique to Luss, we have the small local trial on the eve of the Open," he had explained. "The two trials are run separately and judged by a different judge. Mainly we hold the local trial to encourage younger or newer handlers to have a go in front of friends and neighbors—which is far less daunting and intimidating than walking out in front of complete strangers with some of the best handlers in the country watching."

To get a better understanding of what happens at a trial and what the judges look for, I'd been reading books from Mark's library. By the time the local was to take place, I had filled a small notebook with explanations about each element of the trial and what standards had to be met by a dog to receive a high score. On the afternoon of the trial I sat in the village drinking my usual Lomond Latte and reviewed, for about the twentieth time, the trial elements. First is the "outrun," in which the dog is sent off to circle wide behind the sheep. Next is the "lift," when the dog sets the sheep in motion, followed by the "fetch," as the dog moves the flock steadily forward in a straight line toward the handler. And, finally, there are the dreaded elements known as "pen" and "shed." Although any part of the course can turn into a disaster—knocking off big points from that one-hundred-point starting score—pen and shed can make or break a champion.

"Pen" means exactly what it sounds like. The dog must get the sheep to enter a small pen. And since sheep prefer a spacious pasture to a small enclosure, the pen element provides the perfect setup for a Highland showdown between the herder and those being herded. As for "shed," well, the easiest way I'd found to remember what it means—to separate one or more sheep from the rest—was to think of my favorite scene from *Babe*. Who could forget how Pig executes a perfect "shed" by politely saying: "If the three ladies with collars would kindly walk out of the ring, I'd be very much obliged."

But to be honest, even after reading and re-reading my almost-memorized notes, I still didn't understand the popularity of sheepdog trials. Considered a competitive sport in Britain, the National and International trials are the canine equivalent of the Kentucky Derby, thanks to the BBC show *One Man and His Dog*. It was one thing to see a collie gathering sheep on the hills, relying on its own instincts, running full-out for fifteen minutes or so, as I did with Bobby's dog Lynn at Shantron Farm—that was exciting. But what, I wondered, did millions of people find so enthralling about watching one black-and-white dog after another determine the passage of several sheep across a field and into a pen while listening to strange whistles from a human being?

The local trial was scheduled to begin at seven P.M., a time set so that working shepherds could compete. At about half past six, with Trim and Spot already tumbling around like puppies in the back of the Land Rover, Mark and I set out for the farm where the trial would be run. Mark explained that because restrictions on the movement of livestock were still in force, both the local trial and the Luss Open would take place at nearby Duchlage Farm instead of in the village. This change would affect the trial by including some wild cards. For one thing the sheep to be used belonged to the farm.

"Sometimes it doesn't help when the sheep come from the farm where the trial's held," Mark said. "They know all the nooks and crannies. And these are crossbred sheep, very big sheep. We call them mules. You have to try to slow sheep like this down, but that's not easy."

When we arrived at the farm, Mark, who was chairman of the event, left me alone while he sorted out some last-minute details. For a moment or two, I stood rooted to the spot, trying to decide where to go: to the group of lively, young shepherds—"the boys," as Mark called them—who laughed and tussled with one another as their dogs frolicked in the grass, or to the half dozen attractive, older men lined up against a wooden fence, some with dogs and some without.

I decided to go with the older men–sedate dogs scenario and headed for the fence, taking my place next to a man with gray hair and mischievous eyes that matched the deep blue of his argyle sweater. I leaned back and placed the heel of one foot on the fence behind me, trying to look as though I belonged. As I did this something pushed against my other leg. I looked down and saw a collie with a silky coat and curious face looking up at me, his healthy pink tongue adding a nice splash of color to his overall black-and-white outfit. Without thinking, I leaned over and stroked the top of his head, forgetting the etiquette of not petting dogs at trials.

"Her name is Nan," said the man in the argyle sweater. "And my name is Duncan."

Although Duncan said nothing to indicate I'd made a mistake in petting Nan, I blurted out an apology anyway. "I'm sorry about Nan. I mean, about petting Nan. I know she's not a pet. But she's so beautiful and sweet that I forgot myself."

I could tell he was pleased by my remark about Nan. But like most of the dog handlers I'd met, he modestly downplayed the compliment. "Well, she's casting her coat right now so she's not lookin' as good as she's been."

I asked if Nan had come to the trial as a competitor or as a spectator.

As a competitor, he said. "She's run in other trials. Had a first in one and a second in another. Nan's a bonny dog, but I haven't run her that much, to be quite honest. I'm not really too much of a trial person. I like trials but I'm not competitive."

Duncan asked if I planned to run a dog. His question pleased me, with its suggestion that I was an experienced dog handler. Although I wanted to say yes—just to enjoy the momentary fantasy—I told him the truth, explaining why I was in Luss, staying at Mark Wylie's farm. And naturally I threw in the part about my family being Scottish— a part of the Clan Buchanan—and how natural it felt to be among Scots people.

Duncan listened with what seemed genuine interest and then said, "So, lassie, ye've come home then, have ye?"

In just a few words, Duncan had summed up exactly what I'd been feeling since stepping off the plane in Glasgow. "Aye, that I have," I said. "I've come home."

Just before the trial started, Duncan offered to talk me through some of the specific runs as they took place. I was just about to accept his offer when a man with a pleasantly ruddy face shaded by a tweed cap leaned over across Duncan and introduced himself. "I'm John and you should'na listen to a word Duncan says. I'm the one who should be tellin' you about the dogs." I could tell the two men were friends and that John was up to a wee bit of mischief.

By now there were Jeeps and Land Rovers and pickup trucks parked all along the inside of the farm's fence. Most of them were parked so that the back of the vehicle faced the field, a position that gave the collies waiting for their turn a good view of the action. Some of the dogs were loose, chasing one another like pups across the field, and Trim, one of Mark's dogs, was rolling around in the grass, paws extended into the air. Even workaholic Border collies, apparently, enjoy taking some downtime now and again.

I walked to a spot where I could examine the sheep. Mark was right. Compared to the Blackies and the Cheviots, these sheep were as big as Winnebago motor homes. I worried about Trim and Spot and my new friend Nan and wondered how they'd do up against such "mules."

At seven-thirty on the dot, the judge started the official time clock— each dog had ten minutes to complete his run—and the first handler sent his dog rocketing off into his outrun. The sheep were huddled at the far end of a meadow the size of a football field, almost too far away for the human eye to see. But that's what binoculars are for. So I pulled mine out and followed the streak of black and white accelerating up a hill and then swinging behind the sheep in a wide curve, so as not to spook them. After stirring them into an easy motion, the dog moved up behind the sheep a few steps at a time, stalking them, his rear end high, his head and tail low, the classic Border collie crouch when working sheep.

It was then that Duncan and John started a play-by-play commentary for my benefit. I pretended to know what they were talking about when they said things like, *It was a good lift, that. Nice and slow, didn't make the sheep bolt.* Or, *That dog should'na have stopped on the run-in. There'll be points off for that.* Then I realized I wasn't pretending. I actually understood what they meant.

As the trial progressed I saw that what I had imagined would be a boring sameness of runs—each run just like the one before—was in fact quite the opposite. Each run seemed quite different to me. Some dogs excelled on the walk-in but failed miserably at the pen or shed. Some dogs seemed too forceful, scaring the sheep into erratic chaotic movements. Others were too laid-back and allowed the sheep to challenge them. One such confrontation between four big sheep and one medium-sized dog was as gripping, to me anyway, as the classic "Thrilla in Manila" fight between boxers Ali and Frazier. But unlike the boxing match there was no clear winner in the dog vs. sheep battle. Although the sheep finally were brought back into line, the dog lost a whole lot of points.

When it came time for Mark to run Trim, I asked Duncan to call the action for me. Basically, what it came down to was that Trim was too forceful with the sheep when they first made contact and this unsettled them for the rest of the run, throwing them off line. But Trim did very well at the pen and shed, scoring maximum points for those elements. When Mark ran Spot, it was pretty much the same story: too forceful with the sheep at the start but excellent at the pen and shed. The final trial placement of Trim and Spot would be determined by how well the other dogs did in their runs.

About two dogs later, it was Duncan's turn to run Nan. I watched the two of them as they stood waiting for the judge to push the start button on the time clock. Then with a whistle that sounded like a bird's call, Duncan sent Nan speeding off on the outrun to lift the waiting sheep. So far, so good. But as Nan started to walk the sheep in, the "mules" suddenly just stopped and stood there, refusing to move. This impasse continued until Nan got them moving again, but so slowly that by the time they reached the pen, the ten-minute time limit had been reached.

"What happened?" I asked Duncan when he resumed his place at the fence.

"It's just the sheep," he said. "They're very touchy, not at ease with a dog. And Nan was getting tired, too, the wee dog."

When the competition was over and the four top dogs named, Nan was not one of them. But Spot and Trim were. Spot, with a score of seventy-four, won a second and Trim, whose score was sixty-five, placed fourth. The top scorer was local shepherd John McDougall's dog, Midge, with an eighty-five. But Spot was given the cup for Best Hill Dog, an award given to the dog deemed by the judge to be strong enough to gather and control sheep on an open hill as opposed to an enclosed field.

Mark wasn't surprised that Spot won Best Hill Dog. "Every time I take Spot to trial, someone wants to buy him," he told me as we drove back to the farm. "I've been offered three-and-a-half thousand pounds for him." When I turned to look at Spot in the back of the truck, what I saw was not Best Hill Dog but a dog who, after giving his all, was stretched out, dead asleep. Only an occasional twitching of his legs hinted that in his dreams Spot might be reliving his run with the sheep.

By the time I went down for breakfast the next morning, Mark, his wife, and their eight-year-old son had already left for Islay—the most southerly island of the Inner Hebrides, a short ferry ride from the mainland—with Trim and the Loch Lomond ducks. I regretted not having seen more of Christine, Mark's wife, but since she worked during the day and the family living quarters were in another part of the house, our paths just didn't cross. Still, I'd gotten to know their fourteen-year-old son Lewis a bit and thought he was a terrific lad. It was Lewis who saw to it that I had a fine cooked breakfast before setting out for the Luss Open, which would start at eight A.M. and last until five in the afternoon.

When I arrived at Duchlage Farm with Shona Robertson, the young woman who helped Mark organize the trial, it was just after eight. The parking lot was already crowded with cars and trucks that ranged from the usual beat-up Jeeps to expensive, late-model trucks. I scanned the printed program that listed the names of the thirty-three competitors, two of whom were women, to see if the "dangerous men"—Stuart Davidson and John Angus MacLeod—were on the schedule. They were.

The trial was set up so that each handler ran a dog in the morning session and then another in the afternoon. "Usually you would run the better of your two dogs in the afternoon," Mark had told me the day before. "That's because all the sheep are rerun in the afternoon—which means they've already been round the course and should be better and more familiar with it the second time around. So all things being equal you'd run your stronger dog."

I saw that Stuart Davidson was listed as the second trialist in the morning session and John Angus—as everyone called him—as fourteenth. In the afternoon, John Angus would run his dog near the middle of the group, while Davidson would take his turn closer to the end. Davidson's dog, Kep, had won at Luss the last time the trial was held.

Because the Luss Open was a qualifying trial for the Scottish National in August, I had expected the mood to be more intense than that of the previous night. However, the trial participants struck me as the least flustered, most low-key competitors I'd ever seen in a high-stakes sporting contest. They didn't seem to be nervous or consumed with thoughts of winning. In fact they didn't appear to be thinking about anything at all. And the handlers, it should be pointed out, were pretty calm too. Except for one man who caught my eye.

I'd noticed the tall, gaunt man with sharp features who, accompanied by an especially handsome collie, kept walking back and forth across the field, past the other handlers and their dogs, never stopping to nod or speak. At times he stood by himself in a far corner of the field, in self-imposed isolation. In his tweed jacket and vest, Sherlock Holmes fore-and-aft cap, knickers, woolen kneesocks, and dress crook, the man looked as though he'd answered a call from central casting for a sheep-dog trialist.

"Who is that?" I asked one of the young shepherds I'd met the night before.

"That's John Angus MacLeod," he told me. "He gets very jittery at competitions."

"Is Stuart Davidson here?"

"Aye, that's him sitting with his son Craig in their automobile."

Although I was dying to talk to one of these "dangerous men" about the psychology of winning a dog trial, it didn't seem likely to happen. Certainly, not with John Angus—although I'd been told everyone connected with the trials has a "John Angus story." Approaching a "jittery" handler with a reputation for being testy struck me as a bad idea. But maybe Stuart Davidson might share his views with me. I decided to hang out around his car and take it from there. To my surprise, he actually spoke to me first. Probably because I was standing at the back of his vehicle, sweet-talking his dog Star, who, I was pretty sure, enjoyed the attention.

Although I'd like to claim that Stuart—as my thinking voice now called him—and I talked in depth about the psychological issues involved for dog and trainer in competitive trials, I can't. Still, our brief conversation through his rolled-down car window yielded some insights that I jotted down in my notebook: *Stuart says the challenge to the dog trialist is to beat the sheep. To put them where you want to. Plus winning, of course. He says that at the end of the day, he wants to be the best. And Stuart says his dogs know when they're going to a trial. They know because he's dressed differently.*

When I turned away from Stuart's car, I saw John Angus about ten feet away, leaning on his tall distinctive crook, his dog posed by his side. Without warning my reporter's aggressive instincts kicked in. I went over to him, introduced myself, and asked if he'd mind my taking a photograph of him with his dog. "The two of you look so perfect," I explained.

John Angus said nothing but he repositioned himself and his dog in a way that suggested taking a snapshot was okay. I moved back from him, snapped the picture, and then snapped another one. "Just in case the first one doesn't come out," I said to him.

To my surprise, he spoke. "I'll tell you a story. Once I was winning a trial and an American took my picture. Although I ended with ninety-three points I wasn't in the prizes."

Although the words he spoke were oblique, I knew immediately his remark was a rebuke. I tried to be conciliatory. "Well, I hope you win anyway, even though I've taken your picture."

"Your hope's no use to me," he said sharply.

To be honest, the trial wasn't as much fun after that. Perhaps it was because I didn't have a Spot or Trim or Nan to root for. Or perhaps it was because I worried all day that I had jinxed John Angus. That he would lose—by a lot—and it would be my fault. When I told this story to my shepherd friends, they laughed and told me John Angus always had some excuse ready, in case he didn't win.

Still, I breathed a sigh of relief at the end of the day when the top handlers were announced. John Angus led the list, with a score of eighty-five points. After thinking it over I decided to take the high road and not tell him "I told you so" or anything like that. I decided to look at the bright side of the incident. Along with the many wonderful memories I would take with me from Scotland—of Mark and Anne and Bobby and the collies, of the friendly Scots and breathtaking country-side—one would stand out in its uniqueness.

Unlike most tourists I would return with my very own John Angus story to tell, not to mention an excellent snapshot of one man and his dog.

Acknowledgments

For making this book possible, the author wishes to thank Gail Ross, literary agent and friend, whose continued encouragement and support has been invaluable. I am also deeply grateful to Susanna Porter, my editor, for lending her sensibility and intelligence to this endeavor. And heartfelt thanks go to Kate Medina and Leslie Breed for their continued interest and support.

Above all, I am grateful to my sons, Andy and Sam, who continue to grace my life with their presence, and to my daughter-in-law, Yuko Yoshioka, a wonderful new addition to the family.

ABOUT THE AUTHOR

ALICE STEINBACH, whose work at the Baltimore *Sun* was awarded a Pulitzer Prize for Feature Writing, has been a freelance writer since 1999. Currently a Woodrow Wilson Visiting Fellow, she has taught journalism and writing at Princeton University, Washington and Lee University, and Loyola College. Her last book, *Without Reservations: The Travels of an Independent Woman*, was also published by Random House. She lives in Baltimore, Maryland.

ABOUT THE TYPE

This book was set in Weiss, a typeface designed by a German artist, Emil Rudolf Weiss (1875–1942). The designs of the roman and italic were completed in 1928 and 1931 respectively. The Weiss types are rich, well-balanced, and even in color, and they reflect the subtle skill of a fine calligrapher.